THE STRONGMEN

The Strongmen

EUROPEAN ENCOUNTERS WITH SOVEREIGN POWER

Hans Kribbe

agenda
publishing

First published in 2020 by Agenda Publishing

Agenda Publishing Limited
The Core
Bath Lane
Newcastle Helix
Newcastle upon Tyne
NE4 5TF
www.agendapub.com

ISBN 978-1-78821-275-5

British Library Cataloguing-in-Publication Data
A catalogue record for this book is available from the British Library

Typeset by JS Typesetting Ltd, Porthcawl, Mid Glamorgan
Printed and bound in the UK by TJ International

Contents

Acknowledgements

The idea for this book emerged out of countless conversations and encounters around the world, going back 15 years. These conversations nearly always dealt with practical matters of politics and business, in other words, with concrete problems and how to solve them through action, not with concepts or theories. However, probably more than any book or theory could have done, they offered a window into the politics of strength. They revealed how differently politics can be experienced and lived. I owe a debt of thanks to all those who unwittingly, but no less relentlessly, challenged my assumptions and uncovered a new world.

I am grateful, further, to the people who commented on some or even all of what I have written here. Luuk van Middelaar, supremely gifted writer, sharpened my ideas, helped me recognize pitfalls and provided vital encouragement throughout. Alison Howson, remorseless editor, imposed structure, rigour and brevity. Tim Price has been a companion in exploring the world of the strongman. I have endlessly tested arguments with Simonas Vileikis, astute observer of global politics, leading me to either improve or discard them.

Lucía Caudet read early drafts of chapters, offering a sanity check and the assurance I needed to begin writing in earnest. Finally, I thank Rafael and Mateo, men of action, for enduring a father immersed in thought.

Hans Kribbe
Brussels

Preface

Not long ago, the world's strongmen were only tinpot dictators of tinpot countries. Parts of the world, we knew, remained in the doldrums of despotism. But this formed no particular threat to the West and its ideals. Liberal democracy seemed unassailable in its appeal. Strongman politics, the consensus was, thrived on social and intellectual torpor. Sooner or later the rest of the world would wake up and follow our example.

Today, history looks far less certain, less linear. Bullish confidence in the Western model, commonplace once, has become a curiosity. The strongmen are on the rise in Asia, Africa and even in the West itself. And rather than tinpot countries, they now run some of the world's wealthiest and most powerful states. The technological and military resources the strongmen command collectively, and in some cases individually, exceed those of European and other liberal states by far. The time when strongmen needed to pose as democrats to gain international acceptance is over. It suffices to win the respect of other strongmen.

For Europe, the repercussions of this new balance of power are vast. Since the Second World War, Europe has stood for an idea of global order, on which it also staked its future. According to this idea, multilateral rules can be found that serve the interests of all people, and peace and prosperity come about when those rules are upheld by global institutions of governance. It remains a powerful vision, one that has bought the continent the security and unity it needed. But as a conception of order, rules are no longer the only game in town. The strongmen have their own idea about how the world should be organized. And at the heart of this language of politics and order lie not rules but an idea of strength.

Coming to terms with the politics of strength, with the "grammar of power", as French President Emmanuel Macron has called it, is one of Europe's biggest trials. It is also the central objective of this book. For while the politics of strength continues its rise in the world, our understanding of it lags behind. Dictators, tyrants and despots have always existed, of course. However, the idea that the strongmen are simply mad or evil – psychopaths who cannot be appeased – still goes some way towards summing up the strongman debate. As a result, we confront a political phenomenon that we poorly grasp, or at least not as systematically as it deserves to be.

Understanding the language of strength and power is important for at least two reasons. The first and most obvious reason is that this allows us to get a better grip on who or what we confront in our encounter with men like Trump, Xi or Putin. If we can put ourselves in the shoes of the strongman and see the world as he sees it, we can better anticipate his actions, better make ourselves heard and devise strategies that might allow us to attain our political goals.

The second reason why getting to know the language of power is important is that Europe will have to use this language itself, something the Covid-19 pandemic is likely to make only more pertinent. Increasingly unable to rely on American might, the continent is groping for a doctrine of power of its own. "European sovereignty" and "strategic autonomy" are words on everybody's lips in Paris, Brussels and Berlin these days. Ursula von der Leyen calls her Commission a "geopolitical Commission", words that invoke the idea of power rather than rules. Exploring the language of power, then, will also help chart the continent's own journey, its "re-entry in history", as it might be called. If Europe is to discover its own brand of power and strength, studying the men for whom politics is nothing but power is not an illogical starting point.

This discovery of power is, in part, a personal journey too, one that at the start of the millennium took me from London, where I wrote a doctoral thesis in political theory, to Brussels, a city steeped in rules, and then onwards to Moscow, a city made of power. Working in the private offices of European commissioners for the single market and competition policy, I could observe how the EU was obsessed with rules and existentially unnerved by the language of power and interstate rivalry. Only rarely, I found, was there political debate about whether policies were good or bad as such. If people thought an action or policy commendable, they argued it was contained in an anterior or higher piece of legislation, the inevitable consequence of logically applying rules rather than a sovereign act of power. Only technical and legal disagreement was allowed to exist, never political.

A good example of the EU's fixation on rules was its decision in 2015 to force retailers to attach labels on goods from Israeli settlements indicating that these goods were not "made in Israel" but in illegally occupied territory. It seemed a none-too-subtle hint that if Israel continued building settlements beyond its recognized borders, other trade sanctions could follow.

Rapping Israel on the knuckles was a divisive and political act, however. Israel's prime minister, Benjamin Netanyahu, angrily pointed out that creating special labels for Jews was reminiscent of Nazi times.[1] But a political debate about Israel and the Middle East peace process never materialized. EU trade officials argued the measure simply flowed from labelling regulations put in place in the 1990s to deal with mad cow disease. This was not about being "for" or "against" Israel, they explained. It was only about applying indication-of-origin rules. Made in Israel labels, the fact was, could not be used for goods made elsewhere; they needed to be labelled "Israeli settlement" or "Israel occupied territory". A big debate was unnecessary. It sufficed for the Commission to issue a short "interpretative note", laying out how labelling rules were to be applied, and wave the decision through.

Obviously, no one in Brussels had suddenly been gripped by a desire to more accurately apply its indication-of-origin rules, nor had there been a food scare linked to settlement produce. This was Europe using the power of its market to put pressure on Jerusalem, and to keep hopes for a Middle East peace deal alive. And yet no one would affirm this was indeed what the move intended. Was it the right political strategy to pursue and a sensible use of European power? The question could not even be asked or debated because the decision was not, officially, a political strategy to begin with. It was the outcome of EU rule application rather than of European political agency, an act of power.

After I left the Commission, I began advising the press department of Russia's presidential administration as part of a team of Western communication specialists in 2006. Our goal was to help Russia improve its image in the West by opening up to the international media. Russia and the West were still on speaking terms. Moscow presided over the G8. Hopes about the country's integration into the West were fading, but they had not vanished.

Gradually, the work opened my eyes to how different the world of the strongman thinks and talks. As the relationship between Moscow and the West unravelled, I felt progressively caught between the strongman's language of power and Europe's language of rules. Part of the job was to provide two-way political interpretation, to clarify Moscow's perspective in Europe and to explain Europe's perspective to Moscow. But the barriers both sides had erected against foreign viewpoints proved increasingly insurmountable. In 2014, following the outbreak of the Ukraine crisis, history finally caught up with us and the work ended.

The presidential aides and Russian officials I met over a period of several years were cultured, courteous and alarmingly well informed. They spoke thoughtfully and in fluent English. More than anything they were "political". Europe's idea of the world, they seemed to think, was naïve, oblivious to the cold reality of power. For them, there would always be winners *and* losers, friends *and* foes. Power and agency formed the fabric of the universe. European plans for a new and ambitious trade and partnership deal with Ukraine and other eastern European states "had to be" an instrument for geopolitical interests, specifically those of the US, which when push came to shove had Brussels on its leash.

While at first this sounded preposterous, over time it dawned on me that the Russians might not be altogether wrong. The US did not lord over Europe in any overt way, to be sure, but the thought that our language of rules-based multilateralism glossed over certain realities of power began to look less and less absurd. I could also see why Europe's claim that its integrationist ideals had only winners might appear childishly innocent. In the end, both languages seemed to possess a logic of their own. One perspective no longer seemed obviously false, the other no longer obviously true. The only idea that did seem clearly wrong was that these ways of looking at the world could be hauled through a fact checker and be decisively proved false.

The thing about languages is that they are never either true or untrue. While it is possible to describe trade and cooperation deals in the language of rules, it is also possible to describe such deals in the language of power, as a political instrument of strategy. While it is possible to describe indication-of-origin labels as a form of consumer protection, it is also possible to describe them as a foreign policy tool. Sometimes one language offers better and more pertinent descriptions than the other, but sometimes, also, it is not immediately clear which language is better.

As the philosopher Michael Oakeshott argued, the arguments and reasoning we use in politics cannot be reduced to scientific truth-claims, which can be systematically tested for accuracy.[2] This is because political discourse primarily claims to offer reasons for action, often under time and information constraints. It invokes generic theories of human nature, principles of what is right and fair, and perhaps most of all experience, history and the practical lessons they are believed to contain. Political discourse certainly deserves to be critically analysed and interpreted. One can say of a political language that it prevails, is in decline or is more or less useful in a given set of circumstances. One can also say that, if we were to act on the precepts of a discourse, the consequences would be good or bad. But one cannot easily claim political languages to be true or false.

Looking at our preoccupation with fake news and disinformation, what seems ill-understood is how different languages can sometimes coherently account for the same event. Political events, it might be said, are like the duck–rabbit illusion, which the philosopher Ludwig Wittgenstein made famous. The drawing appears to us either as a duck or as a rabbit. Some see a duck, others a rabbit. But if you look again, the rabbit's ears can be viewed as the duck's beak, and vice versa. Both are possible.

We may need someone to point out exactly how: "The duck's wings are the rabbit's legs while the duck's feet are the rabbit's fluffy tail." But then we are usually able to switch perspective, a so-called Gestalt switch. At first, we may see something that is indisputably a duck. But the same lines, the same "event", we later recognize as a rabbit.

It is the inability to switch perspectives, I believe, that plagues Europe's encounter with the strongmen, but also the continent's nascent efforts to think in the language of power and strength. We impose a particular prism on events, or perhaps spin doctors, think tanks, journalists and Facebook do this for us. Yet we do not consider that other prisms are also possible. Most of the time, we are not even aware that prisms exist at all. We believe we experience the world directly and assume everybody else experiences precisely the same thing. We are rarely conscious of the prisms and narratives that instantaneously colour what we see.

In diplomacy, the inability or unwillingness to switch prisms can be fatal. Reflecting on the 1962 Cuban missile crisis, which brought humanity to the brink of annihilation, as well as the Vietnam War, Robert McNamara, US defence secretary under John F. Kennedy and Lyndon B. Johnson, identified rational empathy, or the lack thereof, as the feature that determined whether US foreign policy succeeded or failed. "We must try to put ourselves inside their skin", McNamara warned in the 2003 documentary *The Fog of War*, "and look at us through their eyes, just to understand the thoughts that lie behind their decisions and their actions".[3]

This, however, is easier said than done. World politics does not consist of a few hastily drawn lines. A Gestalt switch is harder to achieve. In politics, languages come attached with emotive strings. They are interwoven with history, identity and destiny. The more engrossed we are in dispute, the more our prisms tend to narrow, the more we see only rabbits, even if those rabbits are flapping their wings and quacking. Rational empathy carries the risk of being tarred as a fellow traveller or *Versteher*. When emotions run high, the distinction between understanding the adversary and joining the adversary's camp often becomes frightfully thin. I am under no illusion that this book will escape such attacks.

Yet, it is possible to succeed. The goal, obviously, is not to argue that the strongmen are fundamentally correct about the nature of the world. The aim is to make a Gestalt switch, and to experience the world differently. Too little do we appreciate how unique our prism is, that there are different prisms to begin with. This is precisely why the strongmen seem mad to us, and we to them. We then try to make them see reason, and they us. We make reasonable observations: "Hey, ducks don't eat carrots, they have no teeth! Stop feeding them carrots please." And they respond, perfectly sensibly too: "Don't you know rabbits can't swim? You're drowning the poor animal!" We need to rise above such "You say duck, I say rabbit" encounters. We need the ability to switch our perspectives back and forth, the mental agility and moral freedom to describe the world in the language of rules *and* the language of power.

This book is written from the standpoint of such freedom. It takes issue with the view that rational empathy is moral surrender. Dick Cheney, vice president of the United States at the time, was once reported to have said: "We don't negotiate with evil; we defeat it."[4] The strongman, in the Cheney view of the world, need not be understood. He needs to be forcibly replaced, by freedom, truth and reason. Look at the chaos Trump leaves behind in the world. Look at the ramshackle petrostate Russia has become. What logic, what pattern, what Gestalt might one possibly hope to find in such madness and darkness?

Much is wrong with the strongmen. Much happens on instinct. That sophisticated political theories figure high in the thoughts of the strongmen stretches the imagination. But that is not to say that the language they use is devoid of rationality, structure or grammar. Without minimizing their crimes and their flaws, and certainly without joining their camp, the idea that the strongmen offer the world only madness looks increasingly mad itself. The strongman may be the enemy. He may have to be fought. But deluding ourselves about the language of power and strength he speaks, and its coherence and appeal, is arguably the greatest disservice we can do to the cause of freedom.

CHAPTER 1

Introduction: the allure of strength

We have tended to see European history, from the Renaissance onwards, as the history of progress, and that progress has seemed to be constant ... But when we look deeper, how much more complex the pattern seems! And beneath the surface of an ever more sophisticated society what dark passions and inflammable credulities do we find.

Hugh Trevor-Roper[1]

THE AGE OF THE ENCOUNTER

Donald Trump leaned back in his chair and demonstratively folded his arms before his chest. Fixing his glaring eyes on hers, he impatiently listened to her pitch. It wasn't the first time he had heard it, nor would it be the last.

He had rebuffed her petitions on countless occasions and was determined to continue to do so for as long as it would take. Yet this time, in the stately Manoir Richelieu in Charlevoix, Québec, things were different. They had used the summit to gang up on him, the gesticulating Emmanuel Macron, the softly pleading Theresa May, his boyish Canadian host Justin Trudeau and Japan's Shinzo Abe. Their aides swarmed around him like flies. They had set a diplomatic trap worthy of the great French Cardinal himself. And he had walked right into it.

Worn down by their persistence, Trump bitterly signalled his assent to the summit's final communiqué. He had heard enough. Slowly he rose from his chair. Then he stopped, reached into his suit pocket, and nonchalantly threw two Starburst candies on the table. "Here, Angela", he said. "Don't say I never give you anything."[2] He had never placed great stock in the art of losing.

Hustling his way back to the safety of Airforce One, Trump regained his poise. He weighed his options, and decided to rescind his agreement after the fact. "I have instructed our US Reps not to endorse the Communique", he tweeted, before launching another angry missive calling his host Trudeau "very weak and dishonest".[3] Not so bad for a day's work.

It was June 2018 and over a year into Trump's presidency. For the Europeans, the G7 summit was a fiasco. Since his election in November 2016, they had fought to keep Trump inside the global club of democracies, papering over the deep fissure that had opened up across the Atlantic. Tirelessly, they had sought to persuade him of the principles of the liberal, rules-based international order, itself the child of US engineering since the Second World War.

But in Québec those efforts had hit a dead end. What personal capital Merkel, Macron, May and the others still possessed with Trump amounted to the candies he had left scattered on the table. The president of the United States had made it painfully clear he preferred the company of the world's growing legion of illiberal, virile and authoritarian leaders: Russia's Vladimir Putin, China's Xi Jinping, Turkey's Recep Erdogan, North Korea's Kim Jong-un, Brazil's Bolsonaro, Israel's Netanyahu and the Philippines' Duterte. America's old allies he found irksome.

Trump had never made a secret of his desire to smash the rules-based international order that the Europeans treasured so deeply. He angrily sneered at anything that smacked of multilateralism. The European Union, a central cog in that order, became a frequent target of the president's disdain. US presidents always heartily encouraged Europe's economic and political integration. They believed a strong and united Europe would help reign in the Soviet Union. But Trump just as heartily encouraged the EU's dissolution. "The beating heart of the globalist project is in Brussels", Steve Bannon, chief ideologist of the 2016 Trump campaign, once elaborated his thinking. "If I drive the stake through the vampire, the whole thing will start to dissipate."[4]

Already before his election, Trump had fallen in with the Brexit crowd. That year, history seemed on his side. In an interview with Michael Gove – the journalist, politician and Brexit campaigner – Trump went on to describe Brexit as a "great thing".[5] "You look at the EU and it is Germany, basically a vehicle for Germany", Trump opined. "That's why I thought the UK was so smart in getting out … I believe others will leave." Of the so-called "adults in the room" there was no sign. The president-elect's coterie of advisors only stoked the argument with Europe. One confidante called on the markets to "short the euro".[6] Trump detested supranational organizations, he explained. "From the perspective of the US, it is often better to work bilaterally with the individual countries of the EU. Frankly, this often gives us the upper hand."[7]

It was the sort of high-octane power talk, brutally direct, that left Europe paralysed. Trump's America, like Putin's Russia, was going to be the wolf that picked off the sheep. "We love the countries of the European Union", Trump expanded on his thinking later. "But the European Union, of course, was set up to take advantage of the United States. And you know what, we can't let that happen."[8]

Devastatingly, Trump saw no greater reason to confide in German chancellor Angela Merkel, the *éminence grise* of Europe's liberal order, than in Russia's Putin, who openly resents its existence. "Well, I start off trusting both – but let's see how long that lasts. It may not last long at all."[9] In the future, Trump made clear, America's backing would have to be earned. It would have to be pitched for like a piece of squalid, transactional business, by Merkel as much as by Putin. The deeper historical and moral bonds with Europe, so carefully nurtured by US presidents since the end of the Second World War, Trump implacably refused to acknowledge. It was all done nonchalantly, in a way that only a strongman could. And as leader of the world's greatest economic and military power, he was the strongest of them all.

Trump's ascent to power blew apart the hypothesis that had underpinned Western political experience for 70 years: the idea that the world was on a journey to become just like us. Our liberal philosophy of freedom, law and order, we believed, would gradually spread across the globe. All nations would eventually embrace our politics, lifestyle and values. It was an article of deep progressive faith that gave us purpose and filled us with pride. There were parts of the world that were still resistant to our democratic ways. There had been Islamic insurgencies and terrorism. But communism had gone from Europe. China had begun to embrace economic freedom, surely a crucial first step to political liberalism.

The "arc of history", as Trump's predecessor Barack Obama adapted Reverend King's phrase, was bent towards liberal democracy, justice and enlightenment. The pull of Western institutions, superior in every regard, was an irresistible magnetic force to the still oppressed masses of the world. Sooner or later they would rise up and sweep alternative models of government before them. With that, the fate of dictators and authoritarian strongmen, who for so long had provided law and order on the planet, and who still did so in certain underdeveloped parts, would be sealed. Emperors and emirs, kings and khans, shahs and sultans, they were all political relics from the past, destined for history's trash heap. One by one they would fall and vanish forever. It was only a matter of time. And strategic patience.

Buoyed by the downfall of the Soviet Union in 1991, this progressivist philosophy of history was long indubitable in Western circles of influence, and most cogently expressed in Francis Fukuyama's 1992 *The End of History and the Last Man*, a fiendishly clever book, although maligned in intellectual circles. More importantly, the freedom doctrine was never only, or even predominantly, an academic theory. Much more, it was a social and political reality, a collective state of mind, a type of consciousness that pervaded and shaped the discourse of politics for generations. It was what Fukuyama's hero the philosopher Hegel generally referred to as *Geist*.

Not unlike *de fide* doctrine within the Catholic faith, it was a state of mind that could be questioned only at the price of apostasy and excommunication. Its compelling force cut right across the party-political spectrum, from left to right. Certified by a never-ending stream of learned books, think tank reports and editorial comment in the media – and canonized in popular fiction, cinema and television series – confidence in the West's philosophy of order became absolute. Foreign policy was aimed at spreading democracy and human rights to every corner of the planet, precipitating the birth of a liberal world. Europe developed its own brand of the doctrine, plotting its journey towards the integration of the continent. A new "functionalist" discourse would supplant nineteenth-century power politics. So began a new form of international order, one forged by bureaucrats and jurists facilitating economic collaboration, first in industrial sectors such as coal, steel, nuclear power and agriculture, later in the trade of other goods, and eventually in all areas of law and public policy.

Europe's new order was rules based, a community held together by shared standards, legal frameworks and the broader philosophy of liberalism. It allowed for a common market without borders governed by supranational institutions that ensured its regulations applied equally to all. The will-to-power of sovereign states was subjugated to higher reason and law.[10] Interstate conflict was turned into technical dispute, which could be resolved by judges and experts sighting evidence, facts and data. Churchill's United States of Europe was not to be, but the separateness of states was becoming less stark. Supply and distribution chains criss-crossed multiple borders. Citizens moved freely around the continent. They fell in love with and married foreigners. A slow, almost imperceptible thinning of national identities began.

Europe's new concept of international order would radiate outwards to parts of the world still mired in conflict and war. With a religious zeal, the EU promoted its multilateralism in areas such as trade, financial markets regulation and climate change. The *annus mirabilis* of 1989 and the fall of communism ushered in years of remarkable self-confidence, as Europe's rules-based order sped eastwards across Eurasia. "The era of confrontation and division of Europe has ended", the Paris Charter for a New Europe declared in 1990. A raft of former Eastern-bloc countries joined the EU in 2004. Dutifully, the Union's governmental philosophy was taught in academic institutes across the continent, most notably at the Collège in Bruges, the prep-school for EU officialdom. Eventually, world order would just be European order writ large.

For a good 20 years, while there were occasional setbacks, an alternate future remained unimaginable. But then, following a succession of crises, faith in the freedom doctrine began to ebb away. Following the banking crisis of 2008, people turned against the borderless world in which sovereignty appeared to have vaporized. They rebelled against global and EU institutions in far-flung foreign capitals, favouring recipes that promised to restore the power of the state and its territorial borders, as well as the political men and women who prescribed those recipes. The euro crisis of 2010–12 stirred additional anger among voters. Creditor nations in Europe's north felt on the hook for southern profligacy. Southern Europeans, in turn, concluded their freedoms had been sold out to bureaucrats and bankers in Brussels and Frankfurt. In 2015, a stream of refugees and migrants from Africa and the Middle East, on the run from war and poverty, left EU politicians scrambling for a response. In Germany, after her failed grand gesture to take in Syrian refugees, Merkel only barely survived elections in 2017. By contrast, Europe's own strongman, the Hungarian Viktor Orbán, flourished by advocating "illiberal democracy".

As it struggled to grapple with the crises it faced, the EU began to look like an ineffectual construct, its global standing further undercut by the 2016 Brexit referendum. Europe's model of order was contracting, while authoritarian political models felt emboldened. From Moscow to Manila and from Beijing to Brasilia, strongmen rulers seemed in the ascendency. Not only did they succeed in holding on to or claiming power; for the first time in a long time they were able to make normative claims for the illiberal politics they offered. The wind of history once again seemed to fill their sails. Liberalism was the assured future once, but the future now looked wide open.[11]

Western hopes for the spread of liberal democracy were still high in 2011, when Arab potentates faced a tide of popular uprisings. Sweet and seductive, the scent of revolution was hard to resist. But as things turned out, the Arab Spring paved the way not for freedom and the rule of law, but for civil war, chaos and rabid sectarianism, leading for calls for strongmen like Egypt's Abdel Fattah al-Sisi to restore peace and order.

Russia's integration into the Western-led order had once seemed inevitable. But its brazen incursion into Ukraine in 2014 conclusively ended those hopes. While reviled in the West, elsewhere in the world Putin became an iconic figure, the trailblazer of strongman politics. The term "Putinization" has become shorthand to describe trends in countries as diverse as Poland, Hungary, Turkey, the Balkans, Mexico, China, India, Israel and the United States itself. "Saudi Arabia is Putinizing, not Modernizing", one commentator declared following the rise of Crown Prince Mohammed bin Salman.[12] Xi Jinping's brand of politics is "Putinism with Chinese characteristics", another posited.[13]

Recep Erdogan, too, steered his country not closer to, but further away from Europe and its vision of order. When EU–Turkey accession talks finally began in 2005, Europe was in no hurry. It suffered from enlargement fatigue. But it still assumed the prospect of membership would help Turkey modernize and become more liberal. In reality, Erdogan set Turkey on a path similar to Russia's, towards a destiny of the nation's own making, an amalgamation of the secular Kemalist Republic and Ottoman ambitions. Erdogan's aim was not for Turkey to be submerged in Europe's rule-governed order of citizens, consumers and stakeholders; it was to become a sovereign agent itself, the leading power in the region it once dominated.

Further afield, China's rise entailed the economic decline of Europe and the United States in relative terms. But as its economy modernized, it was long assumed, so would its politics and values. Gradually China would open up and submit to the same rules and standards. Xi Jinping, however, hailed the superiority of Confucianist hierarchy and self-sacrifice over Western individualism. He began touting China's governance model around the world as more effective than Western-style democracy, investing billions in foreign infrastructure to back his rhetoric with action. He spoke warmly about multilateralism, but as the restorer of China's lost greatness he envisaged a very different kind of globalization, one that meant to displace the Western model.[14]

Far from being swept aside by the passing of time, it became clear that the new strongmen were bending history's arc in novel directions. Before the *annus horribilis* of 2016, the idea of the inexorable advance of liberal modernity still made some sense. But when the United States, the West's fulcrum, vanished into the vortex of strongman politics with Trump's election, the very idea of the West began to lose its moorings. Europe's crisis was worse than already anticipated, a million times worse. Leaders like Putin, Erdogan and even Xi might have been viewed as passing anomalies, not least because in an alliance with the United States they could be held at bay. With Trump this changed. The Leader of the Free World was now a strongman for whom the idea of leading the world meant "America First".

This new allure of strength became increasingly evident during the initial spread of the Covid-19 pandemic. To be sure, the virus was indiscriminate and pounded liberal democracies and strongman regimes alike. It laid bare the shortcomings of all types of politics, including the politics of the strongman. However, the deficiencies in Europe's model somehow seemed more severe and conspicuous.

The continent claimed to rely on science, reason and rational governance, and was confident it would comfortably defeat the disease. It believed it possessed all the tools necessary to keep the virus at bay: advanced healthcare systems, efficient administrative institutions, the smartest virologists and epidemiologists. Epidemics of this sort happened in faraway countries with shoddy sanitary standards. In the West, there were rules and regulations for this purpose.

At first, events seemed to corroborate this sentiment. At the epicentre of the outbreak were the wet markets of the Chinese city of Wuhan, where local party barons had first attempted to hush up the disease. It was a kneejerk response typical of authoritarian regimes, one that firmly put the onus on Xi. China had allowed the epidemic to balloon out of control, piercing the strongman myth. With its culture of transparency, a similar lapse of judgement seemed impossible in the democratic West, proving its superiority as a system of government.

Western political experts predicted Covid-19 would be China's "Chernobyl moment", the beginning of the end, as the nuclear disaster had been for the Soviet Union in 1986. But when, weeks later, the virus hit Europe with still greater venom, the tables turned in the strongman's favour. The continent's death toll shot up exponentially, and eventually surpassed China's. The early sense of vindication made way for disillusionment. The governance systems the Europeans had put their faith in were slow off the mark and poorly prepared for their task. The EU in particular stood powerless, as its member states closed their borders and pursued their own individual policies. Free movement, the cornerstone of European integration, became its Achilles heel. In Brussels, officials struggled to ensure that medical devices such as ventilators and face masks were made available where they were most needed. Political debates about pooling funds for aid and recovery turned into rows and recriminations, as they had done before.

What made things worse was Xi's apparent progress in containing the epidemic in China, using harsh lockdowns, intrusive monitoring tactics and draconian quarantines to "flatten the curve". After its calamitous start, China's authoritarian model had rapidly gained ground and now seemed more adept at keeping people safe. In the battle of political ideas, it was winning, a perception Xi further bolstered by sending medical kit and masks to Europe and the Western world as a humanitarian gesture.

Not all strongmen acted as vigorously as Xi. Trump's initial response to the pandemic was to laugh off the virus as a hoax, an attitude Brazilian strongman Jair Bolsonaro and Alexander Lukashenko, the longstanding ruler of Belarus, stubbornly persisted in. However, in the light of the EU's impotence, claims that its rules-based philosophy of government remained a beacon to the world looked preposterous. This was a time for action, not for rules. The politics of strength seemed better adapted to the world of Covid-19, in which state borders assumed their old significance, international institutions like the EU and the World Health Organization proved toothless, individual and economic liberties were curtailed, and governments ruled through decrees and emergency powers. As Trump boasted about his presidential powers in the context of the pandemic: "the authority is total, and that's the way it's got to be".[15] In the words of his democratic challenger Joe Biden, the president contended he was "King of America".[16]

WHO IS THE STRONGMAN?

The age of the "end of history" doctrine is over. Europe faces a new and less predictable era, one that has been described as "after Europe".[17] It no longer represents the unopposed universal model towards which the world should develop. No longer can we assume the world will converge in the direction of a single and common end state, a global consensus on the superiority of liberal society and its values. Instead, we face an age of political rivalry and uncertainty, a never-ending encounter between self and other, friend and foe, that still feels new and unfamiliar.

If the idea of world history as the rational evolution towards liberalism is associated with the philosopher Hegel, the age of the encounter might be said to belong to the German thinker Carl Schmitt (1888–1985), who in *The Concept of the Political* (1932) maintained that the future will forever be contested.[18] The only permanent and certain feature of history, Schmitt claimed, is the encounter, the confrontation with "the other", "the stranger" or "the enemy". The partition of the world into friend and foe can take various shapes – ideological, economic, civilizational – but whatever its form, the basic distinction between an "us" and a "them" is engrained in our species. Whenever men declare a universal age of friendship, Schmitt found, these declarations merely turn out to deny the enemy is human or his interests objectively real.

The age of the encounter makes us view global politics in a different light. It forces us to reappraise how we deal with those who are "not us", not Europe or the West. We need not give up our liberal beliefs and values, but we do need to recognize that these may never be shared universally. We need to accept that other futures are possible, and perhaps even more likely to materialize. And to cope with this new uncertainty, alternative languages of political order need to be explored. Old habits of lecturing the world in the language of rules and values increasingly provoke fury and resentment. More importantly, those lectures are being ignored.

No longer can we be precious about who we do business with. Surrounded by a legion of strongmen at the inaugural EU–Arab League Summit in Sharm el-Sheikh in February 2019, European Commission President Jean-Claude Juncker was asked: "Mr Juncker, don't you feel bad meeting so many dictators?" Retaining his cool as ever, he answered: "Yes, I do. But if I'd only talk to flawless democrats, my weeks would be over by Tuesday."[19] World politics, Juncker recognized, does not stop without us. Or as another European leader put it: "Sometimes you have to dance with whoever's on the dance floor. We don't always have a choice."[20]

Our assumption that the strongmen were "on the wrong side of history" and preordained to disappear like the dinosaurs has been proven wrong. If we continue to act on the notion that history has a right and a wrong side, while the "wrong" side is outgrowing us in strength, *we* will be the dinosaurs. It is tempting for Western liberals to wallow in the farce that is "Trumpocracy", to find self-validation in the oafish, boastful and clownish Donald Trump.[21] Casting our encounter with the strongmen as a battle between Good and Evil, Truth and Falsehood, Light and Darkness invigorates our sense of moral clarity. But does it restore our political agency, our power to change things? Calling Trump, Putin or Orbán evil is about as practically useful as an exorcism. Priests performing cleansing rituals to make the world "snap out of it" offer no respite.

What does help is to better understand the politics of strength. If the new pivot of history is the encounter with "the other", as Schmitt argued, then who precisely is the other? Who are these so-called strongmen, how is their type of politics construed and what forms the basis of their legitimacy? What is their philosophy of international order? And no less important: what actually happens in our encounter with the strongmen and how does it shape high-level diplomacy? Why does this diplomacy frequently lead to deadlock and are there ways to avoid this? Perhaps most critically, how is the encounter affecting Europe's own outlook on questions of world order? Indeed, how does it change our view of who we are ourselves?

It is to these questions that this book seeks answers, and it does so by proceeding from three assumptions. First, that the concept of "the strongman" or "strength" coherently groups together the political practices of a range of individual leaders who, while unique in many ways, share a common outlook on political order. Second, that these strongmen are gaining in importance in the world and that, even if their rise is not linear, they currently form essential interlocutors in global affairs. And third, that the type of politics they represent remains poorly understood and its effectiveness and attractions underappreciated.

The success of nativist and populist movements in Europe and the world, and that of Trump in particular, has already led to a burgeoning literature on the crisis of liberal democracy. Haunted by the memory of 1930s Europe, this literature takes the rise of the strongmen deeply seriously. It includes books with evocative titles such as *How Democracies Die*, *The Road to Unfreedom* and *Why Our Freedom is in Danger and How to Save it*.[22] As these titles betray, the dominant approach is prescriptive and intended as a political battle cry. It tends to treat liberal democracy as the universal standard of politics. By contrast, it describes the strongmen as a purely destructive and corrosive force to be thwarted, a gangrenous disease to be expunged from the body politic.

This book tries a different approach. It starts from the thought that, historically, the strongman may have the better claim on providing the standard model of political order, while rules-based democracy merely forms a recent digression from that standard. Given that liberal democracy took root scarcely 200 years ago, and in a few select places in the world only, this claim is not by definition implausible. The type of politics offered by the strongmen (and they are nearly always men) possesses significant pedigree. While only a fraction of humanity has lived in liberal democracies, strongmen and similar authoritarian rulers there have always been, ensuring protection, order and justice long before we could even imagine liberal institutions.

Obviously, this does not make the strongman the more cogent model of politics. However, the fact that again and again people have turned to strongmen does suggest the model possesses a baseline legitimacy and serves a public need. My broader point is that too often we fail to recognize and engage with the case the politics of strength makes for itself, its allure and promise. Instead we tick off a list of symptoms and then look for ways to eradicate the strongman disease, taking for granted that strength is in fact an illness, not a remedy against political ailments itself, as the strongmen and their followers argue.

The surest way to stifle an open-minded analysis is to equate the strongman to Adolf Hitler and Benito Mussolini and the ideology of fascism of the 1920s and 1930s. In her book *Fascism: A Warning*, Madeleine Albright, Bill Clinton's secretary of state between 1997 and 2001, uses precisely this strategy. She writes: "If we think of fascism as a wound of the past that had almost healed, putting Trump in the White House was like ripping off the bandage and picking at the scab."[23]

Yet the idea of strongman rule predates these totalitarian ideologies, and in important ways it runs counter to them. While fascism certainly centralizes power in the hands of one man and places that man above the law, the allure of the strength stems from a different and I argue more primitive source, notably the basic need to provide structure to chaos. The strongman proffers no millennial programme for the total transformation of society into a historical end state of racial or other forms of moral purity. Autocratic and illiberal he may be, but the strongman lives in an embattled, chaotic and post-ideological present, not an idealized future. He promises to use strength and power for secular goals, for the survival of the political community as an end in itself.

Fascism, of course, did once exist, and presumably it could exist again. But if it does, it will not be in the guise of the strongman. It is entirely possible for a particular strongman to flirt with and turn to fascist ideology. But if he does, he will no longer be a strongman; he will be a fascist. While politically it may be expedient to conflate both, conceptually they form different kinds of illiberalism. One form is committed to radical and utopian alternatives to the present; the other stands for a return to order and prosperity in times of turmoil. We may reject either, of course. But it is important to be clear-eyed about what form of illiberalism we face. Sweeping claims that history is no more than a tussle between democracy and fascism lose sight of what makes men such as Putin, Erdogan, Xi and Trump different from Hitler and Mussolini.

That is not to say that the strongman is an entirely new phenomenon. But partly because we tend to fixate on fascism and partly because we long assumed the strongman would simply die out, theoretical concepts we can use to explain who the strongman is are few and far between. Historically, there have been plenty of regimes and dictatorships that could be described as broadly authoritarian and post-ideological, and they can help us understand the strongman politics of our times. Think of the "colonels' regime" that governed Greece from 1967 to 1974, the junta that ruled Argentina between 1976 and 1983, or the *Caudillismo* of hardmen such as Spain's Francisco Franco, Chile's Augusto Pinochet and Cuba's Fidel Castro. Many of these regimes and leaders share features that we can recognize in today's strongmen. However, the latter possess additional attributes that, I believe, mark them out still more clearly.

Scholars of authoritarian politics traditionally distinguish at least three types of dictatorship and authoritarianism.[24] To begin with there are military dictatorships, which grab power by the classical means of a coup d'état and rely on armed force and curfews. Second, there are traditional monarchies, such as the Gulf states of Qatar and Saudi Arabia, which rely on ancestral ties and precedent for their legitimacy. Third, there are authoritarian regimes based on the monopoly of a political party, frequently communist, such as China.

One characteristic feature that sets the strongman apart from these three types of dictatorship is the personalist nature of his power. In one-party regimes, power remains collegial to an extent. Power belongs to the party, not the man. It must be shared with party bosses and is constrained by party rules and procedures. Military dictatorship, in turn, is embedded in the hierarchy and norms of the army, while absolute monarchies, of which there are only a few left, are based on ties of family and custom. In strongman regimes, by contrast, constraints tend to dissipate to a greater degree. Power is concentrated no longer in a party cadre, for example, but in the hands of a single leader who dominates the party and its elite.

Personalist dictatorship, argues political scientist Erica Frantz, forms a fourth type of authoritarian rule, a type that has been on the rise in the world and that remains poorly understood.[25] The collapse of communism has meant the one-party model declined, while in China power now revolves mostly around Xi. Military coups, and the general's regimes they give rise to, have equally become less frequent. While the strongmen may have roots in the military, they tend to be civilians and grow their power by political means, not by means of armed force.

This brings us to the most important and at the same time most puzzling feature of the strongman model: the hybrid nature of its power or agency. As we will see later on, the means and methods the strongman uses to govern are non-institutional. However, rather than declaring the institutions and laws of the state void and claim absolute power, the strongman side-steps these constraints, opting to create parallel structures of government. Outwardly, the strongman always takes good care to uphold the form and appearance of the law, effusively affirming the state's institutional integrity: the "dictatorship of law", as Putin once called it. But in reality, for better or for worse, the strongman relies on extra-institutional and discretionary power to get things done.

Typically, there is never a sudden, violent or advertised rupture with the formal state of law, a single moment at which the constitution is "suspended", the *ancien régime* officially restored. Rather, there is the creeping use of informal and hidden power, of personal strength wrapped in official state processes that are themselves of diminished political significance. This concealed use of informal power turns the strongman into an elusive creature that is hard to pin down. Formally, there is no detectable (let alone binary) difference between the strongman and the leader of a liberal state. There is nothing in the constitutions of Russia or Hungary, for example, that makes Putin or Orbán strongmen. On paper, their job descriptions are similar to those of democratic leaders, not to absolutist kings. They have similar legal powers and similar institutional obligations. They stand in elections, and answer to courts and parliaments.

What, then, turns these leaders into strongmen? The answer is that, while the strongmen have institutions, the practical value and effectiveness of these institutions is limited. The power of the strongman, his strength, essentially emerges outside the framework of law. To be sure, rules exist that formally mandate the strongman to take certain decisions, but his power is not exclusively, or even fundamentally, dependent on such rules. Therefore, it is also less easily constrained by them.

POWER AND THE FRAGILITY OF INSTITUTIONS

If we want to understand the strongman, we need to understand the idea of political agency he embodies, the idea of strength or sovereign power. We need to understand what governing through strength means, what it looks and feels like, as well as why it holds appeal. Part I of this book is devoted to this task. Sovereign power or strength, as I use these terms here, is neither constituted nor constrained by laws and institutions. It is a form of agency that emerges directly and organically from acting and deal making, as well as from communication and representation.

The need for such power, and therefore the allure of the strength, invariably follows from the threat of chaos, from the observation that historical conditions pertain in which the modern state based on laws, institutions and rules cannot guarantee order or stability, conditions Carl Schmitt referred to as "the state of exception" or the state of emergency.[26] When institutional power falls short or breaks down, other forms of agency and power are required, more specifically, of course, sovereign power and strength.

The concepts of law and power are theoretically joined at the hip, part of the Schmittian argument goes. The state can never consist entirely of rules and law. It also comprises constitutive interventions of a sovereign, moments and actions that are purely "political", a decision, an act of creation or improvisation that enables rules-based order to emerge or to survive. In Schmitt's own words, law and power are "secularized theological concepts". Just as the natural universe is governed by rules, viz. the laws of physics, the state is governed by man-made rules, by law. But the reality of law presupposes there exists some secular power that can make law, an act of pure strength that necessarily precedes the law, just as God, according to theologians, precedes the laws of physics. Sovereign power, in other words, cannot be entirely banished. And while it can be used to destroy rules-based order, it is also needed to ensure its continuity.

Accustomed to life in institutionalized and well-functioning states, it may be hard to see why such claims should be true. For many Westerners, rules-based power has become the natural state of the world. Institutions are the fabric of our society, so much so we are sometimes hardly aware of them. From the powers of the prime minster and the queen to those of the traffic warden and tax inspector, our entire order is seamlessly grounded in institutional rules that meticulously assign authority and power to offices and state bodies.[27] This, for example, is how we pass prison sentences, adopt laws, print currency and grant citizenship. What we call politics, on this view, is merely an interplay among an endless series of institutionally created facts: presidential elections, parliamentary motions, executive directives, injunctions, government departments, rights and rulings. And these institutional facts, we assume, are exhaustive of what the modern state is: a finely calibrated and fully automated clockwork that, if all is well, keeps ticking interminably.

Equally self-evident is that institutions help states thrive.[28] States with strong institutions tend to do better than those without. Institutional power permeates the state with legitimacy, efficacy and continuity. It gives the state a visible, nearly tangible presence. It is not because an iron-fisted dictator personally intervenes that the trains depart on time, or that property rights are upheld, allowing the economy to flourish. All this happens because the entire machinery of law and government provides for order independent of a leader's intervention. Nothing delivers stability, justice and prosperity like strong, predictable institutions.

However, while this confidence in institutions may be justified in some states, elsewhere institutional power often fails to live up to its promise. This is not, I believe, because rules-based power is a modern Western invention that loses its beneficial effects when exported to foreign settings. Rather, it is because institutions are brittle and breakable by their very nature and unusually hard to fashion. In many parts of the world, institutional power has never properly established itself in the first place. Rules-based government remains frail and ineffective in those places, and there are no quick fixes. Instead of a rare occurrence, for much of the world the state of exception is an everyday reality.

Following the 9/11 attacks, this deficiency was widely recognized in Western policy circles. So-called "failed states" like Afghanistan, lacking strong institutions of government, were viewed as breeding grounds for international terrorism and organized crime, as well as regional instability, poverty and war. Other labels – "fragile states", "weak states", "quasi-states" – were used to indicate the degrees to which states could fail. The worst, like Libya, Somalia and Yemen today, were unable to even secure their borders or raise taxes. Others struggled to provide important public services and utilities: roads, courts, education, justice and healthcare. Irrespective of these gradations, the notion of state failure went hand in hand with a eulogy to institutional power, viewed as a cure-all panacea. The only thing that was needed was to build governmental institutions for the states that had so far lacked them.[29]

But while strong institutions are undoubtedly desirable, the problem we run into is that institutions cannot easily be "made", that is to say, mass-produced and exported across the world. As recent experiences with state building underscore in Iraq, blueprints and roadmaps for how to build modern states – for "getting to Denmark", as Francis Fukuyama puts it – do not exist.[30] Looking back at nearly two decades of Western efforts to strengthen state institutions in Afghanistan, three-star US army general Douglas Lute, having been directly involved in the attempt, reaches a crushing verdict: "We didn't have the foggiest notion of what we were doing."[31] Institutional government and the rule of law may be the solution, but it is a solution that proves tragically hard to come by. We cannot just "will" institutions into being.

The paucity and fragility of rules-based order leads to a number of hard questions, which we only rarely address. One such question is: if building institutional order is hard and takes a long time, what do we do in the interim? One can argue that periods of chaos, conflict and even violent destruction are inevitable for institutional order to fully develop, and that such processes of historical change may just have to run their course.[32] But that is hardly a satisfactory answer for those who need a functioning government right now, who need security, jobs and good roads and healthcare.

So, what alternative ways of providing for order are there? And who or what is going to deliver it? We also know that where institutions do eventually emerge they are subject to wear and tear, to decay and corruption. They require regular maintenance and every so often a fundamental reboot. However, institutions often prove resistant to reform. Vested interests accumulate at their core and frustrate necessary renewal, a phenomenon known as state capture. Who or what can sweep aside such conservatism? Who can restore institutions to their original purpose?

Finally, because of its deliberative nature, rules-based government may not always be best suited for coping with great shocks, crises and "events", with war, unrest, economic or natural disasters, or indeed epidemics. Rules-based power excels in the day-to-day regulation of civil life, in impartially adjudicating conflict between parties, in making and enforcing laws in predictable and automated ways. Institutions are needed for regulating businesses and markets fairly, for setting interest rates and for overseeing the state's finances. But what if events and crises demand a swift, improvised and decisive response, in other words, a certain concentration of executive power?

In short, the politics of strength emerges because institutions are not always available and because like all types of government, institutional government is prone to failure. We therefore need a contingency plan, and the strongman is that plan. His type of politics comes into its own in the areas where the clockwork state of law struggles to reach. His allure is that when the clockwork stops ticking, the intervention of a clockmaker, as theologians might be tempted to put it, offers the only way to get things going again, the only way to govern and for the state to possess political agency at all.

GUISES OF STRENGTH

How, then, does the strongman govern in the absence of rules and institutions? How does he acquire agency, the ability to act? The simplest answer is that strength equals physical force and that the strongman imposes order on unwilling subjects with the help of police batons and organized violence. "Power grows out of the barrel of a gun", Mao Zedong once said. This still tends to be a popular image of strongman politics, and coercing obedience certainly forms part of how strongmen govern. But then all states rely on coercion at times, including liberal democracies based on law. In such states the use of violence is institutionalized and sanctioned by law, as opposed to in strongman regimes, where it is employed without formal constraints. However, coercion as such is not really what makes strongman politics distinctive.

Coercive force fails to capture what is arguably the most important and interesting aspect of strength or power, which is the ability to act and get things done *as a group*. Power only truly springs up, Hannah Arendt correctly pointed out, where people act and speak together, where they act not as individuals but as a team, and ultimately as a state or a political community.[33] Strength, understood this way, is knowing how to marshal the agency of a community, the ability to act in its name by drawing purely on personal skills, networks and authority, without relying on any pre-existing institutional rules that grant representational authority and legitimacy to politicians. Rather than the barrel of a gun, this is what sovereign power is.

Conceived as such, strength can have many guises. Part I of this book, "The strongman", sketches what I consider to be the four most important of these. The profiles or "mugshots" that result from this analysis depict the strongman from different angles. Combined they offer a new and vivid image of what the politics of strength involves, and a theoretical basis for examining who the strongmen are and why they act as they do, both at home and in the world.

The first guise in which the strongman appears is that of the "Saviour", the man or woman who tames "events" through relentless action, who knows how to subjugate what Niccolò Machiavelli in *The Prince* calls "fortuna", the fickle nature of history and events. The forward flow of time, Machiavelli knew, is fast and unforgiving. States are fragile, never far from the abyss, and they need the dark talents of his protagonist to pull themselves back from the edge. In this guise, the strongman, like Machiavelli's Renaissance Prince, acts first and asks questions later. He does what is necessary, ruthlessly if needed. The Saviour is under no obligation to be moral, although he is sworn to protect the interests of the state.

In his second guise the strongman appears as "Lord", the feudal master of a vast system of personal ties and loyalties employed to govern the country on a day-to-day basis, to get things done even if the institutions of central government are so poorly managed or badly infected by corruption that the state has almost ground to a halt. Strongman rule relies on what I call a "silent" contract. Much like the medieval bonds of vassalage, this contract replaces a faltering institutional order with informal systems based on loyalty and fealty.

Under its terms, personal lieutenants – relatives, friends, old allies – receive powers and resources directly from the strongman. In return they swear an oath of allegiance, meaning they can be called on to work for the strongman, an oath that when broken might lead to retribution, imprisonment and violent death.

In his third guise, the strongman is the "Performer", obsessed with the *mise en scène* of his power as much as its secret machinations. Faltering institutions leave gaps of legitimacy, and these gaps need to be filled with a popular brand of authority based on qualities attributed to him as a person. It follows that power and authority need to be projected and enacted on stage, before an audience that must always be captivated by the performance. The first order of business for any strongman is to ensure he is visible and seen to be calling the shots. There must be no doubt about who is the strongest, who protects the people's interests, who commands the troops. Playing at being a monster does not suffice. As we shall see, a strongman needs to enact different roles to keep his audience spellbound.

In his final appearance, in the international arena, the strongman is the "Duellist". The inadequacies of the institutional order have long been evident in relations among states. While not rejecting international institutions per se, for the strongmen diplomacy is fundamentally a duel, a man-to-man contest of strength and guile. Since each puts the interests of his own state first, relationships among the strongmen are inherently competitive and political. Yet because they are all duellists, a common identity still exists among them, as does an informal ethos that prescribes how their competition is to be conducted. This *code duello* forms the basis of a fellowship of strongmen, a "club of rivals". It allows them to lock horns, while at the same time regard each other as just and honourable.

To avoid any confusion, the idea behind these different guises of strength is not to squeeze individual strongmen into a new typology and then compare these types when measured against a set of other variables, such as their longevity or success. The purpose of distinguishing these masks of power is merely to tease out what I believe to be important strands of the politics of strength, to unveil its essential "grammar". Consequently, these guises are not mutually exclusive. Even though some masks fit some strongmen better than others, the strongmen discussed in this book fit them all. Nor do I advance the claim that the four mugshots outlined here exhaust what may be said of the politics of strength, theoretically or otherwise. What I do hope emerges is a new and rewarding understanding of who the strongman is.

INTO THE DEEP END

This account of the politics of strength further provides fresh insights into what our own encounter with the strongmen involves, namely a clash between distinctive and in many ways conflicting political discourses and prisms. In the encounter we do not merely confront foreign leaders advancing different national interests; we confront sovereign power in its various guises, a different grammar of political order. We meet the Saviour, who is liberated from universal moral norms. We encounter the Lord, who pursues his foreign policy goals by relying on the same principles of tribute by which he governs at home. We meet the Performer, who projects power for a domestic audience and lashes out when "foreign" actors suddenly enter his stage. Above all, we encounter the Duellist, who craves respect and recognition from his opponents, and who turns the encounter into a brawl when scorned.

Part II of the book, "Encounters", recounts the story of these clashes. It shows how international events and episodes that involve Europe and the strongmen, as well as their behaviours and strategies, begin to fall into place when interpreted as a "metagame", as collisions between what I call "the language of rules" on the one hand and "the language of power" on the other.

Narrated in four distinct episodes and chapters, it is a story that involves misunderstandings, intrigue, as well as well-intended diplomacy going astray. It explains how Vladimir Putin, Russia's indefatigable conqueror of crises and events, and the West become embroiled in a conflict over the destiny of Ukraine, a conflict that begins with the birth of a new European *Ostpolitik* in 2008, that descends into war in 2014 and that finally mutates into Putin's attempt to destabilize the *mise en scène* of power of his rivals in the West. It is a story of deception and political trickery, and of indignation and fury, as Europe and Recep Erdogan, Turkey's irrepressible Boss of the Bosphorus, wrestle with questions of self and other, friendship and enmity; in other words, with drawing spatial and political borders around who they are. It is the story of China's strongman Xi, who strides westwards across Eurasia and Africa, converting China's growing wealth into a new global order built on feudal power with Beijing as its centre. Finally, it sets out how Donald Trump bruises Europe into accepting, reluctantly, the codes of the duel as the new basis of transatlantic diplomacy.

If the strongman forms one side of the encounter, there remains one last question. Who is on the other? Who is this "we"? The short answer is all those who remain committed to the rules-based international order and its liberal values. For the purposes of this book, I mostly use the name "Europe" rather than "the West", which for most of us includes the United States, but certainly not only in the narrow sense of the European Union, and even less so of Brussels and the EU institutions. The EU is clearly a core part of what I call Europe. It remains the indubitable pioneer of the rules-based order, its "beating heart", as Steve Bannon calls it. But still, it is only a part, the other part formed by a looser gathering of states, also a club or fellowship of sorts, bound by what is commonly called a shared destiny, by shared liberal principles and goals.

This club of states is physically and historically centred around the European continent. But it does not coincide with the members of the EU or even European countries. The UK, in spite of leaving the EU, is likely to remain part of this club of states. So are countries such as Canada, Australia, New Zealand, Norway and Japan, which are interested in upholding the rules-based order. By contrast, whether Orbán's Hungary still belongs to this club is debatable. When I speak of Europe in the broadest sense of the word I refer to an idea and those who politically back it; a wide-ranging alliance of multilateralists that in this book is personified by its leading politicians: Angela Merkel, Emmanuel Macron, Theresa May, David Cameron, Jean-Claude Juncker and many others.

Does the US not belong to this alliance? As long as Donald Trump resides in the White House this question should, I believe, not arise. For the purposes of this book, in any event, it belongs to the club of strongmen. What if Trump is not re-elected in November 2020? A Democratic administration would be likely to attempt a reset of America's relationship with Europe. However, the idea that with Trump gone the gulf that has opened between Europe and the US would again close itself is far from evident. To be sure, the ferocity with which Trump has sought to smash European multilateralism, to drive a stake through the vampire, will not be easily matched. But it needs to be recognized that not just personal but also structural forces are moving the US and Europe in different directions. America's readiness to prop up the multilateral order with its sovereign power has been declining for some time, and that willingness is not likely to suddenly become much greater again.

Trump or no Trump, the need for Europe to test and upgrade its own political and diplomatic strategies in the age of the encounter is not going to dissipate, and the strongmen form a catalyst for that renewal. The story of the encounter is as much the story of Europe being thrown into the deep end and learning to stay afloat. Bereft of the help of the United States and without safety lines, the continent is forced to confront the maelstrom of events on its own. It forms a test of strength, a "Machiavellian moment", that challenges its political morality to the core. Having previously staked its future on rules,

Europe must now learn to decide, act and "improvise" like a sovereign power itself.[34]

In the encounter with the strongman we see Europe's leaders trying to do precisely that. We see Merkel trying out new and controversial diplomatic tactics with Putin, while we follow Macron's efforts to dazzle and confound Donald Trump with handshakes so masculine and bruising they leave Trump's hand dangling bloodless and limp next to his body. We see Europe's leaders strike dubious power deals with Recep Erdogan and discard principles and dogmas that for decades have formed the core of Europe's language of rules. Finally, we see Europe cobble together a new and political language of rivalry designed to keep Xi's feudal power sufficiently at bay, while also protecting its economic and trade relations with China.

The success of these improvisations may still be erratic. But the direction of this evolution is nevertheless clear. Europe, too, is beginning to discern the allure of strength and power. It is a change that forms a profound departure from its established philosophy of world order. "In a world of carnivores", as former German foreign minister, Sigmar Gabriel, sums up the challenge, "vegetarians have a tough time."[35] To survive at all, he implies, Europe has to become a little carnivorous as well. The multilateral rules and institutions that were once the future are revealing gaps, and those gaps are only becoming bigger. No longer are they plugged for us by someone else. And when rules no longer protect us against rogues, only one thing can: power.

PART I

The strongman

CHAPTER 2

Saviour: in the clutches of time

Fortune ... submits more readily to boldness than to cold calculation. Therefore, like a woman, she always favours young men because they are not so much inclined to caution as to aggressiveness and daring in mastering her.

Niccolò Machiavelli, *The Prince* (1513)

PRINCES AND MOMENTS

When asked by *GQ* magazine which world leader he esteemed most, Nigel Farage answered, "As an operator, but not as a human being, I would say Putin. The way he played the whole Syria thing. Brilliant. Not that I approve of him politically. How many journalists in jail now?"[1] It was March 2014, around the same time that infamous "little green men", in reality Russian soldiers, were beginning to pop up in Crimea. But it did not stop Farage from gushing in praise.

Some two years later, months before he was elected, Donald Trump spoke about Russia's strongman in similar terms.

I've already said, he is really very much of a leader. I mean, you can say, "Oh, isn't that a terrible thing – the man has very strong control over a country." Now, it's a very different system, and I don't happen to like the system. But certainly, in that system, he's been a leader, far more than our president has been a leader.[2]

Later, in response to a question in a televized interviewed about whether Putin ought not to be labelled "a killer", Trump calmly pointed out: "There are a lot of killers. You think our country's so innocent?"[3]

The comments were met with disbelief. Had Putin not just invaded and annexed Crimea? Squashed political freedoms in Russia? Beaten up and assassinated journalists, homosexuals and opposition leaders? Trump's political opponents jumped on the opportunity. Hillary Clinton compared Putin's actions in Crimea to Hitler's in Czechoslovakia. Others followed: Wolfgang Schäuble, the German finance minister, Stephen Harper, prime minister of Canada, US Senators Lindsey Graham and John McCain, Lithuanian President Dalia Grybauskaite. Even Prince Charles had arrived at the conclusion that "Putin is doing just about the same as Hitler".[4] One would have thought the merest hint of an association with Putin, that "thug and murderer", in Senator McCain's words, was an electoral death sentence. Yet here were two political leaders flirting with Putinismo!

As the world was soon to find out, their flirtations with Russia's strongman did not harm their political ambitions one iota. Both men, it turned out, had described an alternate type of admiration for Putin, difficult to capture within our normal discourse of politics. No one, of course, admired Putin because he was a moral man. They valued him for other qualities, those he possessed as "a leader" and "an operative". It was a strong and powerful sentiment. So strong, even, that it made good sense to align oneself with it, as Marine Le Pen later did by visiting the former KGB man before the French presidential elections in 2017. What sense of admiration were they tapping into precisely? By virtue of what reasoning could the tyrant be respected at all?

In order to answer that question, there could be worse places to start than with Niccolò Machiavelli (1469–1527), the Florentine *consigliere* and famed author of *The Prince*, and with what Renaissance scholar J. G. A. Pocock called the "Machiavellian moment".[5] For it is in the cold-blooded yet dashingly magnificent figure of the Prince that the strongman's divorce from political normality is articulated at its clearest, and certainly with greater rigour than in much of the contemporary analysis of strongman behaviour. It is here that we find the first modern attempt to theorize who or what the strongman is, to understand, also, the great pull strength still has over us today.

The Machiavellian moment refers to an epoch in early modern political thinking in which the separation of politics from morality became intellectually defensible. Rulers had always transgressed the boundaries of morality, even by the standards of their time. But theoretically the virtues that lay beyond those boundaries, beyond morality, had not been chartered on their own terms. The shift in outlook began with the reaffirmation of secular political order, the state, as an end in itself. But at the same time, the state was viewed as fragile, as permanently caught "in a stream of irrational and unpredictable events conceived as essentially destructive of all systems of secular stability".[6] The future was inherently uncertain, while order was ceaselessly tested by history and prone to all sorts of crises. It meant that the state needed to be propped up by political ingenuity, courage and skill, beyond the bounds of morality if needed.

This represented a break with the medieval-Christian experience of politics and history as the battle between the Light and Darkness. History had been construed as a "theatre of redemption", as a journey towards human salvation at a prophesied end-time.[7] Politics was merely an opportunity to prove one's worth to God, an occasion to prove the moral purity of one's eternal soul.

But not so for Machiavelli and his contemporaries, such as the writer and statesman Francesco Guicciardini (1483–1540), who began framing the turbulent politics of their day in terms of contingency and the interests of the state alone. If, as historian Jacques Le Goff has argued, the twelfth-century invention of Purgatory carved out the moral latitude for bankers to ply their blasphemous trade and thus gave birth to capitalism, Machiavelli reinvented history as a torrent of random, meaningless events, opening up the moral space for the strongman to conduct his lawless brand of politics.[8] The Florentine perceived order as wrought without a plan, forever at the whim of "events" and upheld by human agency alone, by the business of politics. There would be no Last Judgement, no final moment when the virtuous received their reward and the wicked their punishment.

Grappling with these issues, Machiavelli introduces the concept of *fortuna*, an irrepressible force that might catapult states to the heights of success, but also condemn them to oblivion. As a philosophy of history, it felt plausible enough. Italy seemed trapped in a cycle of rivalry among independent city states and principalities. But if human happiness was entangled with the fortunes of inherently fragile states, what could be done to ensure the state's survival? Could anything be done? Machiavelli compares history to a raging river, a force of nature that can destroy everything before it, but that can also be constrained by dams and canals. According to Machiavelli, for states there are three means to contain the force of events: long-established institutions of government, the moral fortitude of the people, and if neither of these are present, the political virtuosity (*virtù*) of an exceptional leader. Strength, in other words.

27

ACTION EQUALS VIRTUE

Enter the heroic figure of the Prince, or the strongman, a brute force of nature himself. Machiavelli's great protagonist is not to be confused with a ruler whose power is safely cradled in tradition and custom or who derives legitimacy from God. The lone figure of the Prince operates in an atomistic world void of divine or traditional legitimacy, bereft of institutional anchors. In his world religion and bloodlines have lost all meaning. The strongman is a "political innovator", who through intrepid dynamism and action forces historical contingency into some shape or order, who dictates the pace of events even in the most challenging of circumstances.[9]

The ideal type of strongman is that of the founder, a mythical figure who creates a state where nothing existed before, and who depends on his *virtù* or strength alone. Machiavelli cites Moses and Romulus, Rome's first ruler, as examples. In real life, of course, the strongman is always ensnared in pre-existing structures, or their remnants. He emerges as the figure who oversees the root-and-branch transformation of a faltering state, who refounds the state. He is the state's saviour, who at times of great danger secures its future. By sheer necessity, however, the lone strongman operates at the outer edge of conventional moral and constitutional order.

This balancing act on the edge of convention is what makes the Prince such an ambivalent figure, as strongmen such as Putin are today. There is a disturbing sense in which this dynamic creature might deliberately set out to destroy the institutions of the state with the sole purpose of monopolizing power for his own gain, something that would turn the Prince into a tyrant. This is precisely the accusation that our own strongmen face, and often correctly. They manufacture or invent crises only to dismantle democratic and liberal institutions. Turkey's Erdogan, his critics argue, exaggerates the threat of terrorism to purge the opposition. In Hungary, Viktor Orbán whips up fears over Muslim immigration and foreign conspiracies to cement his illiberal stranglehold on power.

But it does not have to be like this. Machiavelli offers a different and more tantalizing perspective, in which the strongman emerges as the necessary, if not deeply estimable, figure who stands between us and destruction. His strongman is the purveyor and guarantor of stability and common achievement. He is the architect, reformer and above all the saviour of states and institutions, who unfazed by danger imposes political order on the terrible forces of chaos. It is a feat that requires unique political skill and judgement. The Prince must do what is necessary, without regard for the truth, life and morality. Effectively, in describing the virtues his strongman needs, what we get in *The Prince* is an entirely new political ethos based on the need "to act", on strength, strategy and reasons of state as opposed to rules and principles.

Like the Farage–Trump position on Putin, Machiavelli's analysis of the strongman is deliberately equivocal. Prime among the virtues of the strongman is the ability to act. Action *is* virtue. The Prince forces *fortuna* onto the back foot. Rather than respond to her outbursts and hissy fits, he initiates. He is bold and welcomes risks. But the Prince is no unsophisticated brute. Power needs to be applied with strategy. Action needs moderation by wisdom, judgement and thought. This, too, is essential to princely *virtù*, although according to Machiavelli action (temperament) and wisdom (reflection) are seldom found in one person. Fortune may indeed favour the bold as a rule, but there are times when caution is the better strategy, and bold action ends in catastrophe. The difficulty for the strongman is to recognize when to assertively move forward and when to hang back. What works in one case, moreover, fails in the other. The strongman must act in accordance with morality and restraint when this is expedient, yet outside those bounds when the situation demands it.

This calculus is further compounded by a public relations dilemma. For a strongman, there is a presumption towards cultivating a reputation of ruthlessness (being feared) as opposed to beneficence (being loved). As Donald Trump once put it: "Real power is, and I don't even want to use the word, fear."[10] But fear only takes the strongman so far. There is, Machiavelli warned, a limit to the usefulness of playing the cold and unforgiving ruler. The hatred and resentment it breeds can get you killed. Roman emperors Commodus and Maximinus were assassinated by their own lieutenants because of their savage tactics. Modern examples of the same – Romania's Ceaușescu, Libya's Gaddafi, Laurent-Désiré Kabila of the the Democratic Republic of the Congo – are not difficult to find. The strongman, then, not only needs to know how to manage affairs of state, but also his reputation. He needs a knack for the dark arts of spin, to know how to "control the narrative". Ruthlessness is a quality the strongman should be known to possess. But in Machiavelli's theatre of terror, the difficulty lies in judging how much nastiness needs to be exhibited, and what needs to stay hidden, presumed and left to the imagination.

In October 2018, Saudi henchmen got this calculus spectacularly wrong when they ambushed and brutally murdered regime critic Jamal Khashoggi, who also happened to write a column for the *Washington Post*. According to graphic news reports, the assassins lured Khashoggi into the Saudi diplomatic mission in Istanbul, suffocated him, and then disposed of his body. What the killers had not realized was that the Turks were bugging the building. When

Erdogan, no friend of Saudi Arabia, gleefully released the stomach-turning detail of what had occurred there, the incident became a textbook case of what might go wrong when too much cruelty is displayed. Crown Prince Mohammed bin Salman's prestige in the world plummeted. Until that time, he had been seen as a youthful modernizer, a progressive reformer and a force for good. Now even Donald Trump, generally not shy of being seen in the company of ruthless strongmen, needed to distance himself from him.

Ruthlessness perhaps best appears as potential that simmers away under a humane, gentle and fatherly surface, ready to be activated when needed, but otherwise carefully concealed. Its presence should be inferred and anecdotal. A reputation of pitilessness is often best upheld by the occasional strategic leak, by subtle innuendo rather than a premeditated, global media campaign driving home the point. It is an image that needs to be softened with the reputation of frankness, integrity and honesty.

Machiavelli would have paid greater tribute to Paul Kagame, Rwanda's brutal but at the same time suave and respected president. Few countries in the world have sunk as deep into the pit of lawlessness as Rwanda in 1994. Three months of tribal madness saw 800,000 men, women and children slaughtered, often hacked to pieces with machetes. Chaos and genocide ruled. The West watched with great moral indignation, but it did not have the stomach to act. Kagame, however, did.

It became a model demonstration of Machiavelli's strongman ethos. In a campaign soaked in blood, strongman Kagame took events by the scruff of the neck. According to UN reports, tens of thousands of people lost their lives in the war. Many more died fleeing the country, hoping to escape retribution. But in the end Kagame managed to end the genocide and constitute his country anew. Since then Rwanda has grown into one of Africa's most effectively governed countries, boasting good economic growth, a much higher life expectancy than before and high literacy rates. Kigali is now one of the continent's best run, safest and cleanest capitals, although government intervention is all pervasive. Plastic bags, which had become an ecological scourge, are banned. Malaria and other diseases were brought under control. The country functions, albeit on the basis of significant foreign aid.

The depth of the lawlessness in 1994, paired with the country's recovery since, has protected Kagame's reputation abroad as well as at home. He has come to be regarded as a cerebral, sagacious, even-handed ruler, in his apparent asceticism vaguely reminiscent of the great Mahatma Gandhi. But he continues to rule with the iron fist of a strongman, tolerating neither dissent nor defiance. "Nation-building is like building a house", he argues. "You start with the foundation before you build the structure. The foundation comprises security, peace, and stability."[11] Journalistic freedom and political opposition are so far nonexistent, presumably held back until the construction works reach their completion. Presidential elections in 2003 and 2010 were won with over 90 per cent of the vote, following which Kagame changed his country's constitution – he says with the greatest reluctance – allowing him to win a third term in 2017.

Occasional chilling rumours circulate in Africa about assassination attempts on political rivals living abroad. Other stories are told of Kagame's pitiless strong-arm tactics and a propensity to fly into rages.[12] But while these stories have earned him a level of notoriety, for his broader stature they are of little concern. They ensure he commands the right level of respect at home, without unduly undermining his reputation. It can be hard to tell the difference between a virtuous Prince and a tyrant. "In all men's acts, and in those of Princes most especially", wrote Machiavelli, "it is the result that renders the verdict".[13] Referring to Kagame's use of strong-arm tactics, Bill Clinton, a staunch supporter, agrees. He simply shrugs, and says: "I suppose I do make more allowances for a government that produces as much progress as this one".[14]

IN THE EYE OF THE STORM

While the Prince stands outside the moral order, he partly lives within it for reasons of expedience and because he has to secure a form of legitimacy among his people and in the world. His divorce from morality is not absolute, not the "anything goes" of relativism but based on his pedigree as a ruler when the state is confronted with instability and risk. This is precisely why Farage says he admires Putin as "an operator, but not as a human being" and why Trump hastily adds the proviso that "*in that system*, he's been a leader, far more than our president has been a leader", adding further that he does not particularly like that system. Their admiration, in other words, is political. It echoes Machiavelli's view, who may have been the first theorist of strongman politics, but who also spelled out strength's limitations.

There is, Machiavelli argues, a particular time and a place for strongmen and their sovereign power, just as there is a time and place for republican government and its rules-based power. As a rule, the latter is superior for a number of reasons. First, republics rely on the joint *virtù* of its citizens and

31

do not have to grapple with succession issues, as Kagame's Rwanda or Putin's Russia will have to. Second, they are also stronger because citizens identify more readily with the state, and are consequently more willing to make sacrifices for it, for example by paying taxes or through military conscription. Third, they are more adaptable because the citizen body contains a diversity in temperaments, whereas the strongman is one person.

But this is of course only theory. In reality, as we saw, rules-based power is fragile. It flowers only where certain fortuitous conditions pertain, where some sense of community, stability and social order pre-exists. These conditions may or may not prevail. They may exist to different degrees. They may again disappear, causing institutions to corrupt. What makes for amenable conditions? According to Machiavelli it is the presence of *virtù civile*, of patriotic spirit, a culture of law-abidingness and traditions of free government. Where factionalism prevails, or sectarianism, economic inequality and ethnic tension, republics easily succumb to disorder. Even while republican government is intrinsically preferable to the rule of a Prince, when these conditions pertain the pendulum of power ought to swing to the strongman, who is much better adapted to austere ecosystems.[15]

The Prince offers what economists would call a "theory of the second best".[16] When equilibrium conditions are not met – when "the material is corrupt", in Machiavelli's own words – we cannot hope to attain the best possible state. However, the strongman can help us obtain a second-best equilibrium. In other words, the sort of government we need is the type of government that is best adapted to its environment. Mohammad Rezā Pahlavī, the Shah of Iran, defended his rule on those terms by saying: "When Iranians learn to behave like Swedes, I will behave like the King of Sweden."[17] Or as Omar Ghobash, a senior Emirati diplomat, puts it: "Freedom of speech has different constraints in different places. Speech in our part of the world has a particular context, and that context can go from peaceful to violent in no time simply because of words that are spoken."[18] Democracy and freedom of speech is not always the right answer. "We cannot duplicate the situation in different regions of the world", as Putin once argued against liberal interventionism.[19]

Because the ecosystem is rarely ideal and, at any rate, changeable, the strongman must be expected to be a frequent feature of political order, to appear and again disappear in cyclical patterns. He is needed as a buttress for the state, to be relied upon, for example, when institutional reforms are urgently needed. Machiavelli writes: "rarely, if ever, does it happen that a state, whether it be a republic or a kingdom, is either well-ordered at the outset or radically transformed *vis-à-vis* its old institutions unless this be done by one person".[20] Republican government, he explains, is lousy at reform because in republics reform always needs broad support, and by the time such support is secured, the damage can no longer be undone. On the whole, reform is better served with a strongman's talent for single-mindedness, his ability to shrug off opposing views and simply dictate his will.

It was a piece of counsel General Charles de Gaulle, already the saviour of France's honour in 1940, heeded during the Algeria crisis of 1958, when displeased but battle-hardened French army officers effectively staged a coup d'état against their government. By that time, the army had been at war with Algeria's independence movement, the FLN (Front de Libération Nationale), for several years. But in their struggle, which was hard and bloody, the French army and the French population in Algeria felt increasingly abandoned by progressive governments and elites in Paris, which they feared were secretly preparing the ground for France's departure, as they had done earlier in French Indochina. In the broader historical context, Algerian independence may well have been inevitable. But that did not make much difference for the Frenchmen and women who for generations had lived in Algeria.

In May 1958, French army officers had had enough. They seized power from civilian authorities in Algiers. They then threatened to do the same in Paris. The country seemed ripe for civil war. It provided the perfect setting for de Gaulle, out of office since 1946, to plot his return to political life and save the republic once more. The general still commanded the loyalty of the rebellious officer corps and of the French people. He carefully made sure to avoid perceptions that he welcomed the coup in any way, or had stoked the fire behind the scenes.[21] But the army instinctively trusted him to do the right thing in Algeria, an impression Grand Charles was equally careful not to discourage. When on 29 May 1958 French President René Coty, under massive pressure by the army, called upon de Gaulle to return to public office, Coty explained he had "turned to the most illustrious of Frenchmen, towards him who, in the darkest years of our history, was the Leader for the reconquest of our liberty".[22]

De Gaulle knew exactly what role he was to play. But the Saviour presented demands. "The degradation of the State is proceeding with increased velocity", he dramatically declared to the Assemblée Nationale.[23] "Algeria is plunged in a tempest of trials and emotions." He would not shirk his responsibility. But in return he would ask parliament for "the means for executing this duty". And those means, the general pressed on relentlessly, were six months of "full powers", a limited period during which he enjoyed the freedom to act with "efficiency, rapidity and responsibility", in other words, with complete discretion.

For de Gaulle, the deeper cause of the Algeria crisis lay in the institutional frailty of executive power in France's Fourth Republic. Its parliamentary system had simply not been able to cope with events. Institutions needed to be reformed. Power needed to be placed in the hands of an executive president, elected directly once every seven years. But to create his Fifth Republic, de Gaulle understood he needed time to govern alone, and on the basis of strength. He needed to sidestep procedures and endless deliberations, and put his plans directly to a people's vote. In the circumstances, parliament could hardly refuse. Jean-Paul Sartre, the existentialist philosopher, declared he would rather "vote for God; he is more modest".[24] But the majority of French citizens did not view the general's single-mindedness as particularly troublesome. Four months later, with the backing of 82.6 per cent of the vote, the Fifth Republic was born. Three months later still, de Gaulle became its first president.

While he could not keep Algeria in French hands, Machiavelli would have appreciated the general's political craft, in which he may have recognized the example of the ancient Romans, who regularly granted men of strength temporary but extra-constitutional powers to protect their republic against danger. While the Romans had finished with the idea of monarchy, they also recognized that, in exceptional times, only power of the sort usually wielded by kings could save the city from going under. And because republics could not have kings, the muscular, swashbuckling figure the Romans appointed to dispense such power was called "Dictator".

The dictator was appointed for six months, much like de Gaulle, and for that period was empowered – let off the leash, so to speak – to use his muscle and guile to ward off a specific threat to the republic's existence, the kind of concrete menace Rome's squabbling senatorial elite was unlikely to be able to see off by itself. The dictator's allegiance, however, remained to the republic and its institutions, his goal merely to defend and restore its laws, not to abolish them. In theory, his sovereign power was always linked to the completion of a concrete and lawful objective, following which the dictator was again to vanish, much like Romulus, Rome's illustrious founder, who legend claims vanished in a whirlwind. The strongman was allowed to act outside the legal order, but only so he could return the state within it.

Machiavelli's own Italy, much later, was famed for its *condottieri*, mercenaries who contracted themselves out to the highest bidder, for example to a city state in short-term need of military muscle on a grand scale. Still later, in the Dutch Republic (1581–1795), the office of *Stadtholder*, a remnant of the Habsburg monarchy, afforded significant executive and nearly regal powers to its elected occupant, the Prince of Orange: a republican strongman in the Roman mould rather than a proper king with absolute power, as could be found in France at the time. As a dictator of sorts, the Prince of Orange assumed importance at times of war and crisis, but at other, more tranquil times his power veered back to the republic's cities and provinces and the institutions that represented the latter. Known as *"Stadtholder-less"* periods, at times the role was left wholly unoccupied.

In these roles, the strongman is a passing figure, called in to expunge a political disease and put the state back on its feet. Any ruthlessness is justified only by its time- and purpose-limited nature. Rather than an enduring alternative to rules-based power, the strongman appears as an appendix to the law, as the state's "fixer in chief". Even in Europe today, caught as it is in various crises, the longing for such a saviour-strongman is often palpable. Describing himself as "a man for storms", French President Macron, an avid student of Machiavelli, consciously styles his image in the Saviour's mould.[25] "If we wish to stabilize political life and get out of our current state of neurosis", he argues like de Gaulle, "it is necessary ... to accept a little more verticality".[26]

DICTATOR FOREVER

How long a strongman can keep his exceptional powers depends on the eco-system the state finds itself in. What happens when those conditions remain poor? Machiavelli considers the scenario in which a people teeters from one strongman to the next, and only knows how to live under strongman rule. When liberated from their strongman, such a people would be like an animal that "brought up in captivity and servitude ... becomes the prey of the first comer who seeks to chain it up again".[27] In such conditions, when an incumbent strongman is overthrown, be it by popular revolt, coup d'état or foreign-led regime change, a depressing merry-go-round of strongmen follows. Order breaks down and chaos ensues, until a new strongman takes power.

A recent example is Egypt, where after 30 long years strongman Hosni Mubarak was overthrown in 2011, only to make place for another, the Islamist Mohamed Morsi, who after just one year was again overthrown by the next, General Abdul Fattah al-Sisi, who today still rules Egypt. Upon his ousting, Mubarak was placed in custody facing a potential death sentence. After he was toppled himself, Morsi was sentenced to death in turn. The list of countries that seems to follow this pattern is long.[28] After the US got rid of Saddam

Hussein in 2003, Khadim al-Jabbouri, a victim of his regime, rejoiced. He took a sledgehammer to Saddam's statue in central Baghdad and helped to tear it down. More than a decade later, he takes a different view: "Saddam has gone, but in his place we now have 1,000 Saddams".[29]

Not infrequently, a new strongman is hailed as a democratic redeemer. But all too quickly he turns out to be just another spin in the strongmen's carousel, which seemingly keeps turning without end. The only way to stop such strongmen cycles, which Machiavelli puts his hopes in, is the more permanent and enlightened rule of the *Dictator Perpetuo*. The best we can hope for, he offers, is that a man of such exceptional virtue and strength comes along "that he can enforce obedience to such a time as the material has become good". The idea is to buy time, large amounts of time, to provide for stability and on that basis make progress by taking little steps. Deo Nkusi, a political ally of Rwanda's strongman Paul Kagame, says: "Changing people here is like bending steel. The people were bent into one shape over 40 years and they have to be bent back. If we do it too fast we will just break them. We have to exert pressure gradually."[30] Boris Titov, Putin's business ombudsman, explains: "Maybe somewhere, some day, when the conditions are right, the 'institutions' will improve. But here and now, everyone will just keep on stealing and taking the riches abroad."[31]

The principal task of the strongman, meanwhile, is to keep order. As conditions slowly get better, he could put in place the rudimentary elements of institutional rule: a professional police force that provides security, courts of law that adjudicate, a government apparatus that gets essential things done, a functioning free market economy. The strategy is to gradually build the state from its foundations upwards, beginning with structures capable of enforcing order.[32] As Paul Kagame argues, you do not begin with the roof.

Whether this could, or even should, lead to something those in the West would describe not just as a state of law, but as a democratic and liberal state, is less relevant for most strongmen. The job of building a state is hard enough, and subject to its own standards of success. Political freedom is a concern for later, if it is a concern at all. The strongman's prime focus is on the economy and on fighting poverty, as it has been in China and other Asian countries. For Lee Kuan Yew, the strongman who ruled Singapore between 1959 and 1990, the central challenge of government was to create the conditions under which standards of living for citizens could improve, something that by all accounts he succeeded in doing. When he came to power, Singapore's annual per capita income was about $400. Today it is over $60,000, making it one of the world's wealthiest nations. Liberal democracy, however, played no role in this success story. "I believe that what a country needs to develop is discipline more than democracy", said Lee, summing up his political beliefs.[33] Liberal democracy, he found, merely leads to "disorderly conditions that are inimical to development".

For decades, conventional wisdom in the West was that by modernizing its economy, China had also put itself on the path to liberal democracy. "Economic freedom creates habits of liberty", US President George W. Bush once put it. "And habits of liberty", he went on, "create expectations of democracy".[34] But while China's economic development accelerated, political reform did not follow. For Xi, political freedom seems a distraction. As for Lee, his lesson to the world is that economic success can and must be achieved within the confines of an authoritarian system. Xi's so-called "China Dream" is to restore his country to the global power it once was. But there is no evidence that by the time this feat is accomplished – according to his estimations this should be in 2049 – political liberalization will follow.

The more pertinent question is whether Xi's personalized power as a strongman will make way for a more institutionalized and collaborative style of government. While Xi may prove right in claiming that economic modernization can be achieved without political liberalization, can his goal be realized without embedding his power in impersonal institutions and the law? On Machiavelli's account, the *Dictator Perpetuo* is destined to become the victim of his own success, eventually. Having navigated the country to calmer seas, and made it rich and strong, a strongman's personal interventions become less critical. Collegiate and rules-based mechanisms of power can and ought to take over, as in times of peace and calm such mechanisms provide for better and more stable government. Power centralized in the hands of one man should be devolved to courts of law and self-reliant bureaucratic systems. In theory at least, the purpose of a strongman is to create the conditions in which his services are needed less, allowing him to gradually retire from frontline politics, something that Singapore's Lee Kuan Yew sought to achieve by taking on new roles as "Senior Minister" and later "Minister Mentor".

In reality, of course, things do not always go according to plan for the strongman. Facing innumerable hurdles along the road, he is forced to hold the reins for longer and longer. Advisors turn into yes-men, dulling the strongman's critical senses, blinding him to reality. Nothing moves without his personal involvement, inducing debilitating sclerosis in the affairs of government. What happens when the strongman dies before the job gets done? The risk is that order again collapses, kick-starting a violent cycle of strongman oustings. Premature death forms the Achilles heel of permanent strongman rule.

Worryingly, strongman rule is a path beset with moral temptation. Everything hinges on the strongman's continued self-discipline, his political morality, his values. There is no built-in insurance against tyrants and "bad Emperors", it seems, other than the strongman's own determination to stay the course, to use his power for the public good rather than his own.[35] Clearly, often this moral discipline proves insufficient. All strongmen start out as Rwanda's austere reformer Paul Kagame or as Lee Kuan Yew, vowing to help their country back on its feet and revive its fortunes. Yet more than a few end up as Zimbabwe's Robert Mugabe, who after nearly four decades of predatory rule and tyranny had succeeded only in enriching himself.

But still, it should be acknowledged that most strongmen recognize that certain standards apply to them, an ethos of sorts. Their claim to power is not a plea for naked selfishness. Vladimir Putin describes his life as that of a "galley slave", as someone who labours for the common interest. This may or may not be reflective of his actual record in office. There are certainly plenty of people who mock the notion. But his self-description does reflect the standards Russia's strongman is apparently ready to be judged by. The galley slave does not row for himself. He toils for the motherland. He rows not for fun, but because he must, out of a sense of duty.

This ethos of the strongman does not coincide with our democratic morality, which easily leads to confusion. In an infamous television interview in 2004, Gerhard Schröder, then German chancellor, was asked whether he believed Putin was *"ein lupenreiner Demokrat"*, an impeccable democrat. It was a tricky question. A flawless democrat Putin was certainly not. But Schröder's policy was to build closer ties with Russia, so he could hardly say so openly. To describe Putin as anything less than a democrat would undermine his Russia policy. So, he took a deep breath and roundly said yes, I am convinced this is the case.[36]

It proved an answer that has haunted Schröder ever since. His dilemma was that Westerners no longer possess the language in which they can say that Putin, while not a perfect democrat, is still a good leader. For them, democracy and human rights have become the *only* political standard. Consequently, for Schröder, Putin just had to be a flawless democrat. Or else he would have qualified as a crook, with whom closer ties would have been impossible. Schröder could have appealed to Machiavelli's language of strength. He could have said: "Putin may not be an impeccable democrat, but he is making Russia a better, more liveable country." However, the language of power and strength has lost normative validity. In the language of human rights and values the West prefers, history bears greater similarity to Pocock's medieval "theatre of redemption" than to the Renaissance prism of history as the uncertain struggle for secular order. You are either a democrat or you are a thug. Other flavours do not exist. It left Schröder sweating in front of the cameras.

The strongman, on the other hand, still lives in Machiavelli's universe of contingency, of order that teeters on the edge of the precipice and that needs to be buttressed by the sovereign power of a Prince. "I am not saying everything I did was right … I had to do some nasty things, locking up fellows without trial", Lee once confessed. But that was not to be the final verdict on his record. "Close the coffin, then decide. Then you assess me."[37] The strongmen, to be sure, are not to be equally admired. There are good and bad strongmen, tyrants. But their demand is to be judged on their own terms. According to the historian Suetonius, at the end of his life Rome's first emperor, Augustus, said: "I found Rome a city of clay but left it a city of marble". This is the standard by which the strongmen want to be judged. As it turns out, many, if not most, fail to meet it, or they succeed only to an extent. They find a city of clay; they leave a city of clay. Or, like the tyrant Mugabe, they find a city of marble but turn it into a city of clay.[38] Yet by their own account, the strongmen do have values. And measured by these values, there are good and there are bad strongmen.

THE FINALITY OF POWER

"As gravity bends light, so power bends time", historian Christopher Clark writes in his book *Power and Time*. Different conceptions of power favour different conceptions of history and time, notions of how past, present and future interrelate. Machiavelli's strongman, the intrepid conqueror of contingency, is the perfect example. His power owes its appeal to the experience of time as a torrent of events in which past, present and future are merely linked by crises and acts of strength. The consequence of grounding strongman power in this conception of time is that calmer epochs logically go hand in hand with a return to the power of rules and institutions. Theoretically, there is no room for a strongman to perpetuate his special powers indefinitely. Conceived as a Saviour, the strongman can never fully liberate himself from the law or from what Machiavelli called the republic that he is supposed to save.

It is this finality that sits uneasily with rulers who seek more permanent and absolute power still. The strongmen of Roman times, the Caesars, already wrestled with this tension. After Rome had been torn to shreds by civil war, and then "saved", its emperors sought to perpetuate their extra-legal powers. But they were held back by the city's old constitutional nomenclature and the traditional ways it regarded sovereign power and strength. For the Romans, only a king or dictator could wield unchecked power. But neither seemed suitable for the scope of the Caesars' ambitions. The idea of monarchy came closest but remained discredited, while the traditional powers of the dictator, seen as a more honourable figure, faced the unwelcome limitation that after six months these powers expired.

Rome's most illustrious strongman, Julius Caesar, having already served consecutive terms as Dictator, coined the new title of "Dictator for Life", a role which his heir Octavian, the later Emperor Augustus, went on to develop. Yet the name remained an institutional anomaly. So, if the emperors were neither kings nor traditional dictators, then what precisely were they? Octavian's answer, like that of our own strongmen, was that there was no real answer. He believed his great personalized power was best concealed by maintaining the pretence that constitutional politics continued as normal.[39] Political backers proposed Octavian take on the name Romulus, to reflect his true power and importance. But the name patently smelled of regal power and so he refused. Instead, Octavian settled on the more humble designation of "princeps", first citizen, which was more in tune with Rome's republican heritage, and then later on Augustus, the venerable one.

The hunger for even greater and truly permanent power could only be expressed in another political discourse, a language severed more radically from lingering ideals of republicanism and the rule of law. Europe's absolutist kings of the early modern period, for example, were able to support their power by arguing they ruled by divine right. Mandated by heaven to govern outside earthly constraints and laws, theoretically they could do so in perpetuity through lineage: the bloodline. Unlike the power of the princeps, their extreme power could be acclaimed as God's timeless will.

Similar aspirations to perpetuity are found in the powers of Mussolini's *Duce*, Hitler's *Führer* and Stalin's *Vozhd*, which are grounded in a different conception of time and history. The totalitarian ideologies of fascism and communism are not the avowal of sovereign power as a temporary "state of exception", to be called upon only in times of need; they are the affirmation of sovereign power as an end state, as the state of affairs when the world reaches its completion. It advances the *Führerprinzip*, the belief in the natural superiority of the single man, a man gifted with mystical visionary and prophetic powers, or touched by a secular God, and therefore destined to wield sovereign power alone. An eventual return to constitutionalism is never fore-seen, a relapse not desirable or even conceivable.

Hitler's Third Reich was going to last a thousand years, without pining for "sleazy" parliamentarianism and other bourgeois restrictions on power. In an address, Hitler's propaganda minister Joseph Goebbels once remarked that the year 1789, which saw the birth of Europe's democratic order with the French Revolution, could now "be expunged from the history books".[40] The Nazis longed for a definitive and total transformation into another social form, for a new and final era in which checks and balances would no longer be neces-sary, the whole artifice of institutional politics irrelevant because there would no longer be interests, perspectives or ideas to be balanced. There would be but one interest, one idea, one form of continuity, which for Hitler was not even that of the nation state, but of the race. And one man alone, he with the sharpest, the farthest, the most laser-like vision, knew best how to promote it. For Hitler, as Clark rightly notes, politics was never Bismarck's "art of the pos-sible"; it was to the art of realizing "*Endzeit* scenarios – *Endkampf, Endlösung, Endsieg*".[41]

It is important that today's strongmen show little appetite for twentieth-century ideology nor for the older discourse of the divine right of kings. They stand closer to Octavian's princeps or indeed to Europe's other great strong-man of republican ilk, Napoleon Bonaparte, for whom expunging 1789 from the history books was never an option.[42] Xi Jinping is reclaiming the virtues of scientific socialism, but in a form that ultimately echoes little of Mao's total-itarian incarnation. The Arab monarchies in the Gulf still claim ties to the Prophet and to the divine, rather than ground their power in the temporary suspension of law, as Egyptian strongman al-Sisi and Turkey's Erdogan do. But their ties with heaven seem increasingly weak. Even the Prophet is no longer intrinsically partial to absolute monarchy as a form of government, as the Shah of Iran found out in 1979.

None of the world's major strongmen invoke the language of monarchy. Hardly a book or newspaper article appears that does not refer to Putin as Russia's New Tsar, Xi as China's New Emperor and Erdogan as Turkey's New Sultan. But these designations get it wrong in one revealing sense, which is that these strongmen categorically refuse to use those names themselves, pre-ferring whatever administrative, humdrum-sounding and transitory title they have been assigned by the legal-institutional order of the state, be it president, chairman or prime minister. Trump says of Xi Jinping: "Some people might call him the King of China – but he's called president."[43] Erdogan claims: "I have no intention of becoming a Padishah, a Sultan".[44] Their reasoning is perfectly clear.

As for Augustus, the language of monarchy is irrecoverable (or, perhaps, *not yet* recoverable) and using it would make them look illegitimate, strangely at odds with the modern state and its elections, parliaments and courts.

In the experience of time that the strongman owes his power to, history does not lead to heavenly or secular salvation of some kind. The river of time, instead, corrodes and destroys. It whittles away at political order and occasionally tears deep holes in the state's hull. The strongman is chosen to repair these holes, to use uncurbed strength to steer the vessel safely through the rapids. Two consequences are inevitable, and they distinguish the strongman from a king. First, he neither "is" the state nor does he own it; he serves the state. In the image of the strongman as the state's Saviour, power and the law are welded together. Second, for the strongman time always runs out. Kings can claim to be politically eternal. But the strongman is mortal. However rocky the passage, however long the journey takes, he faces the expectation that at some point, when times are more tranquil, power must return to where it belongs: in the chains of the law.

CHAPTER 3

Lord: in the shadow of the state

To seek a protector, or to find satisfaction in being one – these things are common to all ages.

Marc Bloch, *Feudal Society* (1940)

THE SILENT CONTRACT

The strongmen govern through strength, not through rules. But what do the politics of strength look like? Why strength? On the whole, European states, which are based on rules, function like well-oiled machines. Their bureaucracies are vast and capable of reaching into the smallest pockets of society. There are rules for the tiniest minutiae of our lives: from the emission levels of diesel cars, to urban planning laws, to the percentage of cacao in chocolate bars. What do we need strength for?

The strongman's answer is that government is not always an efficient and reliable machine. Institutions of government can break or lose their relevance. Great civilizations and states view themselves as eternal. They place themselves at the centre of the world and blindly assume they will remain there forever. But Machiavelli's warning is that they are wrong. If we take the long view, the greatest challenge of order is its evanescence. States are vulnerable to crises, to wear and tear and decay. And when institutions are weak, dysfunctional or at risk, the politics of strength takes over. Formally, rules and constitutions may still exist. A machinery of government may still exist, on paper. But if these structures no longer possess political agency, the ability to govern or change things, strength provides an answer.

One of the sources for the politics of strength is what I call the "silent contract", an informal and covert bargain between the strongman and an elite of powerbrokers recruited by the strongman to help manage the nation's public affairs. It is this band of helpers that, in part, gives the strongman his power, his ability to create and lead an often highly effective system of government in the shadow of the state. And as I will argue in this chapter, the character of this shadow system of government, and the personal and informal ties that hold it together, can be best understood as the ancient principles of feudalism and the obligations between a lord and his vassals.

As the French historian Marc Bloch sets out in his classic work *Feudal Society*, feudalism emerged in Europe as a practical answer to the dissolution of the administrative and legal structures of the Roman Empire. It entailed the radical privatization and delegation of wholesale public power to geographical units smaller than the state.[1] At the head of feudal society stood a king, an emperor or tsar, more generally called a lord or master. However, these kings lacked the tools to govern their lands from the centre. Instead, they devised a system of government in which its basic tasks – raising armies and revenue and dispensing justice – were subcontracted to men who swore loyalty to their masters. Those vassals then parcelled off their powers to still smaller units and estates, led by lower-ranking chieftains, creating a hierarchical chain of personal obligations that stretched from the very top to the very bottom of society, at which stood peasants and serfs.

Europe's feudal order, Bloch explains, found its historical origins in the Germanic war band, the *comitatus*, which was based on a compact between a local warlord and his retinue of war-companions. The latter were sworn to fight at his side in looting expeditions and vendettas. In return for their fighting services, the men received gifts: food, plenty of drink, lodgings, but also social status, influence and, not least, protection. This compact was entered into freely. Recruits pledged fealty to their boss in informal ceremonies, and in turn the latter promised them physical rewards, honour and glory. In the state of political confusion and decay that ruled Europe, the *comitatus* offered an embryonic alternative concept of order, an extra-legal mode of organization that could be used not just for looting, but also as a mutual protection scheme and a form of government. In a world torn apart at the seams, protection became the most coveted good. And if law could no longer provide it, private ties and obligations offered the possibility of a new social equilibrium. As Bloch argues: "Men looked for chiefs, and chiefs for vassals".[2]

Gradually, feudal ties began to pervade all of society. They became the new social norm, around which a political culture grew. Military services evolved into other types of homage. Yet stripped to its bare essence, feudal order still revolved around the same contract. Three important principles underpinned it. First, the king or lord retained ownership of the land as a whole. He was *dominus*, owner. Vassals – dukes, earls and barons – held the land they administered only as tenants and at the king's pleasure (*tenure*). Second, those vassals owed their king an oath of fealty, fees and services (*homage*), while the king owed his vassals protection. Third, the feudal lord was entitled to sanction his tenants and take back their land if they broke their oath or fell short of their duties (*confiscation*).

While hierarchical in theory, relations between feudal kings and their vassals would often be intricately balanced and conflictual. The king would naturally seek to centralize power and maximize his strength. But for his strength he depended on the services and fees received from his vassals. Not yet able to claim absolute powers or govern in the name of God, Europe's feudal kings needed to take counsel and secure the consent of their nobles. Vassals, in turn, would strive to optimize their independence and keep the rents they owed to their *dominus* to a minimum. Some snubbed the king's demands or plotted to get rid of him, giving rise to frequent and violent power struggles.

The balance of power could swing either way. If it swung in the king's direction, he was truly sovereign over his vassals. But if the balance swung the other way, a king might have to negotiate or even beg for his vassals' support. Over the centuries, Europe's kings tended to win this tug of war, reconsolidating power in the centre. The proto-bureaucratic structures of the modern state grew out of the king's court. No longer did knights and fighting men have to be assembled from all corners to fight wars. Standing armies, reporting directly to the king, proved a more potent and reliable military force. Feudal ties increasingly lost their usefulness. Just as feudal society rose with the decline of central government, so it again faded when central authority reasserted itself.

To be sure, by suggesting that the politics of the strongman can, in part, be understood as a feudal system of fealty and homage, I am not claiming the strongman wants to take us back to the dark ages. The world of the strongman is modern, certainly in aspiration. His state may be ineffective and in need of buttressing, but it still is and wants to remain a state. That said, like a feudal lord the strongman needs tools to go around the stuttering machinery of central government. That is the nature of his rule. And the tenure system is one of those tools.

RUNNING ERRANDS FOR THE BOSS

Instead of parcelling off bits of territory to vassals, the modern strongman tends to grant personal tenure over resources of a different kind: government departments, state corporations and the state's enforcement agencies. Typically, the tenure system extends into the private economy, for example when big public contracts are tendered: the construction of hospitals, gas pipelines, major infrastructural works. A businessman who wins a public contract in a strongman regime is not just expected to deliver on its terms. He can be called upon to provide additional and private services. In the silent contract, as we shall see, the distinction between public and private dissolves. A business may be owned privately in terms of the law, but it may at the same time be an instrument of public policy, under the control of the strongman.

Putin's Russia offers an example of how many of its leading businessmen are also running errands for "the boss".[3] This arrangement grew out of the post-communist chaos of the 1990s, when Russia's first generation of businessmen, known as the oligarchs, colluded with Russia's first president, Boris Yeltsin, to sell off the state's industrial crown jewels for a fraction of their market value. It enabled men like Roman Abramovich, the owner of Chelsea Football Club, and the media moghul Boris Berezovsky to become billionaires overnight. In 1995, Mikhail Khodorkovsky, perhaps Russia's best-known oligarch in the West, paid just $350 million for 78 per cent of Yukos, Russia's state oil firm. When Yukos shares were floated, some two years later, the company was worth $9 billion, its market capitalization rising to $15 billion in 2002.[4]

Of course, the oligarchs could not just spend their new-found riches as they pleased. Yeltsin had in effect created a "parallel government", one that was flush with cash and beyond the restrictions of constitutional law. He wanted its power to deal a decisive blow to Russia's Communist Party, his rival in the 1996 presidential election, and secure the future of the nascent democratic Russia.[5] Like loyal vassals, the oligarchs did what they promised. They bought television channels and newspapers and stuffed the pockets of parliamentarians. They enlisted spin doctors to shape mass public opinion in the direction they and Yeltsin favoured.[6]

Victory, however, came at a price. Stripped of its assets, the Russian state looked weaker than ever before. By contrast, a coterie of individuals had become obscenely rich and powerful. What was worse, as Yeltsin's health began to deteriorate, the balance of power decisively shifted towards his vassals. And rather than building the foundations for Russia's liberal future, they used their wealth to fight each other out of the tent.[7]

This changed with the ascent of Putin, who had been handpicked by Yeltsin as his political heir. As soon as he was elected president, Putin set out to remind the oligarchs who was lord and who vassal. He spelled it out over dinner in his summer Dacha in 2000 during what is known as the "barbecue meeting".[8] The oligarchs could keep the industrial assets they had obtained from the state during the privatization. But they had to keep from meddling in Russian politics and more importantly, swear fealty to their new *dominus*. If they refused to do so, they and their businesses would – just like the kebabs Putin was serving – be roasted over hot coals.

The threat of communism had petered out. But part of the oligarchs' wealth, Putin insisted, needed to be reinvested in the country. The oligarchs would formally own their industrial assets as a matter of law, but under Putin's political management they were informally still regarded as state assets, as "Russia Inc.". The oligarchs were free to manage their businesses on a day-to-day basis. But from time to time they needed to report to the Kremlin, to Putin or one of his courtiers, under whose strategic authority their businesses fell. And whenever Putin decided it was necessary, some of the oligarchs' resources would be ploughed back into the country, which remained poor even by Soviet standards.

While shifting some of their capital abroad, and thus outside the Kremlin's immediate control, most oligarchs got the message. It was put up or shut up. Abramovich took on the role of governor of Chukotka, an impoverished part of Siberia so far east it is actually in the western hemisphere. The move was unlikely to have sprouted from personal ambitions to spend time in the region. Battered by Arctic weather fronts all year long, a travel company organizing trips to Chukotka warns: "Coming here, you ... need to be prepared for delays, physical discomfort, terrible weather and all sorts of other problems."[9] Yet it did not deter the aluminium tycoon from regularly making the journey, or more importantly, from funding the constructing of a new airport in Chukotka, as well as hospitals, roads and cinemas.

There seemed to be no clear reason why the oligarch, who clearly preferred looking after his personal pet projects in London and the Mediterranean, had taken on the role. The truth, of course, could never be publicly stated. "Roman's changed the lives of 70,000 people in his province", his spokesman once tried to explain. "They used to be starving and now they all have Dolby Surround Sound."[10] But it was not an attempt to launder his reputation. "For Roman it is not an ego thing", the same spokesman continued. "This weekend, he's spiriting a bunch of poor Russian kids to London to catch a performance of *Mamma Mia*. What a PR opportunity, and I have to sit on it." Nor could the truth be fully stated when Abramovich chipped in to fund the 2014 Olympic Winter Games in Sochi and the 2018 World Cup in Russia. "I don't rule out that Mr Abramovich may take part in one of these projects", Putin once dryly commented on television. "Let him open his wallet a little. It's no big deal – he won't feel the pinch. He has plenty of money."[11]

Russia's largest industrial corporations were neither private nor public; they were in a strange no man's land in between. The primacy, however, had shifted back towards the centre. If the private sector had once stripped corporate assets from the state, the state was now prepared to strip those assets right back. If Russia's new generation of capitalists once co-ran the Kremlin, the Kremlin now co-ran their companies. In the tenure system that Putin had created, it meant property rights were never secure, a fact decried by liberal economists and investors. But Putin argued that the wrongs of the 1990s needed to be righted, and if this could not be achieved within the framework of the law then he was determined to do so by other means. The coerced renationalization of industrial assets Putin deemed a radical and undesirable step. But the informality of the tenure system offered middle ground, a practical alternative that no one could quibble about. There would be no rupture with the rule of law, Putin reassured investors. Rather, the post-communist order would be legitimized with the help of the silent contract.

Putin's homage system delivered, and the contract that underpinned it did not fundamentally change when in 2008 Dmitry Medvedev took over the presidency. What did change was the type of service Russia's young president liked to receive from the nation's oligarchs. A modernizer, Medvedev had great affinity with digital technology, unlike Putin, who had temporarily given himself the job of prime minister. Medvedev understood Russia needed to invest in innovation and decided to throw his weight behind "Skolkovo Innovation City", Russia's plan to create a hub for entrepreneurial and tech talent in Moscow. He hoped and expected Russia's oligarchs would back the plan, thereby catapulting Russia to the topflight of the global digital economy.

Another change was that the oligarchs now needed to serve two masters. Already in Bloch's feudal society, it commonly happened that a vassal owed fealty and homage to two or even several lords. But it was an inherently unstable practice, one that grew into "one of the principle solvents of vassal society".[12] Could a vassal's loyalty be divided? How to choose between several lords, one of whom was certain to feel angered and betrayed? For four years, Russia's oligarchs found themselves in a similar position and, just as in the medieval times Bloch describes, there were no clear criteria for choosing one over the other.

Paying homage was becoming a more complicated business, and ever more expensive. Most observers agreed that Putin still held most of the strings and therefore probably deserved the greater loyalty. However, the future was uncertain, which allowed Medvedev to expand his own networks of allegiance. Who were Putin's men and who were Medvedev's? For some time, this seemed the most important question in Russian politics. Vassals needed to hedge their bets, paying homage to both leaders. Oligarchs who had demonstrated their fealty to Putin by spending fortunes on repatriating Tsarist Fabergé eggs also needed to chip in with funds for Skolkovo City, supporting Medvedev's reformist agenda. Clarity was restored when Putin announced his return to the Kremlin in 2011. Unsurprisingly, the money stream for Skolkovo quickly dried up. In April 2013, its head offices were raided by anti-corruption investigators.[13] From now on, other types of political service were in greater demand.

REPOSSESSION

Errand boys whose loyalty is in doubt, or who in other ways fall short of their obligations, face consequences, and sometimes these consequences are grave. Confiscation of property is only one of the possibilities, and far from the worst. Exile, imprisonment and violent death are others. "Struggles of great feudatories against their kings; rebellions against the former by their own vassals; dereliction of feudal duties … these features are to be read on every page of the history of feudalism."[14] They continue to be frequent still. Punishment is usually meted out in private, as befits the silent contract. But more than occasionally these vengeful episodes bubble to the surface, where they capture the public's imagination.

Having been elevated to the rank of Crown Prince in 2017, one of the first things Saudi Arabia's Mohammed bin Salman, better known as MBS, did was to remind the kingdom's elite of nobles and financiers of the feudal contract that bound them directly to him. His message: breaching the terms of that contract was something they would deeply regret. In a move that has since become known as the "Sheikdown", MBS summoned dozens of Saudi businessmen, ministers and members of the royal family to Riyadh's Ritz-Carlton under false pretences. When they arrived in the five-star luxury hotel, Saudi police stood ready to handcuff them. The imprisoned men, who included prominent Saudi billionaire Prince Alwaleed, were forced to sleep on the hotel lobby floor while the world watched in astonishment. The move sent shockwaves through the Persian Gulf and the world.[15] For a brief moment, oil prices shot up.

As the crackdown unfolded, hundreds of Saudi princes and nobles were held on charges of corruption. It resonated with the nation's mood. Had they not squandered their positions of privilege and wealth on yachts and other paraphernalia, instead of using their resources to strengthen the economy and help the people? It felt as if a modern, progressive and faintly democratic wind was blowing through the kingdom. Fundamentally, however, it hardly mattered what the charges were, and even less whether they were correct. The only thing that mattered was that, for as long as MBS pleased, the men would remain locked up. What mattered was that the crown prince could confiscate their possessions, that to walk free they needed to open their purses and embrace their position and duties in the feudal hierarchy as tenants not as lords.

In the politics of strength, battling corruption is a favourite by-word for weeding out disloyal vassals, and an ideal pretext for purging rivals. When China's Xi Jinping took power in 2012, he promptly ordered a crackdown on corruption, tasking his most loyal vassals to oversee it. Bribe-taking, Xi warned China's elites, was endemic in Communist Party ranks. However, his new anti-graft campaign would tighten the rules and root out the practice. He would both swat "flies", by which Xi meant low-ranking corrupt officials, and kill "tigers", meaning corrupt top officials. "Power should be restricted by the cage of regulations", Xi said, stating his intentions.[16]

And so it began. Charges of embezzlement, bribery and abuse of power landed Bo Xilai in jail, China's former minister of commerce. Bo had been destined for a dazzling career in the Politburo. Because of it his loyalty was in doubt. Stories about Bo's abuse of power started to appear all over China's media. His wife was accused of having murdered a British businessman. Soon, others received the same treatment. In the past, too often we looked away from graft, Xi cautioned. It would no longer continue. "The weapons of criticism and self-criticism should be well-wielded, with some spice to make every party official blush and sweat a little", the strongman said ominously in 2014.[17]

Obviously, Xi was not just chasing ghosts. Corruption levels were undoubtedly off the chart. But was it coincidence that some of his keenest rivals ended up in prison? In the strongman's war on corruption, a noble and popular cause, the question is never whether its victims are guilty. One can readily assume they are. The question is why some are singled out for investigation while others are not. The answer, of course, has everything to do with who enjoys the strongman's protection. And that in turn depends on who pledges his fealty to the strongman and dutifully pays his dues.

In Russia, oil tycoon Mikhail Khodorkovsky went to jail for tax fraud in 2004. He languished there until Putin decided to release him weeks before the Sochi Winter Olympics in 2014. In the meantime, Putin renationalized his oil company Yukos, renamed it Rosneft, and appointed one of his most trusted vassals, Oleg Sechin, to oversee it. Khodorkovsky became an icon in the West, where it was acknowledged that his incarceration had nothing to do with tax fraud. When Putin came to power, Khodorkovsky reinvented himself as a liberal. He cared little for legal principles when Yeltsin's silent contract made him a billionaire in the 1990s. But knowing Putin would be a less pliant master, belatedly he became a convert. Under the rule of law his obligations of fealty and homage did not exist. The West began to regard Khodorkovsky as a Soviet-era dissident who had been locked up for his liberal values. The truth was more mundane. Unlike model vassal Abramovich, Khodorkovsky had reneged on the oath he had once taken, and now he had been repossessed.

Other oligarchs falling short of what they owed to their new lord faced similar sanctions. Boris Berezovsky, who claimed he had personally recommended Putin to Yeltsin as his successor, soon realized the terrible mistake he had made. At first he tried to play the part of Putin's older brother, a father figure and a mentor. But Putin quickly brushed the notion aside. Berezovsky was to kneel to the Kremlin's new overlord like everyone else. Forced to flee Moscow for London, where he obtained asylum and fought legal battles with other Russian oligarchs, he continued plotting and scheming against Putin, until ten years later his money ran out. Bankrupt and out of options, in 2013 Berezovsky belatedly threw himself at Putin's feet, begging his *dominus* for clemency and protection, which he sorely needed. In a handwritten letter to Putin, the wayward vassal spoke of his great desire to finally be allowed to return home.[18] It was a plea that Putin, in no mood for mercy, left unanswered. He did make sure the existence of the letter became public. Not much later Berezovsky was found dead in his house, according to UK police reports by hanging.

SILENCE IS GOLDEN

While the strongman uses feudal principles to govern, unlike Bloch's medieval lord his hybrid regime must reconcile those principles with the rule-governed state and its institutions. Theoretically, both systems can never coexist in the same political space, which is why the silent contract between strongman and vassal is and must always stay silent, allowing the state to uphold the appearance of legitimacy and rectitude.

The silent contract's secretive workings are not dissimilar to the codes of the Sicilian Mafia. The Mafia, Diego Gambetta has argued, emerged in the nineteenth century when ancient feudal structures on the Italian island had evaporated but the state and its new enforcement arms were not sufficiently strong to provide the sort of protection that Sicilians needed.[19] The Mob stepped into the breach, acting as third-party guarantor of commercial contracts and other deals. Its involvement ensured traders would stay good to their word. Who would try to rip off a business partner if the transaction was underwritten by the Mafia? Its services, Gambetta argues, fulfilled a genuine need for a while, but they obviously infringed on the theoretical monopoly of the state. The only way for the Mob to exist was not to exist, at least not publicly.

Like the Mafia, the strongman conducts the feudal part of his business clandestinely. And just as in the Mafia, there is no place for whistleblowers. The strongman, then, relies on two chains of command, two budgets, two enforcement regimes, one covert and one visible power structure. This duality of the informal and formal, of the secret and open, is what makes the world of the strongman hard to read. If we only look at institutional processes or only listen to what the strongmen say aloud, we can never grasp the entirety of what goes on. In the strongman state, different realities overlap and alternate. Two political games, two sets of norms, are at play at the same time: the legitimate and the clandestine.

In practice, it means the strongman governs "à la carte". He chooses to assign some governmental tasks to the informal homage system, ordering vassals to get the job done while other tasks are allocated to the formal institutions of the state. Liberal states govern from a set menu. "The rule of law, it is not an option, it is an obligation", European politicians declare. "Democratic values and the rule of law … are not 'à la carte'".[20] The strongman, on the other hand, benefits from options to get things done. The rule of law is one, the silent contract is another. And if the latter form of governance offers the best result, why not use it? That is not to say the strongman can openly avow such a choice. The state can be side-stepped, but it can never be side-stepped *openly*. The silent contract can only be reconciled with the state through deniability. Its sin lies not in the act but in getting caught. And when that happens, complications invariably follow.

The tension between these incompatible norms of governance, and the at times strained effort to manage it through secrecy, is not only noticeable in how strongmen like Putin or Xi govern. It haunts all organizations that rely on feudal networks of fealty and reward. One non-state example is FIFA, the Zürich-based global body that governs world football, and that under the presidency of Sepp Blatter, a feudal lord of sorts, saw its silent contract spill into the public domain. The consequences proved dramatic.

For 17 years Blatter ruled football like his own fiefdom, rewarding loyal vassals and punishing those who were not. Hailing from a remote village in the Swiss Valais region, Blatter had always been oddly out of touch with the norms that prevailed in urban Europe, arguing once that women should play in "tighter shorts" to boost the game's popularity. For the 2022 World Cup in Qatar he advised gay people to "refrain from any sexual activities". As a communicator Blatter possessed only modest talent. But behind the scenes his political abilities flourished.

It was a skill set he had learned from the Brazilian João Havelange, who himself had become FIFA president in 1974 by defeating Englishman Stanley Rouse in a vote. Europe's football powers had long hoovered up all the key jobs in world football. But as the body grew, Havelange knew power was shifting towards the South and East. The Europeans could easily be beaten as long as non-Western football associations stuck together. Tirelessly he travelled around the world to cobble together an alliance of loyal backers. It enabled him to dominate FIFA for a quarter of a century. Henry Kissinger, acting as lobbyist for the US bid to host the 1986 World Cup (which ended up going to Mexico), once sighed that FIFA made him "nostalgic for the Middle East".[21]

Blatter called Havelange "the patriarch".[22] When he took over from the Brazilian in 1998, football had become big business. Blatter made sure plenty of the money found its way to the local barons who ran the football associations of Africa, Asia and Latin America. For the first time, he brought the World Cup to Asia (2002), then to Africa (2010), to Russia (2018) and finally to the Middle East (2022). In return, he kept raking up votes inside the organization. Within a few years, Blatter had built a seemingly unbreakable chain of fealty that stretched down from the Swiss Alps to the low-lying plains of Africa and Asia. Politically, the system was stable albeit at the displeasure of the Europeans.

But all that changed when the wheeling and dealing inside FIFA became public. Rumours of FIFA football barons taking bribes had long been doing the rounds, but as long as they were only stories Blatter seemed unperturbed. However, when in 2010 FIFA voted to award the World Cup to Russia and then to Qatar rather than to their rivals England, Spain and the US, the nature of its governance model could no longer be hidden. How could the tiny Gulf state, with temperatures as high as 50°C, ever have been chosen to host soccer's World Cup? "It would have made more sense to hold it on an iceberg", a British newspaper wrote, "with polar bears as goalposts, or hold it upside-down, or in a tank of piranhas, or on a cloud."[23] Stories of vote-buying spread like wildfire.

FIFA's reputation was shredded, at least in the West. Later, after he had been toppled, Blatter said the decision for Qatar had been the turning point. It was the moment the gloves came off. When they were still in contention, the Europeans had played along with Blatter's game. Prime Minister David Cameron openly applauded Blatter's contribution to the game. After the England bid collapsed, Cameron demanded his head.[24] Investigations into the awarding of the World Cup to Russia and Qatar proliferated. Secretly recorded conversations between FIFA barons swiftly found their way to the media. Blatter had often lovingly spoken of "the FIFA family". Now FIFA was branded a mafia family, with Blatter starring as the Godfather.

Blatter responded by starting his own internal inquest, still hopeful he could deflect the criticism, further cementing the loyalty of his vassals. In 2015 FIFA needed to elect a new president. In light of the scandal there seemed no way that Blatter could be re-elected for a fifth time. But in FIFA's homage system the importance of rules was only relative. What mattered more were loyalty and protection. Blatter's rivals realized this too. Dutchman Michael van Praag emphasized that the global development of the game was his priority, hoping to secure African and Asian votes. However, van Praag wore his reformist heart on his sleeve. He tried to beat Blatter by promising to inject rules-based northern discipline in FIFA. Under his guidance, the World Cup would be awarded on the basis of objective rules and carefully designed suitability criteria.

FIFA was literally being torn apart between two systems of governance, one based on rules and the other based on strength. As long as Blatter's silent contract had been kept under wraps, that conflict had been manageable. But now that everything was out in the open, one or the other needed to give way. Blatter refused to be cowed. When in April 2015 he travelled to the Caribbean to canvass for votes, he was treated to a hero's welcome. Fawning delegates hailed him as "the father of football". Osiris Guzman, president of the Dominican Republic football federation, compared Blatter to Moses, Lincoln, Churchill and Martin Luther King; and in case the message had not gone through, to Nelson Mandela and Jesus as well.[25] Back in Zürich, the outcome of the vote never seemed in doubt. "I am a mountain goat that keeps going and going and going, I cannot be stopped, I just keep going", the 79-year-old Blatter told a Swiss newspaper.[26]

But then, two days before the vote on 29 May 2015, FIFA was reminded of why some things can only be done quietly. At 6 am, Swiss policemen raided the Baur au Lac hotel in Zürich, where FIFA executives were staying for the vote. Seven of them were held on charges of fraud, racketeering and money laundering. In an attempt to shield the men from the press, hotel staff held up white bed sheets as the FIFA executives were led to police cars. The election descended into farce, but went ahead. Blatter comfortably secured a majority for another term. FIFA's silent contract still remained strong. However, as an organization that operated in the public world of law, it neared collapse. "Why would I step down?" Blatter still asked sheepishly, expressing his support for the police investigations.[27] But it was obvious they were coming for him next. Having lorded over a global system of patronage for 17 years, the mountain goat had finally run out of options. Three days later, on 2 June 2015, he announced his retirement.

HANDING OVER THE CROWN

In Bloch's medieval Europe, the continuity of political order was underwritten by the hereditary principle. Feudal bonds and obligations were transferable from one generation to the next, without interruption. When a feudal king died, society did not collapse, having to be reconstituted all over again based on new oaths of fealty. Obligations of homage and tenure passed on directly from father to son, or at least stayed within the family.

Operating in the modern world of law, today's strongman is not so lucky. Without the hereditary principle, the continuity of the silent contract is always in question. What happens when a strongman loses in elections? His formal powers as president or prime minster are easily transferable, of course, as they are embedded in his office. But the silent contract is personal, and the strongman's sudden demise at the polls means its obligations are instantly rendered void. Insofar as it depends on the silent contract, society faces collapse. A new strongman is likely to purge old vassals from the positions of influence they retain, replacing them with men and women loyal directly to him.

Such ruptures are moments of great political danger, instances of regime change rather than a change of government. The stakes are high for all. Having lost their protector at the top, uncertainty reverberates down the chain of vassalage. Jobs are no longer certain. For some, retribution or prison looms, a fate that may only be avoided by making big pay-offs to the new ruler or exile. In short, when a strongman faces competitive elections, much more is at stake than the office of president or prime minister. The future of an entire political substructure is on the line, a state of affairs that risks great instability and conflict. Arguments against free elections have been made for less.

In 2015, the former army general Muhammadu Buhari caused an upset by defeating Nigeria's incumbent president, Goodluck Jonathan, at the ballot box. It was an astonishing and historic result, and testament to the fact that Jonathan had truly made a meal of things. No one in Nigeria had ever managed to oust an incumbent president in elections before. Like most African rulers, incumbents knew a trick or two to decisively stack votes in their favour. In a nation that had seen its share of coups, millions held their breath at what would happen next. It was not a given that Jonathan would voluntarily cede power. Buhari had campaigned on a pledge to fight corruption harder than ever before, an obvious threat to Jonathan and his countless vassals, many of whom hoped he would conjure up a reason for declaring the result void. Jonathan decided it was not worth risking a civil war and retired from public life. His loyal vassals needed to make their peace with a new lord. And that meant pulling out their wallet.

Most strongmen try not to let it come to this point, and mostly they succeed. They make sure they win votes, usually by big margins. When they reach the end of their presidential term limitations, if these exist, they sidestep or abolish them, as Rwanda's Paul Kagame did, or Vladimir Putin and Recep Erdogan in Russia and Turkey.[28] Such practices come in for Western criticism, but this censure typically overlooks the fact that while the cliff edge of an election presents few obstacles for the handover of institutional power, it is unsuitable for handing over the feudal power on which order is in part based. The latter requires a personal and familial touch, and above all time. Neither losing an election nor death in office is an option. Instead, succession is a gradual process that needs to be judiciously managed, often a complicated and tricky task.

With the hereditary principle having lost its legitimacy, there can be no automaticity. A successor needs to be groomed to step into the leader's shoes when the time comes, although most assuredly not before. The overall goal is to transfer the loyalty of the most strategic power brokers in the country – in the armed forces, the intelligence apparatus, the media – to the new man at the top. The heir apparent needs to know who owes what to whom, so he can use the homage system to good effect. The egos of vassals eyeing the throne for themselves need to be mollified, or dealt with in less forgiving ways. The power of rivalling factions may need to be rebalanced or reined in. Jobs may need to be reshuffled. Inevitably, some vassals will have their noses pushed out of joint. As long as they are few, the risk can be managed.

In a system of governance anchored in verbal commitments, trust forms a vital ingredient. Credible assurances need to be given by the heir apparent to his barons and other senior vassals, as well as his predecessor, or they are likely to rise up against their new lord. Once power is transferred, promises made are promises kept. It is one reason why it is risky for the retiring strong-man to disappear from political life instantly. The more prudent model is to gently retreat from public life, to step away from the day-to-day affairs of government, while carving out a role in the background to serve as the silent contract's guarantor and prop up confidence in the ability and fidelity of his successor.

Given the importance of trust, it should not come as a surprise to still see family ties play a significant role in the handover of strongman power. Even if the hereditary principle of feudal society has lost its normative force, its rationale is still evident. Who else can we trust more than family? What else better guarantees continuity?

Little can be said with certainty about the forces at work in leadership suc-cession in North Korea, but one thing seems sure: not Marxism, but family ties constitute the glue that holds Pyongyang's oppressive regime together. For the last 70 years the nation has been run by one family, the Kim dynasty, which has passed on power from father to son over three generations. Current ruler Kim Jong-un took over from his father in 2011, who had inherited power in 1994 from Kim Il-sung who rose to power when Japanese rule ended in 1945. That not all members of the Kim dynasty were to be trusted became apparent in February 2017, when Kim's half-brother, a one-time rival for the throne, wound up dead at Kuala Lumpur airport in Malaysia, widely believed to have been poisoned on the orders of his sibling.

Family ties are rarely far removed from strongman power, and the feudal features of the silent contract explain why. In 2018, Recep Erdogan appointed his son-in-law, Berat Albayrak, minister of finance in his cabinet, and some-times whispered of as his successor. Grace Mugabe, known as "Gucci Grace" for her expensive tastes, was being readied to take over the presidency from her husband Robert Mugabe, 40 years her senior. She might well have succeeded if, in 2017, Zimbabwe's generals had not decided they had had enough of the Mugabe family. Even Donald Trump has given senior White House positions to his beloved "First Daughter" Ivanka and her husband Jared Kushner. "If she ever wanted to run for president", Trump once commented about Ivanka, "I think she'd be very, very hard to beat".[29]

Not all strongmen turn to their immediate family. Vladimir Putin is known to be ferociously protective of his two daughters and family, who he keeps out of the media and political life. China's Communist Party provides a more organized mechanism for succession, a pipeline of leadership candidates slowly drifting to the party's top ranks. The rise of contenders in different party roles makes it plain who is in the line of succession. Since Xi harbours no plans for imminent retirement, currently the pipeline lies dry. But when he does decide to step back from power, these party structures, if they stay intact, could help him organize the handover. It is an institutional asset that makes one-party rule less vulnerable than one-man rule.

However, only some strongmen are able to rely on such party structures. When he was adopted by Boris Yeltsin as his son and heir, and at once thrust into the Kremlin hot seat, Putin came out of nowhere. Today, no one other than Putin knows who he might pick as his heir apparent, or indeed when he will do so. In January 2020, Putin unexpectedly announced proposals for amending Russia's constitution. It led to feverish speculation that a handover plan had been set in motion. Some thought Putin intended to step back from the presidency at the end of his mandate in 2024 to assume a role of mentor and arbitrator of last resort, following the example of Singapore's Lee Kuan Yew. It proved speculation of the sort Putin did not welcome, and when loyalists in the Duma proposed an amendment that would allow him to remain in the presidency until 2036, it was the perfect opportunity to quash such idle talk. "I'm sure that we will do many great things together", Putin said, welcoming the proposal, "at least before 2024. Then we'll see."[30]

THE MICE AT PLAY

The silent contract leaves no paper trail, let alone archives. It is held together by informal obligations. A vassal's word is his bond. As a system of government, this makes the silent contract hard to coordinate and manage, particularly if it grows in scale. By definition, the homage system can never be bureaucratized and "organized". Information cannot be centrally stored. For outsiders, the system's most important power brokers may be difficult to even identify. They do not necessarily hold senior rank or official rank in the state at all. They may be friends, mentors, businessmen or family members. What successful courtiers have in common is infinitely more powerful than institutional seniority: personal access, the strongman's ear. Courtiers always reside in the king's proximity. In the nexus of political whispers that surrounds the strongman, they are conduits for passing information up and down the feudal chain.

Invariably, however, information from the very top is fluid, imprecise and scarce. It means homage systems are rarely just top down. They are also bottom up. Waiting for the strongman to request a specific service is too passive a strategy. Vassals keen to demonstrate their loyalty need to be entrepreneurial. They need to constantly renew their value proposition and create demand. As communication lines to the top get cluttered, this inevitably involves second-guessing what the strongman wants. This is a risky business. Who knows what the strongman truly covets? Pushing gifts in the strongman's direction – watches, yachts, villas – is easy, but unlikely to impress by itself. The challenge is to offer him things he does not already have. If a thousand years ago a vassal needed to offer his lord military muscle, today's vassal is a supplier of diversified political services: funding a political party, a national prestige event, bailing out a plant or organizing foreign influence campaigns.

Constraints on the flow of information are one reason why the silent contract becomes hard to control as it sprawls and gets bigger, until eventually it grows so large it can no longer be controlled at all and its vassals merely run errands of their own. Putin's silent contract, which has dramatically bulged over the years, offers an example of what can go wrong.

Putin's political strategy was to rein in Yeltsin's oligarchs by forging a rival group of vassals that controlled the state's enforcement agencies. Then he pitted both groups against each other. He engineered a system of checks and balances not in the state, but in the shadow of the state, where barons and vassals controlled public resources and assets as a form of tenure received from their lord. The oligarchs held Russia's strategic industries, while Putin's new enforcement barons, the so-called *siloviki* or hardmen, ran the state's policing arms. Only with policing bodies snapping at their heels, Putin knew, did the oligarchs have reason to be frightened. Economic power competed against the power of physical force, the power of money against the power to lock people away. It placed Putin in the imperial position of the Great Arbiter at the top, from where he could oversee the dogfight and guard the system's balance.

It seemed a shrewd plan, although not one without downsides. As his vassalage system grew bigger, playing the role of arbiter proved increasingly hard. In Russia's feudal *sistema*, competing groups of vassals ceaselessly lobby for Putin's blessing, using whatever conduits they have at their disposal. Usually the Great Arbiter takes his time to make up his mind. Often, he appears uninterested and tells feuding vassals to sort out their differences among themselves. As a consequence, disputes tend to rumble on, until they are either settled or spill into the public domain. Ironically, the strength of his enforcement barons in these vendettas has allowed Putin to occasionally cast himself as the protector of private property and individual liberties. But this protection rarely stretches very far. Putin has left it up to his war band of enforcers to check the economic power of the old oligarchs. But who checks the powers of his enforcers?

One common assumption is that Putin does so himself. Nothing ever happens in Putin's vassal system without him having ordered it, this view holds. But given the scope of the system, and the constraints on information it labours under, it seems more plausible that, more often than not, vassals initiate their own actions, sometimes to impress their master, but more likely to simply settle their own petty scores. Having acted first, they then wait for Putin to respond. Different possibilities exist. First, he does not notice. Second, Putin approves or he turns a blind eye. Third, he urges for the matter to be settled by negotiation, an apparently much-loved tactic. Fourth, he disapproves and sanctions his enforcement barons for their stupidity or selfishness. But since Putin rarely opts for the final option, the freedom the latter have won is considerable.

In an extraordinary example of score settling, in 2017 Putin's own minister for the economy, Alexey Ulyukaev, was convicted to eight years in prison. Ulyukaev had made the mistake of objecting to a sensitive business transaction supported by Oleg Sechin, boss of national oil company Rosneft and widely considered to be the most powerful of all the hardmen in the president's private war band. Few in Russia's high-flying elite dare cross swords with Sechin, who back in the 1990s, when Putin was still a deputy mayor in Saint Petersburg, had already acted as his local errand boy. By contrast, Ulyukaev was a mere minister, a state bureaucrat without personal ties to Putin himself.

Against Sechin he never stood a chance. Relying on connections in Russia's enforcement apparatus, he devised a sting operation in which he offered Ulyukaev a $2 million bribe to lift his reservations to the business deal he needed approved. Hosting the minister for a meeting in his office, Sechin pointed to a basket stuffed with artisanal sausages, his so-called peace offerings. Take the sausages, Sechin gestured, wearing a wiretap to record their conversation. When on leaving Sechin's office federal agents inquired what the minister might be carrying in his suspiciously heavy gift basket, sausage was not the only thing they found.[31]

One might have expected Putin to mediate in the vendetta between both men, stopping it from playing itself out in a court of law, which it eventually did, and therefore in public. Perhaps it is what the minister thought would happen. If so, he should have thought again. Little comes between Putin and his barons, certainly not in the public arena. Ulyukaev kept protesting his innocence, saying he never knew what was in the bag other than sausages. Perhaps he was correct. The trouble was, he could not convince Putin to over-rule his trusted errand boy.

Putin's hands-off approach to such vendettas has become a leading fea-ture of how he manages Russia's silent contract. It is only normal for vassals to compete among each other, Putin appears to believe. Is feuding not what vassals are meant to do? May the best one win, his attitude appears to be, as long as these contests do not come in the way of important state business. Unfortunately, they frequently do.

On 4 March 2018, Sergei Skripal and his daughter Julia were found slumped unconscious on a park bench in the medieval town of Salisbury, where he had lived since 2010. Skripal was a former Russian intelligence officer who had once betrayed his fellow Russian spies, served time in prison for it, and then, following a spy swap, settled in the UK. It did not take long for medics to discover the Skripals had been poisoned by a highly toxic, military grade nerve agent called Novichok, a chemical weapon that could be traced back to its origins in Russian facilities. Men in green biohazard suits fanned out across Salisbury's parks hoping to prevent further contamination, while authorities ordered people who had been to the restaurants and pubs the Skripals had visited to wash their clothes. The attempted assassination, it became obvious, had placed the entire town of Salisbury at risk.

It made a strong diplomatic response inevitable. Within days, Putin had a ballooning international crisis on his hands. Three months before Russia was due to host the World Cup, the timing was disastrous. Boris Johnson, for-eign secretary at the time, lashed out calling Russia a "malign and disruptive force".[32] Other Western nations rapidly joined his condemnation. Putin, of course, denied any state involvement. But Prime Minister Theresa May made it clear that for the UK only two things could have happened. Either some of the Russian-made Novichok agent had been stolen and then used by crimi-nals, or this had been a premeditated attack by the Russian state.

What May did not mention was that in a system where formal and infor-mal types of government operate in parallel, and not infrequently at cross purposes, matters need not be quite as clear cut. The third and arguably most plausible explanation of what had occurred in Salisbury was that members of Putin's feudal war band had simply decided to act on their own instincts, as they had been allowed to do before. It is certainly much harder to imagine that Skripal's assassins, who have since been identified as Russian secret agents, went through official or even unofficial channels to get Putin's sign off for their hit job, than that they acted on their own impulses. That spies settle old scores with traitors is rationally understandable, as is a desire to do this in gruesome ways that have a chilling effect on other defectors. What is not rationally understandable is how Putin, who looks after bigger interests in the world, might think the attack to have been a smart move.

In response to the crisis, some two dozen Western countries expelled over 150 Russian diplomats and adopted other penalties against Russia. But while naturally Putin kept denying Russian agents had been behind the assassination attempt, Putin's real message to the world was more nuanced. The world of international spying, the former KGB man argued, had its own norms and practices. Spies will fight out vendettas and they will always continue to do so. However, such account settling, he went on, should not impinge on important matters of state. "I'm talking to you as an expert, believe me", the strongman said. "We need to cast off this fluff and get down to business."[33]

But the weakness of Putin's argument is that use of nerve agents on foreign soil is not so easily cast off as "fluff". More generally, Putin's laissez-faire approach to conflicts inside Russia's feudal *sistema* fails to acknowledge the extent to which the brazen methods of his war band have come in the way of business and matters of state already. Known as corporate raiding, Russian businesses small and large recurrently complain of being hustled by enforcement officers for financial gain with apparent impunity.[34] In the system of checks and balances that Putin engineered, the problem is that the power to lock up people has emerged triumphant, meaning the system is now defunct.

Occasionally, the Great Arbiter still does his job, such as in June 2019 when Russian journalist Ivan Golunov was detained by Moscow City police on what were widely believed to be fake charges of drugs trafficking.[35] Golunov had been investigating corrupt business practices in Moscow's funeral industry. It had not made him new friends in the city. But the case against him stank so obviously it created an uproar even in the Kremlin-friendly media. Three Russian newspapers ran editorial articles with the headline: "We are Ivan Golunov". To everybody's surprise, within days the criminal charges against the journalist were dropped, after what appeared to have been an intervention from the top. "Mistakes can never be ruled out", Dmitry Peskov, Putin's spokesman, confirmed.[36] Clearly, power did not go entirely unchecked. That was the good news. The bad news was that the strongman had needed to step in at all. Golunov's future would have been bleak without it.

Why did it come to this? The answer is not that the silent contract is fundamentally deficient. Exactly the opposite is the case. At least initially, the politics of strength is all too effective. If you need to get something done fast and without hassle, without people meddling, what better solution than to use your own private errand boys? Raising taxpayers' money for a particular project causes political headaches, slows things down, gets citizens upset. It invites media and parliamentary scrutiny. Sidestepping such mechanisms and releasing the same funds through private channels makes everything easier.

The seductiveness of the politics of strength lies precisely in its immediacy, in the direct and personal sense of control it affords. But this immediacy and speed also points at its inherent limitation, which is that it is accident prone. One can use strength to achieve certain things, but one cannot use it for everything or all of the time. Putin compares government based on strength to "manual control", as opposed to relying on institutional processes, that is to say, autopilot. Strength gives the opportunity of driving at great speed, rather than being taken around at 30 miles per hour in the back seat of a self-driving limousine. Grabbing the wheel may be necessary at times and hard to resist – perhaps particularly for someone like Putin, who is known to literally take his presidential limousine for an occasional spin – but it is a choice that invites risk and danger. There are no built-in speed limits or fail-safe systems. For some time, things may run smoothly. However, when traffic becomes dense and the road winding, inefficiencies creep in. Information becomes scare. Oversight is lost. As a result, poor decisions are made. Eventually, drivers tire and lose control.

Strength must be used sparingly and in a controlled way, with a view to switching to autopilot sooner rather than later. When the feudal kings of medieval Europe wrested power back from their vassals and eventually centralized, rationalized and bureaucratized it in the state, they did so for the obvious reason that it turned them and the state into more powerful and effective agents, both domestically and internationally. Rules-based power may be slow, sticky and frustrating, but when the scale and sophistication of social organization increases, its great virtue is that it continues to cope. This is the appeal of rules-based order. For the strongmen it may be hard to recognize this and let go of the wheel but the best among them find the inner strength to do so.

CHAPTER 4

Performer: the *mise en scène* of power

Reputation of power is power.

Thomas Hobbes, *Leviathan* (1651)

Authority is the possibility of acting without making compromises.   Alexandre Kojève, *On the Notion of Authority* (1942)

THE STRONGMAN'S TWO CONTRACTS

He did not wear a fake beak, a newspaper later joked. But he was dressed in baggy white overalls, big black goggles and black gloves. The birds, robed in their own white and black plumage, needed to recognize him as one of their own. They were to follow his lead as he, Vladimir Putin, president of the Russian Federation, took to the skies in a motorized hang-glider.[1]

It was autumn on the Siberian steppe. The skies were leaden. The first snow would be falling soon. The plan, concocted by the president's image-makers: to lead the flock of cranes, hatched and raised in captivity, into the air and start their natural migration cycle to warmer places further south. They only had to follow the big bird. He knew where to go.

The stunt was pregnant with political symbolism, an attempt to highlight Putin's prowess as the nation's leader. And that proved to be its undoing. Because when Putin took off, the cranes stayed put. On his first attempt, one bird followed. Later, five. The other birds looked on in bemusement. Strong winds, an ornithologist explained apologetically. But it could not stop people from mocking the publicity stunt as a spectacular failure.

Inadvertently, Putin had underlined something pertinent about the nature of power and strength. While, obviously, there are mechanisms for coercing compliance in all states, the power of a leader also depends on his ability to secure *uncoerced* compliance. Putin's aides on the ground could have scared the cranes into the air by flapping their arms around. His security detail could have fired their handguns into the air or unleashed a pack of dogs. But while this would surely have chased all birds in the air, such force would have profoundly altered the meaning of the stunt. The use of force would have merely accentuated the limits of Putin's power. It would have laid bare a painful lack of authority. For having authority over your flock precisely means *not* having to force it to move.

One common view of the strongmen is that their power is always "hard", based on brute force and violence. The strongmen lock away opponents and stifle freedom of speech. The images of tanks in Tiananmen Square are etched into the consciousness of an entire generation, as are those of riot police on Bolotnaya Square in Moscow and Taksim Square in Istanbul. The strongman, this view maintains, governs without the consent of his people. Is this not supposed to be the whole point of strongman politics?

In *The Dictator's Handbook*, political scientists Bueno de Mesquita and Alastair Smith argue that the key to autocratic rule is simple and universal: secure the backing of supporters with guns. Step one, get the money. Step two, use it to buy the loyalty of an armed cadre. This makes step three, keeping the people at large in check, child's play. As long as you have five backers with guns, their argument is, anyone can control a room filled with 100 people. The only question is: who grabs the guns first? "Paying supporters, not good governance or representing the general will, is the essence of ruling."[2]

But while this explanation of power may be appealing in its simplicity, it is also wrong. To be sure, paying off hardmen with guns will boost the chances of anyone staying in power. But what this model describes is a quite peculiar sort of state, one that solely relies on tanks rolling through streets and soldiers enforcing curfews, and not on popular support at all. Perhaps dictatorships of this kind once existed or still exist. But the strongmen use more sophisticated and political tactics. They resort to tanks and guns when needed, but they also resort to elections. They claim to be operating within the framework of institutions and the law. And they also claim to represent some version of the general will. It is true, of course, that the strongmen rely on an informal system for procuring helpers or vassals based on inducements, as we saw in Chapter 3. But this "silent" contract is only one of the legs their rule stands on.

The other leg is the strongman's contract with the people, and it is the opposite of silent. In fact, it is a kind of contract that might be compared to the agreement that exists between an actor on stage and the audience that observes him in the theatre. The strongman, I argue, derives his strength from performing a particular role in a piece of drama, and from the people – the audience – agreeing to assign certain qualities, abilities and powers to him, at least for the purposes of the play. And the type of role that the strongman needs to perform to obtain strength is that of a person with authority, the sort of person people follow willingly, just as willingly as they follow the orders of a policeman, teacher or doctor.

This performance is important because it undergirds the strongman's power not just with elite but also with popular backing, which comes in handy when elites and vassals get ideas of their own. It is often assumed that the biggest problem autocrats face is keeping the people in line, for which they rely on the support of elites. For the strongman, reality is often very different. Their biggest problem is keeping elites in line, and for this they need the support of the people.

This, of course, was already the strategy pursued by Julius Caesar, the icon of Roman strongman politics. Caesar's goal was not to enlist the help of Rome's patricians and senators to keep the people under his thumb. His plan was the opposite: to use his popular backing to vanquish the senate, which stood in the way of his political ambitions. As Donald Trump might have approvingly said, Caesar's idea was to drain the swamp, to appeal directly to the city's poor for power and legitimacy.

In Caesar's case, of course, it did not end well, or even in impeachment. He was murdered by angry Roman senators armed with daggers. But his death removed any remaining doubt about who the strongman's true enemies were. Caesar's political strategy was sound. What the strongman failed to realize was how deep the swamp really was, and how much the toads in it wanted him dead. That, at least, was the conclusion his great-nephew and heir Octavian arrived at. Having routed the armies of Caesar's assassins in battle, Octavian went on to eviscerate Rome's elites, killing 2,000 of their ranks. As a message, he found it resonated. The people's backing made his power as Rome's Imperator unassailable, and from this position of utter dominance Octavian shrewdly pledged to restore the senate to its former glory. It was a move that again pacified the city's elites and that gave his strength and authority its famed longevity.

Like Octavian, the deftest of the strongmen make sure their strength is neither exclusively based on the loyalty of vassals nor exclusively on popular support. They prop up their rule from both ends, enabling them to play off one against the other. It makes for smart politics. If elites and vassals become disgruntled or greedy, the strongman can rely on his popular authority. A leader who enjoys popular legitimacy is not easily deposed. He is properly empowered to act. "The men who have changed the world", Napoleon knew, "never succeeded by winning over the powerful, but always by stirring the masses".[3] By contrast, a strongman despised by his people is vulnerable to palace coups. He needs to make concessions to keep his elite backers satisfied, as he depends on them. And those concessions render him weak.

The strongman is not a democrat. But his power benefits from setting the idea of "the people" against the idea of "the establishment". The strongman likes to play the people's tribune, who lives and thinks as they do, who understand the people's problems, its urges and longings, and who speaks its language. He may or may not actually be a man of the people, but his strength feeds on the impression that he is, and on the ability to drum up angry crowds of loyalists in the streets or furious voters in the polling booths. Not all populists are strongmen. But more than a few strongmen are populists. The elite's betrayal of the people, as Catherine Fieschi writes in *Populocracy*, is "the teleological myth that fuels populism".[4] It is also a trope that strongmen use to shore up their power.

On the night of 15 July 2016, Recep Erdogan demonstrated the great power of his contract with the people, defeating a coup d'état staged by elements in the military. At first the coup seemed to follow the standard playbook. Soldiers had been dispatched in helicopters to capture or more likely murder Erdogan, who was staying in a holiday resort on the Turkish coast at Marmaris. In the meantime, the putschists had ordered tanks and other military hardware onto Istanbul's streets. It was intended as a public display of strength. Troops blocked the Bosphorus Bridge connecting the city's Asian and European shores. There was, of course, no greater point to the blockade, other than the mere fact that the plotters had the power to do so. Helicopter gunships and fighter jets patrolled the skies at low altitude, so they could easily be heard. The parliament in Ankara was bombed. It was the political theatre that all coups require, with targets picked for their symbolic value. All the Turkish people needed to know was: now we are in control.

The plotters seized national television station TRT, making its news anchor read out a prepared statement confirming the military had deposed Erdogan. The Islamist Erdogan had a long and complicated history with the Turkish army, the traditional hotbed of Kemalist secularism, and it seemed as if he had now lost its trust. Erdogan, moreover, had been waging an aggressive purging campaign against the followers of an erstwhile political ally, the Imam Fethullah Gülen, many of whom occupied elite posts in strategic sectors of influence: the judiciary, the government apparatus, the media and also the army. This senior cadre, a ragtag coalition of Islamists and secularists, had now turned against the strongman.

For a while it looked as if there was no way back for Erdogan, who for all people knew was already dead. But while the plotters had taken control over state-run TRT, they had inexplicably failed to take private news channels and social media off the air too. It proved a costly mistake that enabled Erdogan, who had escaped his assassins by the skin of his teeth, to address a message to Turkey's population from a hideout. Using a phone to establish a video connection with a Turkish television station still on air, his words and image were broadcast across the entire country.

It was at that precise moment that the coup failed. The footage, first, showed Turks he was still alive and free. But it also allowed him to appeal to his huge popular support base, which started to gather in Turkish streets and squares in ever growing numbers to face the rebel soldiers. In the tense stand-off that followed approximately 250 citizens were killed, martyrs according to Erdogan. But in the end it was the soldiers who backed down. No longer in control of the guns, Erdogan's contract with the Turkish people had saved him. When Erdogan returned to Istanbul Ataturk Airport some hours later, the coup had already imploded, leaving the country's elites to lick their wounds.

The strongman's position of power had not only held, it had emerged stronger and revitalized. Directing his wrath at Turkish elites, it meant Erdogan was now able to dramatically step up his purging campaigns. A state of emergency was declared and later renewed. Tens of thousands of army officers, civil servants, lecturers, journalists and businessmen either lost their jobs or were held on charges of terrorism, even if little or nothing connected them with the coup attempt directly. As for Octavian, proscription lists seemed nothing if not logical to Erdogan. The disease needed to be expunged from the body politic. Power needed to be consolidated, limbs cut off to stop the rot. What gave the strongman the strength for doing so was his contract with the people.

PROJECTING STRENGTH

The idea that a strongman's strength emanates from the use of theatre and representation, and the implicit contract between the performer and his audience, seems odd and strangely contradictory. However, the notion goes back at least to the writings of Thomas Hobbes, who in his *Leviathan* (1651) maintained that such a contract was inherent in the very nature of political power. At a time when parliament began to assert its political rights against the king, Hobbes' politics were decidedly royalist, arguing for the concentration of power in the hands of a sovereign ruler. But whereas other thinkers framed the king's absolute power as a divine gift from the heavens, Hobbes' argument was devastatingly modern and secular. For him, the king owed his powers to the blessing of the people.

It was a radical idea, one that posited the world as essentially disordered and atomistic, a place in which life – in the infamous phrase – was "nasty, brutish and short".[5] But precisely because of this, individuals had good reasons to submit to a sovereign ruler who would establish a system of government and law and protect them. And for Hobbes, this ruler was the king.

What left his fellow royalists stunned, and distrustful of his argument, was that Hobbes' sovereign was at one and the same time the creation of the people as well as the people's absolute master. The idea of a contract made order look unstable, which in reality of course it also was. What if people tore up this contract? How even to imagine its existence? Avoiding such questions, contemporary thinkers tend to view the social contract from a normative slant, as a pure thought experiment to ascertain what obligations we owe to each other and to the state.[6] However, another way of thinking about the idea of a contract – and the one followed here – is that it captures how strength comes about, and also how it might again dissolve. Power, this argument goes, is a "social fact", the product of social convention, of collectively assigning functions and meanings to particular types of behaviour.[7]

In general, social facts are everywhere around us, and they are social because they involve a group of people ascribing a particular status, function or meaning to a thing, place, person or action. A handshake, for example, is a social fact, a type of behaviour that we commonly agree acknowledges someone's social standing. Walls and fences are social facts, as we understand them to demarcate private spaces and property. A one-dollar bill is a means of payment because we agree it is. It would only be a worthless piece of green paper otherwise.

Usually we do not verbally or even consciously "agree" to assign representational meanings to things and people. Social facts are not first put to a vote. We construe them unthinkingly and out of habit. We experience social facts simply as facts. We instantly recognize a one-dollar bill for what it is, for example. The joint act of awarding a particular status to dollar bills remains implicit and unspoken. It suffices for us to observe that the bill looks like and behaves like a one-dollar bill.

Take the example of a police officer who is called to an altercation between neighbours in the middle of the night. Having surveyed the situation, he orders one of the neighbours to turn down the music and the other to go back home. Both do as they are told. The peace is quickly restored. Why do the neighbours obey? The answer is that they assign a particular social status to the police officer. They view him as an agent of the law, and as such he needs to be obeyed. The policeman's authority, that is, results from a social transaction in which the neighbours confer power on him. Moreover, this power emerges organically and merely by the policeman displaying types of behaviours, markers and postures that elicit obedience in his audience. The police officer wears a blue uniform and addresses the neighbours sternly. It allows the audience to instantly recognize who and what he is, and that he must be obeyed.

Power, then, requires the performance of an act and an audience that recognizes its performer as someone they need to obey. In other words, while Hobbes may not have shown that the power of kings or strongmen ought to be absolute, he did arrive at an important lesson about the nature of power, one that contains the secret to how strength is obtained, kept and also lost. That lesson is that power is a performance, an act, something that needs to be made visible and projected to an audience.

In its most simplistic form this theatre involves showing off brute strength. If in a schoolyard enough boys perceive another to be superior in physical strength, even if their perception is based only on bluff or swagger, his strength becomes real. Ever more boys will flock to him pledging their loyalty, either because they fear reprisals or because they seek help, safety or simply rewards, and they think – rightly or wrongly – that he can provide those. As the number in his crew grows, so does the boy's power. Able to command the collective muscle of a group, he can now begin to make a real difference. He can bully other boys. He can project even more strength, exude more confidence, something that will attract yet more followers.

We might compare power to digital platforms such as Facebook, Uber or WhatsApp. What such platforms require is scale. There is no point in joining Facebook if no one else is a member. But once the number of people in a social network increases, so do your own reasons for joining. Once almost everyone uses a network, joining becomes almost inescapable. The great challenge for social networks lies in attracting a critical mass of users, after which growth becomes exponential, self-sustaining and often leads to a position of market power. Such "network effects" play an important role for the strongmen too.

They also require a critical mass of clients. And they also strive for monopolization. Once the number of a leader's supporters reaches a certain threshold, his power starts growing exponentially, while rival leaders are either crushed, bought out or give up. And so the strongman assumes his dominance.

To start such positive feedback loops, reputation is everything. The paradox of power is that you must be known to possess it in order to get it. In politics, as in business, you must have clients in order to acquire them. Someone who understood the principle of network effects well was the Nigerian politician Bola Tinubu, the former governor of Lagos and a senior figurehead in the country's ruling All Progressive Congress (APC). While a major power broker from Nigeria's populous south-west, when Nigerian President Muhammadu Buhari took power in 2015 Tinubu's political luck ran out. Regarding himself as Buhari's kingmaker in the south, Tinubu thought he had earned for himself, or loyal followers of his, a senior post in government. But Buhari adroitly manoeuvred him to the political sidelines, favouring others.

Empty handed but undeterred, Tinubu concluded that if he was not going to be given power in the form of a real job he had better make one up. He understood he needed to project power. He needed to retain his reputation of influence if he wanted to remain a player in Nigerian politics at all. And so Tinubu began styling himself as "National Leader". The job of National Leader did not exist. One could not be elected or appointed National Leader. However, that did not stop people in his entourage from addressing him with that title whenever they had the opportunity. And sure enough, it did not take long for the media to begin reporting about him as "APC National Leader Tinubu".

Some Nigerian politicians thought Tinubu had gone mad. But in fact it was the opposite: he had grasped the true nature of power, the importance of theatre and representation. What party rules or the constitution actually said about jobs and titles only mattered so much. What mattered as much, if not far more, was the projection of power. If enough Nigerians would call, treat and look up to him as National Leader, if he could get that label to stick in everyday use, then legal formalities were not important. De facto he would be their National Leader.[8]

Unfortunately, as a social fact, strength is also inherently unstable and prone to collapse. Negative feedback loops exist too. Once sufficient people come to believe a strongman is on his way out, even if this perception is based on rumours that are false, his power is likely to fade rapidly. Anticipating he may soon no longer be able to protect them, followers coalesce around a new protector. Even the slightest rumours of illness can start a period of deep political uncertainty.

Nothing is more dangerous than the strongman's prolonged absence from the public eye. In April 2018, reports started to circulate that General Khalifa Haftar, the military strongman who ruled the city of Benghazi and much of eastern Libya, had been taken ill in a Paris hospital.[9] Haftar, it was alleged, had suffered a massive stroke. Predictably, it sent his followers into a frenzy of speculation about who might succeed him. The rumours spread fast and seemingly uncontrollably. Some suggested the strongman had slipped into a coma, others that he was already dead. For days, verifiable information about Haftar's condition was unavailable, stoking fears of further infighting in a country that was already deeply fractured. Then two weeks later, as if risen from the dead, Haftar casually and confidently strolled down the stairs of a private jet in Benghazi, declaring he was perfectly fine. Those responsible for spreading false rumours about his health, he added, "will answer for them in the appropriate way".[10] Things quickly returned to normal.

To stamp out negative feedback loops, strongmen resort to harsh and especially public reprisals for those who display signs of disloyalty. This puts hesitating followers in an awkward spot. Jump ship too early, you pay the price for treason. Jump ship too late, you go down with the boss. In politics, timing is everything. When Dmitry Medvedev was elected Russian president in 2008 and Putin became prime minster, Russian officialdom agonized over whose portrait to hang on their office walls. Customarily it would have been the president's. This time nobody was sure. How long would Medvedev last? Some decided the safest course was to simply stay on the fence: they put up both.

Born out of perception and social reputation, rather than hard and objective fact, power is a transitory phenomenon. It can vanish in the blink of an eye. However, if properly nurtured it can last for decades. Strongmen require their clients' confidence, just like banks do. As inherently unstable institutions, banks project strength and stability with grand architecture to instil confidence in their clientele. A run on a bank can start for no good reason at all. A few clients empty their accounts on the basis of a rumour. Then some more. As word spreads a tipping point is reached, after which it becomes an avalanche. Perception is all that matters here. The most solid of banks will go bust if its clients no longer believe it is solid. And so it is with the strongmen. Confidence must be maintained at a high level. Strength must be on full display, while anything that undermines the image of strength must be squashed.

Power, for example, becomes fluid when large numbers of people openly display dissent in mass protests, as Hosni Mubarak found out in Egypt in 2011.[11] As the number of protestors goes up and up, and the protests are not broken up, the regime's image of strength is revealed as illusionary. This is what brought down the Berlin Wall in November 1989. Its fall began with large crowds chanting "we are the people" all over the country. Unable or unwilling to forcibly stop the protests, the German Democratic Republic deflated like a punctured tyre. Its projection of power was no longer believable. Riot police stood down, convinced of the futility of using force. Moscow had made clear it would not interfere. After ambiguous comments made by officials at a press conference in the afternoon of 9 November, protestors in Berlin just walked through decades-old checkpoints into West Berlin as if they no longer existed.

The large anti-China protests that swept Hong Kong in 2019 posed a similar threat to Xi Jinping. The question for Xi and the strongman in general is how to stop things from getting to the tipping point when confidence in their strength dissipates and followers switch their loyalties to a rival. Resorting to force is the obvious option, but not always the most attractive. Alternatively, crowd estimates can be downplayed or media coverage of the protests manipulated. On 1 July 2019, Hong Kong police put the crowd at 190,000, while the protest's organizers put the number at half a million.[12] Who truly knows how many took part? Imagery of half-empty parks and streets can be used selectively to suggest a slump in turnout. Counter-protests can be organized, showing the regime's support base to be strong and loyal. Sometimes a strongman may also wish to inflate crowds to accentuate his power. This is what Donald Trump tried when he claimed more Americans had attended his inaugural address in Washington in January 2016 than any such address before.

The *mise en scène* of strongman power can range from the subtle to the not so subtle. As a rule, the more client confidence is at risk, the more brutally and violently power needs to be showed off, to quell any doubt. The point about violence is rarely violence itself. It is the image of strength it communicates. New and aspiring strongmen must prove their strength in particular. Mohammed bin Salman's "Sheikdown" in 2017 seemed designed as an extravagant piece of theatre. The House of Saud does not have to wash its dirty linen in the Ritz-Carlton, frequented by foreign VIP guests and businessmen from all over the world. Photos were leaked to foreign media of the detained princes sleeping on the hotel's floor.[13] The show of strength drew criticism from the West. But the young prince was merely following the strongman playbook. He needed to project power. He needed to show he was serious and in control.

Brutality has always been a favoured communication tactic for autocrats. When confronted with rebellious towns on his conquests, Genghis Kahn is said not only to have razed them to the ground, but to also make sure the world knew about it, in particular other towns on his path of conquest.[14] At the height of his Great Purge, Stalin ordered so-called enemies of the people executed at a rate of 1,000 per day.[15] In North Korea, Kim Jong-un had his defence minister executed by anti-aircraft guns in front of a crowd of onlookers, according to South Korean intelligence reports. His crime was to have fallen asleep in a meeting with the president, an act of defiance that naturally could not go unpunished.[16]

The trouble with such tactics is that paranoia only begets more paranoia. Followers fear they will be purged next, feeding precisely the conspiracies these tactics seek to prevent. When in 1953 Stalin suffered a stroke at night, he lay unattended on his bedroom floor until late into the next evening, reportedly in a puddle of his own urine. Guards, doctors and even Politbureau members did not dare enter his room for fear of disturbing his sleep, and being purged for it. Or maybe they just decided to let him die, to be rid of the paranoid tyrant.

Narratives of legitimacy matter, and thankfully there are also less violent ways of projecting power. Strongmen who sit comfortably in the saddle, who have already shown they will do whatever it takes, try to make their strength appear not just overwhelming but also rightful. It was precisely this transition – from governing through fear to governing through authority – that Octavian made, and that made him famous. As one historian of Rome describes the change: "The murderousness of the young Caesar's early career had been the measure of his weakness, not his strength … The surest buttress of power was his *auctoritas* – and the surest buttress of that was his ability to serve the Roman people as the restorer and guarantor of peace."[17]

Augustan *auctoritas* remains the holy grail of strongman government, the basis of its durability. And to achieve the transition that Augustus made, a strongman needs to hone his dramatic skills and assume the guise of a more sophisticated and honourable persona. Visibility is a precondition for success. The pressures on the strongman to be in the spotlight are no less intense than for democratic leaders. He must be talked and written about, be unfailingly present at the centre of events. For the strongmen, all the world truly is a stage. And on that stage, they must endlessly display demeanours that exude authority: wearing uniforms and robes, giving instructions to underlings, pointing out directions on maps, speaking earnestly into phones, inspecting the troops.

To achieve this visibility, Augustus had coins minted with his image, sending a powerful message to the remotest corners of the empire, a practice all Roman emperors would later adopt. Statues of Augustus, in different poses – as the military commander, the great statesman and the father of the nation – proliferated under his reign. He literally rebuilt Rome in his own image.[18] Architecture and construction, bath houses and aqueducts, entire cities served as the permanently visible reminder of his power and greatness. Temples, monuments and arches commemorating his deeds drowned out older imagery. Augustus became synonymous with Rome. He authored an autobiography, *Res Gestae Divi Augusti* (The Deeds of the Divine Augustus) and acted as the patron of the arts. He nurtured relations with the country's finest poets and writers: Horace, Virgil, Ovid and the historian Livy, who would go on to amplify his image as Rome's wise and just strongman.

While the technological means to secure visibility have changed, today's strongmen still use similar tactics. Strewn across the Middle East and Central Asia are large billboards with the emblazoned photographs of local strongmen. Their stately portraits adorn the walls of uncountable buildings, offices and schools. Kazakhstan's strongman Nursultan Nazarbayev ordered a brand-new capital city, Astana, to be built on the country's barren northern steppe. When in 2019 he announced he would slowly step back from power after nearly 30 years of rule, the city was promptly renamed as Nursultan.

Further south, in Ashgabat, the capital of Turkmenistan, strongman Saparmurat Niyazov, having crowned himself Turkmenbashi (Father of all Turkmens), had a massive gold statute built of himself that rotates to always face the sun. Saddam Hussein's image could be found on the inside of Iraqi wrist watches, so that whenever Iraqi's glanced at the time, they were reminded of their leader. Biographies are written for the strongmen, PR stunts organized. Documentaries are commissioned, political rallies organized. Spin doctors monitor and guard the leader's image online. When memes started to go viral that likened Xi Jinping to Winnie-the-Pooh, the gentle but gullible teddy bear, Chinese censors responded without mercy. They blocked Pooh from China's digital network.[19] Westerners thought it was petty. But for Xi it was no laughing matter.

The strongman is not a man; he is the image of a man, a story told once and then endlessly told again. Imagery, drama, this is what power is made of. If the Romans relied on coins, architecture and poets to enact that drama, today's strongmen seek to control what the mass media say about them, either by outright censorship or by contriving for loyal friends to acquire influential media outlets, which is what Viktor Orbán has aimed to do. Digital and social media offer an additional means for the strongman to be ever-present and for the drama to play out in public. The question is no longer how to make the leader's story visible; it is what his story of legitimacy should be. If a strongman's authority is forged in drama, what are the performances and narratives that elicit the obedience from his audience?

KOJÈVE'S THEATRE OF POWER

An answer to this question is provided by Russian-born Frenchman Alexandre Kojève (1902–68), whose seminars on the philosophy of Hegel decisively influenced the intellectual scene in Paris after the war. Later, Kojève became a feared trade negotiator for France and the European Economic Community in Brussels, the precursor to the EU. Recalling his reputation, a diplomat once commented that "When Kojève arrived, he triggered panic in the other delegations."[20] US officials referred to the Frenchman as "the snake in the grass".[21] As a political thinker, Kojève owed his fame to having coined the idea of "the end of history", later popularized by Francis Fukuyama. Less well known, but no less interesting, is his short work *The Notion of Authority*, which he wrote in Vichy France in the 1940s, a period when history seemed very far from over.[22]

Kojève believed there were four "pure" types of authority, or in the language of the theatre, a cast list of four basic personae or roles that political leaders could perform to project power on stage: master, father, leader and judge. These four roles were not exclusively intended to be performed by strongmen or other autocrats. Rather, Kojève seems to have thought that the characters or narratives he described exhaust the entire theatre of power and authority, and that politicians of all kinds and persuasions are simply enacting different variations on these roles to strengthen their hold on power. Moreover, politicians are certainly not limited to a single role. Accomplished actors mix things up. They switch from one character to the next, offering their audience a performance that always keeps it enthralled.

The master

The first role Kojève distinguished is the part of "master", the warrior or daredevil who puts his own life on the line. The master is ready to assume the risk of getting hurt or even killed. Those who obey him, typically, are more cautiously inclined. They prefer to wait, are themselves too scared to act, and consequently they follow their master's lead. The master resembles Machiavelli's Prince, the man who is always on the front foot, imposing his will on events, who, as Kojève puts it, "knows how to act", is "capable of taking a decision", "gets down to business". On the other hand, the master is not known to be "reasonable" and "careful".[23] He cares neither about the past nor the future. His business is the present.

The master is often a strongman's first and most comfortable guise, and his appearance is invariably linked to danger and crisis. When Egyptian general

Abdul Fatah al-Sisi seized power in 2013, like so many strongmen he did so in the role of action hero. His mission was immediately clear to his audience: save the nation from the bedlam created by the Arab Spring. Al-Sisi had planned his entrance wisely, with due appreciation for the subtleties of the drama. Before making his move, he waited until things had become sufficiently bad under the elected Islamist Mohamed Morsi. When he acted, few in Egypt quarrelled with his decision to arrest the president and suspend the constitution. The politicians had messed up. Now the generals needed to clean things up. The West did not like al-Sisi's methods. But it liked Morsi's methods even less. It was the right play at the right time, and flawless in its performance.

The fact that al-Sisi had been Egypt's top-ranking soldier proved invaluable for the role. He already possessed the looks, talk and gait of the fearless warrior. He merely needed to walk onto the stage and maintain his customary appearance of resolve. The uniform meant the audience could instantly recognize the character that was now claiming a place in their story and the type of authority he exerted over them. On the whole, they liked what they were seeing. The general denied having political ambitions for the future. His job was in the present. He needed to neutralize a threat, restore law and order, then the political process could resume as normal. But as calls for him to stay and lead the nation grew louder, al-Sisi became a politician himself. In 2014, he was overwhelmingly elected president.

Other soldiers have used the dramatic power of their uniform to assume the role of master in times of revolution, turbulence and crisis, as did arguably its most illustrious performer in the modern age, Napoleon Bonaparte. Returning from heroic exploits on the Egyptian battlefield in 1799, Napoleon's authority had grown so strong that his presence in Paris alone almost sufficed to snatch power away from the republic's civilian government. "It was not the return of a general", a fellow officer commented, "it was the return of a leader in the garb of a general."[24] It made Bonaparte's ascent inevitable, culminating in the coup of the Eighteenth Brumaire. Military force was hardly necessary to complete the putsch. The republic's government felt it in their bones: the people would follow Napoleon's lead, not theirs.

The number of military strongmen and autocrats to first emerge on the political stage in the guise of the warrior is high, from Spain's *Generalísimo* Francisco Franco to Venezuela's Hugo Chavez, Chile's Augusto Pinochet and Rwanda's Paul Kagame. But the role of the swashbuckling action hero can also be claimed by civilians. Putin mastered the part better than most former generals will ever do. He placed himself right at the heart of every national crisis, showing fearlessness and defiance in confronting adversity. It made for a stark contrast with the ailing and inebriated Boris Yeltsin. The war in Chechnya provided a useful backdrop. The first thing Putin did was to fly in a fighter jet to Chechnya where he toasted to victory. "His campaign was the war in Chechnya", one Russian political consultant recalls.[25] "He was young, doing things, moving, meeting with people. It was all unusual for a leader. He could walk and talk." Putin's public persona seemed to match that of iconic Soviet-era action hero Max Otto von Stierlitz, Soviet Russia's James Bond, who in a 1970s television drama risked his life as a special agent operating undercover in Nazi Germany.

Like all good spies, Putin was a superb actor.[26] His salty language left little room for doubt. "We will chase terrorists everywhere", he once declared. "If we find them in the toilet, excuse me, we'll rub them out in the outhouse. And that's it, case closed."[27] When in August 2008 fighting broke out between Russian and Georgian military in South Ossetia and Abkhazia, a fuming Putin flew straight from the Beijing Olympics to the front line, threatening to hang Georgian President Mikheil Saakashvili "by the balls".[28] In the summer of 2010, scores of Muscovites saw their homes go up in flames in bush fires. Again, daredevil Putin was on site to assist firefighters. Vowing to see people's homes rebuilt, he had video cameras installed to personally monitor the progress construction workers were making.[29] If for once there were no fires to fight, holiday snapshots would depict Putin wading through wild rivers with fishing rods or racing cars.

The father

The second character is that of the father, whose authority is rooted in the past, more particularly in the act of founding. The authority of the father is the authority of the cause over the effect, of the latter submitting to its creator or "author". To oppose the father, as Kojève puts it, "would be a reaction against oneself, a kind of suicide."[30]

Having founded Apple, Steve Jobs possessed a type of authority that no one else in the company could even aspire to. Even after he died, his authority remained intact. Indeed, as Kojève points out, "the orders of a dead father are respected better than the ones he gave during his lifetime".[31] Heirs can assume this authority by showing they act in the father's spirit and name, by being faithful to his intentions and values. The authority of the father, in other words, can be passed down the generations until it becomes the authority of tradition, of history and those who represent it.

Obviously, the role of the father is best performed by strongmen who can claim to be responsible for foundational acts themselves, mythologized episodes of national suffering, struggle and ultimately achievement. Such strongmen typically award themselves the grand title "father of the nation", a status they keep until their deaths, and even after. Turkey's Mustafa Kemal became "Ataturk" (1881–1938), Father of the Turks, and founder of the modern Turkish republic. Singapore's Lee Kuan Yew (1923–2015) led Singapore to independence and then to economic success. Lee governed his country for three decades. After he stepped down as prime minster, his paternal authority as founder alone ensured he remained the leading political force in the country, which is currently ruled by his eldest son. Kazakhstan has its own father of the nation in Nursultan Nazarbayev. Thriving on his authority as founder, his power remains strong and dominant, even outside of presidential office.

Not all strongmen, obviously, can claim to be founding fathers themselves. What they can do is perform the role of "son" and hence appropriate the father's authority. To achieve this, the ruler needs to align his image to that of a founding figure from the past, professing to take forward his legacy and vision. Occasionally, Xi can still be seen in a grey Mao suit, giving expression to the regime's continuity and his authority to lead it in Mao's name. The son of a senior party official in the days of Mao and later Deng, Xi's is one of China's so-called "red Princelings". His roots and credentials can be traced back to the revolution's early origins. He seems destined for greatness and power.

In North Korea, an entire cult of personality has been built around the state's first leader and war-hero Kim Il-sung (1912–94), who was declared "eternal president of the republic" in 1998. The memory of his great deeds, as those of his son Kim Jong-il, is carefully kept alive at schools and by hundreds of statues that are scattered across the country. North Koreans are obliged to hang official portraits of both rulers in their homes and face stiff penalties if they fail to do so.[32] It allows current ruler Kim Jong-un to govern under the authority of his venerated father and grandfather.

Family ties may be helpful in gaining authority, but they are not essential. More important is the continuity of the regime. For the Islamist Recep Erdogan, the role of the son poses clear difficulties. While Erdogan does not entirely eschew the memory of Ataturk, his own rise to power in 2003 broke with Kemalist secularism. Erdogan does not reject the modern Turkey that Ataturk created, but the version of it he advocates differs in important ways. It makes identification with the republic's great founder less than evident.

Similar ruptures have not stopped Putin from trying to assume the mantle of his nation's forefathers. Whereas Yeltsin wanted to remove Lenin's embalmed corpse from his mausoleum in Red Square, Putin ordered Lenin to stay where he was, a fresh coating of embalming liquid added every now and then.[33] In 2000, Putin restored the Soviet anthem, even though he had its words altered. Apart from its obvious faults, he argued, the Soviet Union achieved great things: the defeat of Hitler, Sputnik, Russia's global strength. In 2005, Putin went on to describe the collapse of the Soviet Union as "a major geopolitical catastrophe", a comment that, as he since explained, was meant to deplore the end of Russia's global power, not of communism. He never fails to stand up for Russia's historic record in the battle against Nazism and its reputation as one of the Allied powers.

Putin's unrepentant posture towards the past struck a chord with his audience. But he understood he could hardly cast himself as the pure progeny of Joseph Stalin, and even less that of the agitator Lenin, whom he once accused of having placed "a time bomb" under the Russian state.[34] The authority of history could only be fully galvanized by going back still further, to Russia's imperial past. In 2011, Putin unveiled a statue in Moscow built in honour of Pyotr Stolypin, the tsar's prime minister who was murdered in 1911, and he lauded Stolypin's legacy of reform in speeches. Russia's economy had grown faster than anywhere else back then, Putin gushed.[35] But then Lenin pushed the country onto a different path, one leading to disaster.

Returning to the presidency in 2012, Putin increasingly spoke about the importance of patriotism, family and church, forging a moral alliance with Patriarch Kirill. Ostentatiously, he visited Mount Athos in Greece, centre of Eastern Orthodox monasticism. He criticized permissive lifestyles in the West and signed a controversial law that banned advocating for homosexuality. Hundreds of years ago, the founders of the nation had a vision of Russia becoming Europe's "third Rome", the world's new epicentre of Christendom. Now, under his rule, that time had come, Putin seemed to be saying.

The leader

The third role is that of leader, the man who possesses the ability to see further into the future than anyone else. The leader knows what the future holds in store, he can therefore "anticipate" and tell others where to go. His authority, as Kojève makes clear, is the authority of those who can see over the blind. "The person who realizes he sees less well and less far than another readily allows himself to be *led* or *guided* by this other person ... He follows the other 'blindly'".[36] Leaders typically formulate projects, set goals and give instructions, which those who have less information follow.

For centuries, kings sought to strengthen their authority and legitimize their directives by employing sorcerers, prophets and priests able to divine the future. Before they decided to ride into battle, the ancient Romans consulted the college of augurs, priests who, by studying the behaviour and flight patterns of birds, could tell whether the gods approved of their war plans or not. If their prognostications were favourable – and smart emperors always made sure they were – it made it easier to lead the nation into war. Later, leaders turned to philosophy, economics and science to boost the authority of their commands and projects. Dialectical materialism allowed Lenin to foretell capitalism's collapse and point the way to the workers' paradise. His great powers of foresight, eventually bundled in his *Little Red Book*, turned Mao Zedong into "the Great Helmsman", able to steer his people into the Great Leap Forward, safe in the knowledge the nation would land on its feet.

For the strongman, who as we saw is no ideologue, defining projects and visions is often difficult. The strongman's authority is often at its greatest when the nation needs masters and warriors, when the world is in turmoil. Once stability returns, what then? Al-Sisi's uniform stood him in good stead when Egyptians needed someone to clean up the politicians' mess. But how often can the nation be saved from religious extremism, terrorism and crisis? Today, Egyptians demand change and a better future, as they had demanded from al-Sisi's predecessor Mubarak in 2011. To keep his authority strong, al-Sisi the master needs to become al-Sisi the leader, someone offering a vision and a plan, who leads the way and beckons the people to follow.

This transformation can prove difficult even for the greatest. Winston Churchill, a strongman in some ways, owed his authority to the war and to a powerful rendition of Kojève's master. His command of oratory turned him into the indispensable saviour not only of the nation but of the Western world as a whole. Offering nothing but "blood, toil, tears and sweat", and of course victory, his words and voice projected precisely the sort of defiance, bravery and resolve needed to unite the country. However, as de Gaulle found later in France, with the end of the war came the end of the warrior's brand of authority. The audience had grown tired of action heroes. It wanted politicians capable of formulating plans for the future. It demanded leaders with vision. It was a role Churchill mastered less well. In Britain's first election after the war, in July 1945, he lost the premiership to Labour's Clement Attlee, who promised Britons the welfare state and social justice.

Putin equally grapples with the future. The future is divisive, he found in his first published article as acting president.[37] Twice in the last century visionaries had promised change in Russia, in October 1917 and in the liberal

1990s. And twice, the result had been disaster. The change he promised was that from now on there would be no change, only solidity and stability, job and pension security. On television, Putin is astoundingly good at rattling off growth forecasts, inflation figures and employment data. The future is in safe hands, he wants the audience to know. As a performance, however, the prospect of stability grew tedious, especially for the young. When in 2011 critics jokingly compared Putin to Soviet leader Brezhnev, who had overseen an epoch in Soviet history notable for its stupor, a Kremlin spokesman replied that Brezhnev "was not a minus for the history of our country, he was a huge plus".[38]

Putin's understudy, Dmitry Medvedev, gave a more boisterous performance as leader when he became Russia's president. In September 2009, he set out his vision in an article in *Gazeta* entitled "Go Russia!", and it was all about change.[39] It proposed modernization far more radical than Putin had ever done, a cultural transformation. "Bribery, theft, intellectual and spiritual laziness, and drunkenness" formed the real legacy of Russia's imperial and communist past, Medvedev argued. He stood for a youthful, professional and urban future. He ardently embraced digital technology, travelling to Silicon Valley for ideas. He addressed the nation, not on television, but through a video blog. He worshipped swish Apple products, and made sure the whole world knew about it. Observers were quick to see a political rift. In fact, there was no rift. The introduction of the Medvedev character, which was judiciously staged by Putin, only broadened the Kremlin's narrative of legitimacy. It added a type of authority that Putin lacked.

More commonly, the strongmen vision of the future involves restoring the nation's sovereignty, greatness and respect in the world. When Donald Trump holds forth about "making America great again", that is his idea of the future. He posits a bygone golden age of national sovereignty, which was followed by a period of decline and weak presidents who chained America to international treaties. Trump's project is to break free of those chains and lead the United States back to the top. When he rips up climate, trade and arms control agreements, this is Trump pointing the way forward.

Putin discerns a very similar national project and a future in which Russia will regain the standing of superpower it enjoyed since 1945 but squandered in the 1990s. His project is to ensure that Russia will once again be respected in the world as the sovereign power it was, in particular by the US. When Putin brought Crimea into the Russian Federation in 2014, it was an astonishing act of the warrior's chutzpah, but also of leadership, arguably his crowning performance in the role. He had literally managed to transform the country, made it greater even in a physical sense. Rarely had his authority as a leader been greater.

Xi's "China Dream" offers the precise same narrative of humiliation and renewal, even if it measures progress in centuries rather than decades. Once the greatest civilization on earth, but then surpassed by the West, Xi's plan is to make China the world's greatest civilization again. Military parades and displays of state-of-the-art weaponry and technology are used to highlight the strongman's vision. Xi talks with a swagger rarely encountered among his predecessors. "No force can stop the Chinese people and the Chinese nation forging ahead", he predicted at the seventieth anniversary of the People's Republic in 2019, as the world watched hypersonic drones and intercontinental missiles roll by in Tiananmen Square.[40] Not the US, but China would be at the top of the world.

The judge

The final persona in Kojève's theatre of power is that of the judge, whose authority is that of a "respected arbiter", of "impartiality", "objectivity" and "disinterestedness". Rather than joining the melee, the judge elevates himself above the battle. He places himself "outside time", outside history. He has no interest in outcomes or ties to the feuding parties. The judge never acts or takes part. He stands aside and observes, he regulates and judges. In football, a referee gives up being a player himself. The players consider his decisions as final precisely because he does not take part in the game. Referees are allowed to make the occasional mistake, but they are never allowed to lose their disinterestedness. If they do, they lose their authority.

Nelson Mandela's unique personal strength as a political leader in post-apartheid South Africa was based on the authority of the judge, his perceived ability to stand above the parties and to reconcile them. At a critical time in the 1990s, he used this image to lay the foundations for the new South Africa. As a young African National Congress (ANC) activist, Mandela had been anything but an impartial referee. He had been a player and a warrior, rebelling against apartheid by blowing up essential facilities and infrastructure. However, when it arrested Mandela in 1962, unwittingly the regime greatly augmented his authority. While other ANC soldiers took his place in battle, Mandela found himself jailed on Robben Island, a place so desolate it really did seem to exist outside of time. It was the solitude and austerity of his cell, which can now be visited, that helped him cultivate the authority of the disengaged judge. It projected an image of wisdom, integrity and calm. After his release in 1990, Mandela honed this image, using it to win the trust of white South Africans. Among other things, he did so by publicly cheering on the South African rugby team, which at the time was strongly associated with the country's apartheid culture. It showed he now truly stood above the parties. Had Mandela remained a player, it is difficult to see how apartheid might have ended peacefully.

On stage the persona of the judge, while powerful, is normally a good deal less dazzling than that of the master or the leader. A referee ought not to make headlines. His presence is subtle, often hardly visible. But at the same time it is unmistakable. Judges mostly stay silent. Their expression remains blank and detached. While others talk, plead and agitate, a judge listens and takes notes. But when he makes up his mind, one thing is always certain: his rulings are final.

Putin the judge does not act or take part in anything. He is neither liberal nor conservative. He stands aside, coldly observes and judges from afar, without emotion. In frequently televised meetings with ministers or other senior officials, Putin typically asks for a state of play report. As they talk and talk, often nervously, attentively he listens, frowning, looking severe. When they finish, he asks a surprisingly pertinent question. Under the stifling lights of the television cameras, the senior officials break out in a sweat, stuttering some words back. Then, pithily, the ever-cool Putin gives his Solomon's verdict.

Judges are detached from disputing factions, and Putin has been wary of tying his fate to any political party. Like a latter-day "good tsar", he floats above them, placing himself above the state by arbitrating in conflicts between citizens and local authorities. Every year Putin hosts *Direct Line*, a four-hour live phone-in show. It is Russia's answer to America's town hall meeting, and an opportunity for ordinary Russians to vent their anger at incompetent authorities and to petition the president for justice. As they plead their case, Putin thoughtfully listens, raises an eyebrow, then nods while scribbling notes – one imagines of the type "follow up with" – before dispensing justice on the spot. Squirming in front of a television screen somewhere, local officials know there can be no further appeal.

In the theatre of power, the role of judge may be the hardest to master. Certainly, not all strongmen possess the judge's authority or can even aspire to it. Erdogan is still the streetfighter who risks life and limb by challenging the army's stranglehold on Turkish politics. When he rose to power, he fought for the rights of religious and working-class Turks from Anatolia, so-called black

Turks. For a brief time, Erdogan went to prison, like Nelson Mandela. But they let him go, and so he stayed in his role as warrior.

Likewise, Donald Trump relishes a dogfight, and never places himself above it. He plays the warrior who always wins because he is tougher and meaner than anyone, and because he is not scared to break the rules when these come in the way of achieving his and America's goals. Ironically, by flouting institutional norms and other political codes of propriety, Trump only grows his authority, his reputation of strongmindedness. Fearful of scandal and prosecution, others get scared and hold back. Trump is the guy who never flinches. It explains why impeachment by the US House of Representatives in December 2019 left no dent in the president's approval ratings. In fact, over the period his impeachment hearings ran those ratings only went up.[41]

Successful performers, Erdogan and Trump show, need not master all of Kojève's roles to obtain strength, and they certainly do not need to perform those roles all of the time. That said, the ability to perform different personae will certainly add to the longevity of a performer's career. As on any stage, to keep the audience hushed and subdued, or to make it shout and agitate, the performer needs to be versatile and mix up his imagery. Times change, and audiences change too. They call for new heroes and new narratives. Performers need to adapt and innovate, or else the public will not only hanker after new characters, but also for new performers. One way or another, the strongman's job is to keep the audience spellbound. The strongman's contract with his people depends on it. As does his strength.

CHAPTER 5

Duellist: the fellowship of foes

An enemy only exists when, at least potentially, one fighting collectivity of people confronts a similar collectivity. The enemy is solely the public enemy.

Carl Schmitt, *The Concept of the Political* (1932)

A CLUB OF RIVALS

In the end, it took only five seconds to decide he liked him. After decades of deal making in the real estate business it was not difficult. "It's my touch, my feel, that's what I do", Trump said. "I think very quickly I know whether or not something good is going to happen. And if I think it won't happen, I'm not going to waste my time."[1]

It had not looked quite so easy one year earlier, when Kim Jong-un was busy testing his long-range missile capability over the Pacific Ocean, a projection of his strength and power. In August 2017, Trump still tweeted that North Korea's nuclear threat "will be met with fire and fury the likes of which the world has never seen".[2] And Kim, who Trump liked to refer to as "Little Rocket Man", responded by calling the president a "mentally deranged dotard".

War had seemed unavoidable. But when both leaders met in June 2018, on the island of Sentosa off the coast of Singapore, the turnaround was dramatic. When Kim had first floated the idea of a summit, foreign policy experts in Washington quickly agreed it would be a disastrous move. Trump's secretary of state Rex Tillerson, part of the "axis of adults" in the White House, advised against it. Any deal would need to be minutely prepared by professional negotiators. How else had Obama been able to get the Iran nuclear deal agreed?

But Trump rated himself as the world's number one dealmaker. The Iran deal he considered "the worst deal ever". Tillerson, previously the CEO at ExxonMobil, was summarily sacked, by tweet. The president had decided to stonewall his foreign policy mandarins. For Trump, what mattered more than professional advice was his personal relationship with Kim. "This is all about leader vs leader", he explained his motives to White House aides. "Man versus man. Me versus Kim."[3]

When during the summit preparations Kim threatened to pull out of the meeting, Trump responded with a personal letter. "I felt a wonderful dialogue building up between you and me", the president wrote warmly, "and ultimately, it is only that dialogue that matters."[4] Soon things got back on track. "Meetings between staffs and representatives are going well and quickly", Trump tweeted days before the summit, "but in the end, that doesn't matter."[5] Everything, Trump made clear, depended on how he would size up Kim. Was he a man he could do business with? For that, all he needed was to look Kim in the eye.

"Great personality and very smart", Trump summed up his impressions after the meeting.[6] "A very worthy, very smart negotiator, absolutely." Trump had liked what he had seen. "I think he trusts me and I trust him." In an interview with Fox News, the president enthused: "He is the head of a country, he's the strong head, don't let anyone think anything differently. He speaks and his people sit up at attention. I want my people to do the same."[7] Later, he said he was only joking.

Trump's critics were less awestruck. What had actually been agreed, they asked? Was there a timetable for further negotiations at least? Trump had few answers. For him, however, they were the wrong questions. What he had wanted to assess at the summit was whether he and Kim spoke the same political language of strength, whether Kim was a man of his word, an opponent worthy of respect. And his answer to that question could hardly have been clearer.

Trump's bonhomie with Kim, as with strongmen such as Putin and Erdogan, puzzled the world, not least America's traditional allies in Europe, who received a decidedly frostier reception. "No one knows", *The Economist* wrote in November 2019, "why President Donald Trump is so fond of autocrats – including his 'friend' Muhammad bin Salman, 'highly respected' Viktor Orbán, beloved Kim Jong-un and of course Vladimir 'so highly respected' Putin".[8]

But once we look at the philosophy of strength and power, which all strong-men hold in common, reasons readily suggest themselves. For as we saw, in politics strength is never just naked, physical force, severed from all social ties and obligations. Strength is fundamentally relational and contractual. And beyond notions of how the strongman relates to the power brokers in the state (as a lord to his vassals) and to the broader public (as a performer to his audi-ence), it contains a fairly precise idea of how men of strength ought to relate *to one another*. Strength, this idea goes, is not just an instrument. It is an ethos, a political language with its own grammar, and because men like Trump and Kim share this language, it is not surprising they get along with each other.

The notion of the world's strongmen joining hands in some global "fellow-ship of strongmen" may still sound improbable. Populism, observers point out, makes for a poor adhesive for global cooperation. "Leaders who believe in the separateness of nations above all else will always have trouble co-ordinating", argues Janan Ganesh. "The prospect of a new world order built around their shared preferences seems far-off", he concludes reassuringly.[9] Can an inter-national alliance of nationalists be stable? Are the strongmen not destined to fight each other out of the tent?

Looking at the trade war and geopolitical rivalry between the US and China, it is hard to contest the world of the strongmen is an inherently conflictual place. However, what binds the strongmen together in their contest, is not friendship, but a particular sort of enmity. The crux of this enmity is that it is governed by certain behavioural codes and norms. The strongmen, I argue, relate to each other as duellists, as adversaries in a contest bound by the codes of the duel. A duel is adversarial, but it is not a pub brawl or a cold-hearted assassination. It is a contest governed by mutually recognized norms, by what used to be known as the *code duello*. Some behaviours and forms of combat are off limits, while others are allowed and even encouraged. The strongmen are rivals, and their fellowship is therefore a club of rivals, but it is still a club. And every club has its codes and norms. Its members have something in common. They agree on particular things, not least that rivals are worthy of respect.

THE JUST ENEMY

This ethos of strength is still best articulated by the German jurist and thinker Carl Schmitt, who in *The Nomos of the Earth* (1950) traces its origins to the emergence of Europe's modern state order in the sixteenth and seventeenth centuries, a period when the universalist ideal of Christendom made way for a vision of the continent as carved up in states that were sovereign over a clearly defined territory. Crucially, to avoid war this geopolitical carve-up of the continent into territorial states trumped Europe's religious differences. *Cuius regio, eius religio* became the governing principle of international order. He who rules the land also decides its religion and morals.

The consequences of this shift towards geospatial order were huge and fundamentally altered Europe's concept of international politics. In Christendom, what separated "us" from "other" in the world had been religion. It did not matter where people came from. What mattered, as we would put it today, were their values. It meant there could only be one kind of enemy: the heretic who rejected the moral teachings of God and Church. And heretics, obviously, required no special treatment. They were not to be negotiated with or afforded respect but to be judged, sentenced and deradicalized like delinquents, criminals and terrorists.

But as Europe began dividing itself in "us" and "other" along territorial lines, a new and essentially political ethos needed to be developed, one that set out how foreign states and their citizens and rulers were to treat each other. It was only the rise of modern spatial borders that made foreign policy and international law – what jurists called the *jus inter gentes* – necessary and thinkable in the first place. A novel notion of the enemy made its entrance, not of the heretic but of the foreigner, the ruler or citizen of another territory, entitled to laws, customs and values of its own, and therefore obviously to be treated quite differently.

The great question, of course, was how. If sovereign states were to determine their own laws and religious affairs, foreign relations could evidently not be guided by moral-theological doctrine. But what practical principles or conventions still could?

The theoretical innovation that enabled an answer to this question was the personification of the state, which came to be regarded as a moral agent in its own right, with interests and entitlements of its own.[10] Moreover, states were presumed to exist on a higher plane of history, enjoying an existence for hundreds if not thousands of years. They were, as Edmund Burke argued, what connected past and present, the dead and the living. States compelled us to take the long view, to consider their "eternal" interests, which stretched further forward in time, much further than individual interests.[11]

The idea of the state as a being with stand-alone interests later spooked utilitarian and liberal thinkers. But it provided a vital premise of the modern state and the international order that was based on it. It had major repercussions for the ruler's position too. If Europe's feudal kings once claimed the land as their private property, the personification of the state suggested the land belonged to the state, to a public entity in and of itself. While a king still *ruled* the land, he no longer *owned* the land. He was its servant. "Warriors!", Peter the Great thundered to Russian troops at the battle of Poltava (1709), "here is the hour that will decide the fate of the fatherland. You should think that you are fighting not for Peter, but for the state, entrusted to Peter, for your kin, for fatherland."[12] As the state's highest representative, Tsar Peter commanded its administrative machinery; he raised fiscal revenues, instructed armies and other useful servants, but they were no longer *his* revenues, *his* army and *his* servants. They were and always would be the state's.[13]

In practical terms, it meant *raison d'état* became the unique guiding principle in foreign diplomacy. The state could now be viewed as a neutral and continuous entity, as an abstract state of law, a *Rechtsstaat*, with "public" or "national" interests distinct from the private interests of its ruler and citizens.[14] Foreign policy essentially needed to serve those interests, which meant growing its strength, power and wealth. To prevent a permanent state of war among power-hungry states, Europe further required a system of security to guarantee the peace, which emerged in the form of the Westphalian balance of power. Stability arose not because the Pope functioned as arbiter of last resort, but because the power of one state could be neutralized by the power of another. If one state threatened to become too powerful, others would clip its wings and restore parity, if necessary by forming temporary alliances.[15]

As important, Europe's new state order allowed forms of diplomatic courtesy to emerge that facilitated negotiation and deal making at summits.[16] Foreign relations were construed not as a rivalry between individuals, but between the states they were appointed to speak for, abstract entities – "France", "Britain", "Prussia", "Russia" – with their own means and interests, not to be confused with the private means and interests of the men who merely led them. As long as rulers or their ambassadors were rational, it hardly mattered who spoke on behalf of a state. It was pointless to vilify, assassinate or imprison foreign rulers or their diplomats. They were only the state's messengers. It meant disputes between states could be settled in cordial and gentlemanly fashion between men who at a deeper level shared the same vocation, who were morally equal and could even develop a certain camaraderie.

Built into the new order was a new sort of distance, a moral buffer between the public affairs of states, to be conducted on one plane, and the private affairs of men, conducted on another. The civilizing force of the modern state system, as Schmitt saw it, lay in its central idea of the foreigner as the *hostis justus*, the "just enemy". In contrast to personal quarrels and enmities, the public enemy was never to be hated or castigated as traitor, moral villain or (war) criminal. The enemy was merely doing his job, which was to advance his country's "eternal" interests like all rulers did. Moreover, while states would have opposing interests, such interests were not assessed on the basis of a higher, substantive moral theory. The idea of foreign policy and war as the crackdown on evil, as the great battle for truth and justice, was incompatible with spatial order.

Indeed, war came to be viewed as a contest between combatants who were equal in honour. One combatant might be stronger than the other, but neither side was "just" or "unjust" in the nature of their cause. War and foreign diplomacy more generally were merely mechanisms for states to decide their differences, to "test their strength" in contest. However, what did matter was that this mechanism was curtailed by procedures and norms, just as the duel or sportive contests were curtailed by norms of honour, respect and fair play. It was only when those norms were breached by one of the parties that the notion of a "just war" could still be entertained.

Rivalry was integral in Europe's state system, it was the essence of the game of politics, as Schmitt understood better than most. But it was enmity of a constrained kind, and based on a concept of how the game needed to be played, as well as how adversaries needed to be treated. There was to be no "total war", no all-consuming "clash of civilizations" of the kind that Samuel Huntington would prophesy later.[17] What clashed were interests measurable in wealth and power. Contest or interstate war could never be avoided, but spatial order would at least "bracket" war in ways that holy war against heretics or wars in the name of universal values could not.

THE *CODE DUELLO*

The strongmen are often said to conduct foreign policy on the basis of naked power and selfish interests and never on the basis of principles, norms and rights, other than the right of the strongest. The truth is that the language of strength preferred by the strongmen points not to an absence of norms but to an alternative set of norms, a combatants' ethos that provides a different etiquette for how combatants and contestants in global politics should behave. We may not like this ethos, or fear it will push the world over the brink, but the *code duello* is no empty shell, no mere excuse for blatant usurpation and dominance. In some ways, it is a highly prescriptive code, and when its principles are broken, it triggers a fierce and indignant response.

Equal recognition

The most important norm in the strongmen's fellowship is the right to recognition and respect as equals. Recognition is the prerequisite of club membership, the right to call yourself a player and a strong leader. Consequently there is no greater insult, no greater breach of etiquette, than to deny a strongman recognition, to not give him the honour he is due as a leader. Importantly, no strongman is morally more deserving of respect than another in the fellowship. All are players in the same game. Some are strong, others less so, but no contestant is morally superior. Everyone is merely trying to do the same, namely, win.

Trump, Putin and Xi exemplify this behaviour and give each other the recognition and respect they desire. Relations between them are warm and personable. They find it easy to "click", in spite of their differences. What the club of strongmen offers, other than man-to-man contest, is space for displays of appreciation and bonding – normally of the male variety – over cigars, sports, cars and fine wine. It is a place where personal "chemistry" is encouraged, not just in private but also before the cameras of the photographers, where sharing gifts and tributes means so much more than sharing values, where lavish banquets are arranged, special honours bestowed and jokes and anecdotes exchanged instead of finger-wagging sermons.

When strongmen meet, awkward and ill-tempered press conferences and other hostile displays in public are avoided. The hard business of diplomacy, the duel itself, often takes place out of sight altogether, and may be conducted in a matter of minutes. What precedes and follows it may seem trivial but is crucially important: extensive banter, manly atmospherics, warm words, high praise, ecstatic backslapping for public consumption. The strongmen know how to respect each other's *mise en scène*. They understand the need to project power, to uphold an image of strength and equality. They talk each other up, rather than down.

When, in November 2017, Trump visited Philippine strongman Rodrigo Duterte, the media followed the encounter between both men with more than usual interest. Not long before, Duterte had spectacularly fallen out with President Obama, who had publicly rapped Duterte on the knuckles for the summary execution of suspected drug traffickers. In return, the Philippine leader had called Obama a "son of a whore", who as far as he was concerned could "go to hell".[18]

With Trump, known to be less concerned about the rule of law, the mood was expected to take a turn for the better. Already before his trip, Trump had congratulated Duterte by phone on his "unbelievable job on the drug problem". Once Air Force One had descended through the clouds and touched down in Manila, the transformation was palpable. The rapport between both men was instant. "It's a red carpet like nobody, I think, has probably ever seen", Trump remarked. "And that really is a sign of respect, perhaps for me a little bit, but really, for our country."[19]

Instead of highlighting the right to a fair trial and due process, as Western non-governmental organization (NGOs) had begged him to do, at a press conference Trump followed his own instincts: "Rodrigo, I would like to commend you on your success as ASEAN chair at this critical moment of time … The show last night was fantastic. And you were fantastic."[20] The body language was fraternal and warm. While human rights activists cringed in despair, it was a triumph of strongman diplomacy. Prodded by reporters, the White House later issued a terse statement confirming that human rights did "briefly" come up in the talks. But Philippine officials still saw it differently. The drugs issue was discussed, they confirmed, but only at Duterte's initiative, adding: "The US president appeared sympathetic and did not have any official position on the matter but was merely nodding his head."[21]

Supportively nodding one's head is precisely what club protocol dictates when niggly domestic issues around the rule of law come up. Any other response will cause offence and risks denying the respect rivals are due. "There are some bored foreigners, with full stomachs, who have nothing better to do than point fingers at us", Xi Jinping once commented. "First, China doesn't export revolution; second, China doesn't export hunger and poverty; third, China doesn't come and cause you headaches. What more is there to be said?"[22] *Schnauze halten*, as former German chancellor, Gerhard Schröder – frequently seen in the company of strongmen – puts it.[23] Keep a lid on it. It is advice Trump rarely strays from. When in March 2018 Xi abolished China's presidential term limits, Trump merely joked: "I think it is great. Maybe we will give it a shot someday."[24] The massive anti-China protests that swept Hong Kong a year later, he dismissed as "riots". "Hong Kong is a part of China", Trump explained, "they'll have to deal with that themselves."[25] It was a position that Xi heartily endorsed.

When insulted, insult back

By contrast, European leaders ignore the *code duello*, and this ignorance is never more evident than when they start berating the strongmen for their human rights record or something else that contravenes the liberal vision of order. They behave condescendingly rather than respectfully. They treat the strongmen as junior league aspirants instead of equal club members.

Such admonitions often take place in public. For their part, Western leaders need to leave a visible trace of having "promoted democracy". It is what earns them the moral right to do business with the strongmen to begin with. Media are briefed that human rights "will be discussed" or "are on the agenda". What that means in reality is often less clear. An in-depth exchange of positions? Or just mechanically riffling through talking points, performing a cleansing ritual that paves the way to more pressing business? Invariably, what is more important is how things are perceived. And if that perception is not to the strongman's liking, he uses his own tactics to contain the damage to his reputation.

At the Saint Petersburg G20 summit in September 2013, David Cameron needed to wait until deep into the night for this cleansing ritual to take place. Cameron had championed same-sex marriage at home and aimed to hold Russia to account for its dismal record on LGBT rights. Like a tiger stalking his prey, he had been hunting for the right opportunity to raise the topic. But discussions about the Syrian crisis dragged on. He needed to be patient. When at 2.30 am he managed to pin down Putin at the painstakingly restored Peterhof Palace, the conversation did not go according to plan. British accounts of what happened described it as a "bickerfest", both men furiously lecturing each other. "They are acting like executives at a sales conference who have stayed up too late at the bar", a British newspaper wrote.[26] According to off-the-record Russian accounts, a fed-up and tired Putin finally cut the debate short with a joke: "Do you want to go to bed with me, David?" Kremlin press briefers could hardly stop slapping their thighs the next day.

Similar antics are often played out in joint press conferences, for example when Western leaders are asked whether they raised issues of human rights and values. Trapped in front of the cameras, it forces the strongman onto the defensive. One popular technique to nevertheless appear strong is for the strongman to bat the ball right back, a tactic sometimes described as "Whataboutism". It restores the level playing field, the club rule that all members are morally equal.

When European leaders question Turkey's democratic record, Erdogan retorts by rubbishing Turkey's opposition as national traitors. Then he takes aim at Europe's record on religious rights, accusing its leaders of branding all Muslims terrorists. Who are you, he is saying, to lecture me on democracy? What about the treatment of refugees? What about anti-Semitism? What about police violence against the *gilets jaunes* in Paris? Whataboutism aims to deflect not to refute accusations. The tactic exposes the accuser's hypocrisy, the existence of double standards. It proves we are all equal, that nobody is a saint. It is through the act of interrogation that one party gains the upper hand, that a relationship of equals is turned into hierarchy. Superiors demand explanations. Subordinates answer for their behaviour. So, what better way to restore moral parity than by posing some pointed questions of your own?

Alternatively, when lectured a strongman can feign boredom and indifference, a subtle tactic President Obama ascribed to Putin in the summer of 2013. "He's got that kind of slouch", the president coolly observed from the East Room of the White House, "looking like the bored kid in the back of the classroom."[27] Putin, Obama offered, was the type of schoolboy who defied the teacher's authority by pretending he had not heard his instructions, the kid who sought to level the relationship with his intellectual and moral superior by dropping out of school, by dispensing with its social hierarchy altogether.

However, for Putin mounting the pulpit himself still offered the more effective response. Barely one month after Obama's observation, Putin lengthily admonished him in a blistering opinion editorial, which of all times and places appeared in the *New York Times* on 11 September. "We are all different", the righteous Putin snarled back at Obama, who he accused of exceptionalism, "but when we ask for the Lord's blessings, we must not forget that God created us equal." The insolence left Washington's foreign policy establishment frothing at the mouth, making Obama, not him, look weak. It was much to the strongman's delight.

The art of the deal

In the fellowship of the strongmen, diplomacy is informal, personal and paperless. Binding legal texts may eventually have to be hammered out. International agreements may at some point have to be implemented and monitored by international bureaucracies. But all this takes place at a secondary level, the level of pen-pushers *applying* rules, which the strongman can suspend or revoke with the stroke of a pencil or an early morning tweet. The strongmen act on a higher and political plane, which is essentially personal and informal. They *make* deals, rules and treaties. Or indeed they *unmake* them, as Trump did with the Iran nuclear deal in May 2018 and with the Paris climate change agreement in June 2017.

The art of the personal deal, or the "parley", is strongmen diplomacy in its purest sense. It involves the cultivation of direct and personal relationships of one ruler to another, without mediation by formal structures and technical expertise. Strongman diplomacy is top-led and disconnected from what state officials are working on down the chain. Floating above the machinery of government, the strongman cuts his own political deals, before he seals them with the shake of a hand or the nod of a head. In practice it leads to a style of high-level diplomacy that feels chatty, masculine and amicable, but also amateurish, colloquial and improvised.

Personal diplomacy, as we already saw, lay at the basis of Trump's nuclear overtures to Kim Jong-un. It also inspired his impromptu decision, made during a phone conversation with Erdogan in October 2019, to withdraw US forces from the Syrian/Turkish border, clearing the path for Ankara to invade parts of Syria and establish a buffer zone between Turkey and Kurdish militias, which Erdogan viewed as a major security threat. "POTUS went rogue", one US official described the moment.[28] The president had cut himself loose from all conventional diplomatic channels. A massacre of Kurds loomed. But Trump preferred to rely on his own instincts and relations with Erdogan. "Let's work out a good deal!", he wrote in a personal letter to Erdogan. "You don't want to be responsible for slaughtering thousands of people, and I don't want to be responsible for destroying the Turkish economy – and I will … Don't be a tough guy. Don't be a fool!"[29] To some, the letter looked like a prank. The diplomatic tactics he had used were "unconventional", Trump later acknowledged. But a deal to contain the conflict emerged days later, so he could argue they had worked. "You're going to have to let them fight for a little while", said the president, explaining his approach to Turkey and the Kurds. "Like two kids in a lot, you gotta let them fight, then you pull them apart."[30]

To make personal diplomacy possible, Trump knows how to cultivate warm personal ties with fellow strongmen, how to establish trust with even his greatest of rivals. In April 2017, just weeks in office, Trump invited Xi Jinping to his Floridian Mar-a-Lago club, his "winter White House". It did not take long for the two men to strike a chord. During dinner, Trump informed Xi that he had just ordered the US navy to fire 60 Tomahawks at Assad's Syria. It was appreciated, a personal token of trust. "Good, he deserved it", Xi reciprocated.[31] "He's so smart", Trump told the media after Xi's visit.[32]

The return visit in November 2017 was billed by Beijing as a "state visit plus", showering America's new president with honours rarely seen by foreign dignitaries. One year earlier, China had denied President Obama the traditional red carpet welcome at Hangzhou Airport. Its ground crew had mysteriously run out of rolling stairs for disembarkation, media reported. Obama had been forced to "go out of the ass" of Air Force One, as US officials describe a rarely used exit from the airplane's underbelly. But for Trump, all the stops were pulled out.

The president, in the meantime, continued to lavish praise on "his friend" Xi. "You are a very special man", the construction tycoon told his host, who during the Cultural Revolution was forced to farm crops with his bare hands and sleep in a cavern hewn out of stone. While in his campaign Trump fulminated against America's trade deficit with China, he now declared: "I don't blame China. Who can blame a country that is able to take advantage of another country for the benefit of its citizens? I give China great credit."[33]

Back home Trump was criticized for his "grotesque adulation" of China's strongman. Xi is "playing Trump like a fiddle", a foreign diplomat sneered.[34] Experts ruled the visit a political and moral disaster. But Chinese state broadcaster CCTV, a mouthpiece for the Communist Party, found little to grumble about. Trump, it concluded, "has given China what China wants, which is that respect on the global stage, as the other preeminent nation".[35] The strong rapport between both men did not mean, of course, that their rivalry was over. But the connection between them made it possible for the strongmen to do personal deals. They see eye to eye and consider each other worthy of the fight. They may be foes, but they are honourable foes, and duellists above all.

Privileges of power

For the strongmen the basis of world order is spatial: the hard and physical separation between mine and yours – boundaries, walls, fences, customs booths – and how you govern what is yours is of no concern to me, just as it is of no concern to you how I organize what is mine. However, for the strongest of the strongmen, staying out of each other's hair quickly becomes staying out of each other's backyard or neighbourhood too. States and their rulers may be equal in moral terms, but they are certainly not equal in terms of power and size. And in the conflictual world of the duellist, special strength leads to special privileges, to special zones of influence in which big states have informal power over the foreign affairs of smaller states.

It drove Schmitt to the view that the modern world would ultimately not be organized in separate territorial states but in *Großräume*, in Great Spaces, concentric spheres of influence in which a multitude of states oriented themselves to a leading state at their centre. His concept was modelled around the example of the Monroe Doctrine, which held that foreign powers (other than the US itself of course) had no business in the Americas, which in practice meant Latin America. To Schmitt, the doctrine suggested that *Großräume* were held together by the "political idea" advanced by their leading power, which then "radiated" into the greater space around it.[36] This "idea" also distinguished leading powers from each other. Foreign interference was excluded, and the relations between various Great Spaces as such remained political, in other words governed by the *code duello*. However, within Great Spaces it was a different story. Borders between states were no longer entirely impenetrable by foreign influence. Rivalry, moreover, made way for economic interconnectedness based on a common political idea.

Spheres of influence may not strictly adhere to Westphalian norms, but in the club of rivals they are a fact of life, a norm of realpolitik accepted in practice, as are other privileges of strength. In October 1944, at a parley with Stalin in Moscow, Churchill proposed carving up the Balkans into British- and Soviet-dominated spheres. He did not waste time. "How would it do", he asked Stalin, while quickly jotting down the names of various countries on a half sheet of paper, "for you to have 90 per cent predominance in Romania, for us to have 90 per cent of the say in Greece, and go fifty-fifty about Yugoslavia?"[37] Having finished, Stalin glanced at Churchill's list, along with the percentages of influence. Then he took a pencil and summarily ticked it off for approval. "It was all settled in no more time than it takes to set down", Churchill recalled in his memoirs. The offhand manner by which they had decided the fate of entire states left Churchill feeling slightly uneasy, and he proposed they burn his sheet of paper. But there was no doubt in his mind that his deal with Stalin was fundamentally correct and legitimate.

The League of Nations, created after the First World War, had been intended to usher in a more equal world, without privileges for the strong and powerful: a rules-based world. But the US refused to join, and the league suffered an ignominious fate. After the Second World War the US did join the United Nations, as did the other victorious powers, but only after the UN formalized their privileges in the form of a Security Council veto. Franklin Roosevelt felt less sanguine than Churchill about carving up the globe into spheres of influence, but the world, he accepted, would essentially be run by the strong.[38]

In the fellowship of the strongmen, size and power remains nothing to be squeamish about. There is a natural pecking order among duellists, a division in great powers and client states, in duellists big and small. It is something all members have to accept. My nuclear button is "much bigger and more powerful than his", Trump once said of North Korea's Kim Jong-un, before they struck up a more amiable relationship. "And my Button works", he added.[39] Others express themselves with more tact. Little is usually gained by humiliating smaller minnows, by rubbing it in. But size matters, it can hardly be denied.

Spheres of influence are buffers that enhance security. Big geopolitical hitters prefer to keep other big hitters at a safe distance. This is one reason why great spaces arise. Powerful strongmen can ill afford to see their neighbours fall under the sway of their rivals. It is why they exert a degree of influence over their neighbourhood themselves, and also why this is considered legitimate. In a world in which political rivalry is inherent, messing around in someone's backyard is an obvious provocation. It is "not done", a sign of disrespect. And if one nevertheless goes ahead, the only logical outcome is trouble.

Regional influence need not be based on coercion or be synonymous with colonial exploitation or enslavement. Force may be used in extreme cases. But usually *Großräume* are built on more subtle types of influence that result from economic and cultural connectedness, from feudal arrangements in which a central power offers protection, market access or investment in return for a client state not collaborating with its rivals.[40] Nor are great spaces necessarily exclusive, preventing client states from developing trade and economic ties with other great powers. However, the influence such ties give rise to needs to remain small in comparison to the influence the dominant regional power possesses. To use Churchill's language, it must remain well below 50 per cent.

When the influence of a rival strongman exceeds a certain threshold, countermeasures become unavoidable. By shoring up Russia's influence in the former Soviet space, for example through the Eurasian Economic Union, Putin does what any strongman would do. He thinks in terms of percentages. He tries to prevent Russia's neighbours from falling under the sway of other powers. As a general policy, no duellist could reasonably reject it, a fact that Trump confirmed when he gave Erdogan the green light to establish the buffer he sought in northern Syria. "For many, many years Turkey, in all fairness, they've had a legitimate problem with it", Trump justified his move, referring to the areas controlled by the Kurds. "They've had terrorists, they had a lot of people in there that they couldn't have … and they had to have it cleaned out."[41]

Would the US tolerate rivals such as China and Russia meddling in its own backyard in South America? President Obama had suggested it might. "The era of the Monroe Doctrine is over", his secretary of state, John Kerry, announced in 2013 with fanfare to the Organization of American States Conference. "That's worth applauding … That's not a bad thing", he added, evidently not getting the roar of approval from the audience he expected.[42] But Trump, clearly, holds a different view. In April 2019, lashing out at Venezuelan dictator and "Cuban Puppet" Nicolas Maduro, his national security advisor John Bolton confirmed as much. The Monroe Doctrine, he bluntly declared, was "alive and well".

CLASH OF CLUBS

As with all clubs, the strongmen's fellowship is not held together just by what its members share, but also by the confrontation with other clubs. And no club is more different to the fellowship of strongmen than the club of European leaders. For Europe, the world is not stitched together by the duellist's code, but by higher, universal values, by substantive laws that guarantee the democratic and human rights of everyone, everywhere. In Europe's world, order is not spatial, it does not come from territorial states, or at least not entirely so, but also from a supranational community and its institutions. Somewhat akin to the Pope in Christendom, this community claims the moral authority to judge whether states and their rulers are right or wrong in their cause. It can authorize intervention and impose penalties to bring infractions to an end.

The international community's most concrete manifestation remains the United Nations and the 1948 Universal Declaration of Human Rights, as well as the panoply of bodies that support it such as the Human Rights Council in Geneva and the International Criminal Court (ICC) in The Hague, which prosecutes state officials for crimes against humanity. However, just as often coalitions of states, nearly always with Western states at their core, claim to be speaking and acting on behalf of the international community and the liberal values it supports.

Who gets to play Pope is crucial, but no less important is that the notion of a global community of faith clashes with the combatant's ethos of strength. It does so in ways that make the world both less as well as more conflictual. Less conflictual, because this global community is not a club of rivals but a club of friends. Among its members, basic agreement exists about how states should be organized and also how the liberal world is to be structured around rules. As a consequence, for example, spheres of influence are no longer necessary. In a world without rivals they become a logical absurdity. A buffer against what?

But at the same time liberal universalism renders the world more adversarial. Because when the enemy does appear, he no longer does so in the guise of the duellist, worthy of respect and hence bound to certain codes. He becomes an enemy in a deeper and total sense, defined not in spatial or political terms – the ruler of a foreign state – but in moral and human terms. The enemy is a transgressor of universal moral laws, and therefore evil. And the codes of the duel, which bracket and civilize conflict, do not apply when we fight evil.

The frequent confrontation with Europe's ethos of rules provides a powerful adhesive for the strongmen's fellowship, united in its wish to put to rest any notion that it must answer to a higher moral authority. For the strongmen, the sovereignty of the state really is the sacred bedrock of everything. "Russia has been and always will be a sovereign and independent state", Putin argued in his State of the Nation Address in 2019. "This is a given. It will either be that, or simply cease to exist."[43] Strongmen like Putin adore their veto in the UN Security Council, but they are less enamoured with the rest of the UN bureaucracy. As John Bolton, then still in the White House, remarked about the ICC: "We will not join the ICC. We will let the ICC die on its own. After all, for all intents and purposes, the ICC is already dead to us."[44] Or as Trump advisors once summarized his political philosophy: "We're America, bitch."[45]

What explains this angry revolt against global institutions? Part of the answer, as Schmitt noted, is the idea, entrenched in spatial order, of the state as a person with stand-alone interests, as a community that must never be "diluted" because it forms an end in itself. By allowing the state and its borders to become porous, the fundamental notion of a "we" and a common good becomes porous also. States provide the ability to speak, decide and to act together, as one people. And by diluting the state, the ability to act as one is also diluted. The entire idea of spatial order unravels from there.

The other part of the answer is more mundane and political, namely the belief that the notion of a universal community based on rules remains a sham, even in its liberal and secular incarnation. The international community, this view maintains, merely refers to the West, and in Trump's version of the argument it refers to an even narrower conspiracy of liberal elites. Human rights only appear as political pretexts, for example for toppling strongmen whom the West considers to be mischief-makers. Yesterday Gaddafi, tomorrow who knows who? "Whoever invokes humanity wants to cheat", as Schmitt once paraphrased the philosopher Proudhon.[46] Having appointed itself as judge, jury and executioner, the West only uses international rules and values to legitimize the pursuit of its own interests, or so it is claimed.

It is for similar reasons that men like Xi and Putin take a suspicious view of the myriad bodies, mostly created and dominated by the West, that provide the infrastructure for globalization: the International Monetary Fund (IMF), the World Trade Organization (WTO) and standard-setting bodies in digital communications technology as well as a range of other crucial industries. Having access to this entire infrastructure has become essential to economic success, and precisely because of this, whoever controls these networks can use them as a political disciplining tool. International influence, the strongmen also know, is less about military might than about the ability to grant or deny access to enabling infrastructures, payment networks, shipping lanes, supply chains, key technology and knowledge, and even to global sporting events.

Having unearthed an enormous doping scandal in Russia in 2015, international athletics bodies began banning not just some, but all Russian athletes from international contests, including the Olympic Games. In one sense, the sports federations were clearly only applying their anti-doping rules. But Putin's foreign minister, Lavrov, argued something more sinister was going on, a Western-led effort to use its dominance in global sports federations to besmirch Russia's good reputation. "They can't beat us fairly", Lavrov bitterly complained, so they aim below the belt.[47] Was it only a figment of his imagination? Perhaps it was. But as the litany of economic sanctions against Russia showed, globalization was a mixed blessing, at least as long as rivals acted as the gatekeepers to its benefits.

For a duellist, forever entangled in a contest with rivals, such vulnerability is hard to endure. Each time the West freezes an adversary out of the global trade system, it provides an additional reason for creating alternatives or at least for reform. In a club of rivals, the technologies and networks that enable global trade and cooperation need to be organized in ways that guarantee they will not be used to extort concessions, just like the UN Security Council offers such reassurances to its veto powers. If such assurances cannot be given, duellists who can afford to do so have an incentive to build their own international banks, payment systems and digital networks, something that Xi is actively doing. Of course, those who cannot afford to do so, and they will be many, are less fortunate.

What connects the strongmen is not just the duel, but also a powerful sense of unfulfilled entitlement, the longing for global respect, which it does not receive from Europe or the West. What gives the fellowship of strongmen its cohesion, and its force and energy, is a moral anger, the feeling of having been wronged, of having been denied a place at the top table, which the West reserves for itself. Apart from foes, then, the strongmen are also victims, at least in their own eyes. They may never be friends, but there is one common cause they pursue: a world in which they get the recognition a duellist is due.

Intermezzo: metagames

During the Cold War there was an accepted vocabulary between the sides. There was a game, there was an accepted game. Now the danger is there is no order. There is no accepted language. We are not talking the same language.

European diplomat, anonymously, in
The Guardian, 24 October 2016

Call it a prism or a language, an ethos or a narrative, or simply a game, but the strongman believes the world is organized around sovereign power, structured not by rules but by his freedom and ability to act without those rules. He sees order emerge out of dynamism and action, the nurturing of ties of homage and fealty, the projection of strength, and the ethos of the duel. His language of power is based on a loosely cohering set of analytical and normative judgements that highlight the importance of states, borders, spheres of influence, personal diplomacy and rivalry, as well as informal but universal codes of respect and equality that enable deal making with political rivals.

It is a prism that contrasts sharply with how most Europeans regard political and global order, which for them fundamentally is, or should be, organized not around strength but around the power of institutions that apply the same rules to all, the strong and the weak alike. Europe's language of rules renders the separateness of states far less absolute and less political. It maintains that beyond the strongman's code of respect there are more comprehensive values and standards that determine how states are to behave, including towards their own citizens. International conflict, on this view, is structured less around the spatial distinction between states and more around the distinction between those who abide by the rules and those who don't.

The difference between these two prisms – the language of power and the language of rules – explains the incompatibility of temperament that exists between Europe and the strongman, and why the encounter between them tends to be grating and fruitless. It is those languages themselves that clash in the encounter. For Europe's leaders the confrontation with the strongman is a confrontation with the immoral and the unsavoury. To negotiate and shake hands with a strongman is a soiling business. One does not negotiate or sit down with thugs; one reprimands, sanctions and educates them. For the strongmen, in turn, having to deal with European pedants is insufferable, not just because they show no respect, but also because they make them look weak. And for a strongman, the appearance of weakness is deadly.

Instead of managing global conflict and solving problems, Europe and the strongmen spend most of their energy on managing the fact that they do not share the same political language. Churchill and Stalin were able to settle on their "percentages agreement", which helped avoid a future war between them in the Balkans. British and Soviet interests clashed on an epic scale, as did their values. But both men still possessed the same concepts and language of diplomacy. Their agreed world order was structured around power. There was sufficient respect and trust between them to make a personal and informal deal. They could settle their differences, as far as this was possible, because they agreed what they were fighting over: territorial influence in the Balkans. They were enemies, but enemies who agreed to play the same game, pursuing purposes that were conflicting but still commensurable at a deeper level.

Today, Europe's encounter with the strongmen is not nearly as straightforward. Diplomacy is not so much a game as it is "a clash of styles of play", and a dispute about the definition and the rules of the game itself. The encounter, it could be said, is a game about what game we are playing, a perplexing quarrel about what we are quarrelling about. In this metagame, one player, the strongman, remains convinced he is participating in a game of strength and power, governed by the *code duello*. However, the other player, Europe, sees itself taking part in a different game, one of how to uphold and guarantee the rules and values of a legal and moral order. The strongman believes those rules and values are fake. He believes the real, underlying game is that of competing powers. The second player, however, believes that the power game has become obsolete. The intransigence of the strongman baffles and bewilders, his cranky arguments sound like the rants of a madman. However, to the ears of the strongman, Europe's vocabulary of rules, rights and principles sounds no more coherent. Each appears to the other as irrational, mistaken and dangerous: as tone deaf.

In Part II, we follow how this metagame unfolds by looking at Europe's encounter with arguably the world's most important strongmen: Russia's Putin, Turkey's Erdogan, China's Xi and America's Trump. We see how these encounters lead to confusion, mistakes and anger. In Chapter 6, Europe's encounter with Vladimir Putin is shown to be a deeper conflict about what constitutes "foreign meddling" and "forbidden space", areas in which foreign powers may not interfere. In Europe's encounter with Recep Erdogan, examined in Chapter 7, the language of rules and frontiers jostles with the language of power and borders. Chapter 8 shows how Xi Jinping advances a model of global "connectivity" based on the principles of feudalism and strength, which clashes with Europe's vision of global integration based on rules. Finally, in Chapter 9 we see how, in Donald Trump, Europe's leaders encounter a US president who turns the diplomacy of the duellist into an art form, preferring "the deal" over the Atlantic treaties and institutions on which the continent has staked its future for three generations.

Moreover, these encounters show how the language of power and the politics of strength are in the ascendency. They reveal how Europe tries but is no longer able to impose its preferred language on the encounter, a state of superiority it long considered only natural. Rules-based order has not suddenly become obsolete, just as the language of power has never been fully obsolete either. But the balance in the world is shifting. Putin's Russia possesses sufficient strength to shrug off Western sanctions and retaliate in kind. Erdogan no longer needs or wants EU membership and instead uses Europe's admonitions to mobilize domestic support. Xi leads a bourgeoning economic and technological superpower, while Trump leads the United States, the military superpower Europe still depends on for its security.

While Europe still tries, often frantically, to conduct its affairs in the world with its language of rules, the encounters with these men show how hard and ultimately ineffectual this has become. They reveal how the continent is increasingly compelled to play by the rules of power itself, to act with strength. Europe's encounter with the strongmen, it appears, is also an encounter with itself, the story of the continent's own journey, its struggle with rivals and events that are new and dangerous. It is the story of how Europe is beginning to look at the world through the prism of power, and at itself as sovereign and strong.

PART II
Encounters

CHAPTER 6

Putin: recognizing forbidden space

They must have really lacked political instinct and common sense not to foresee all the consequences of their actions.

Vladimir Putin, speech on Crimea, 18 March 2014

REACHING BREAKING POINT

The strongman and his guest nip at their water. They are talking, listening, joking even. At least they pretend to be. It is June 2013 and Germany's Angela Merkel and Vladimir Putin of Russia are sharing the stage at Russia's premier economic forum in Saint Petersburg, the country's great Window on the West. The setting is sublime. The stucco-fronted Neva embankments glow in the pink orange hue of the midnight sun, leaving the city frozen in a no man's land between day and night. It is a world that inexhaustibly fuels encounters in cafés, parks and restaurants.

In reality, the encounter between both leaders is less enjoyable. A row is brewing over German artworks looted by the Red Army in 1945. The relationship has been bad tempered for some time: frustrating, infuriating and sometimes barely manageable. A sense of foreboding ought to have filled the Saint Petersburg air. Instead, light-heartedness prevails. People have become used to Western and Russian politicians squabbling. *Plus ça change.*

But as summer slips into autumn, and autumn into winter, something does change. It happens where it always would happen: in the borderlands of

Ukraine. The *casus belli* is an ordinary EU trade and partnership deal, about to be inked by Kiev. It is a bilateral agreement in the standard Brussels mould, part of its neighbourhood strategy towards the east. Yet the agreement triggers a chain of events that ends Europe's post-Cold War security architecture and claims over 13,000 lives.

What we witness in Ukraine is more than a shooting war; it is Europe's ethos of rules sparring with Putin's ethos of strength, specifically its proviso that special areas and "spheres" exist – forbidden space – where a duellist may not strike, compete or interfere. The domestic affairs of states, in particular elections, most obviously belong to this forbidden sphere. However, as observed already, for the duellist the ban on interference by rivals often extends beyond his own borders and into the strongman's neighbourhood. In Putin's estimation, the West has been edging into this territory for years, and mostly getting away with it. But in Ukraine, the country that Russia regards as intimately linked to its own destiny, the strongman starts to assert himself. At first, he does so by dramatically raising the stakes in Ukraine. Then he strikes at the heart of the West's own forbidden space, its democracy. Convinced that the West is trying to foment unrest even in Russia itself, he decides the time has come to give it a taste of its own medicine.

DUEL IN THE BORDERLANDS

When in 2008 the Europe Union launched its new *Ostpolitik*, the Eastern Partnership, nothing suggested war would be its outcome. It was the year Dmitry Medvedev moved into the Kremlin. And Medvedev was a man to Europe's liking, a stickler for rules like itself. Europe's idea was to integrate post-Soviet states more closely into the Western order, but without immediately offering EU membership. The plans were based on vintage European recipes: remove trade barriers, dilute borders, drop visa restrictions, then stitch everything together with common market regulation and other types of rules. Integration would follow organically.

The idea that the Eastern Partnership encroached on "power privileges" that Putin claimed for Russia was not seriously entertained. The West, of course, had not forgotten the continent had once been divided into spheres of influence. But with the end of East–West enmity in the 1990s, the logic of rivalry that justified such great spaces had been overtaken by history, or so Europe believed, and replaced with the logic of rules. Who could possibly oppose more free trade and greater economic integration? "This project is not against anybody, whoever thinks it is against somebody is wrong", EU High Representative Javier Solana said in May 2009. "We have explained this to the Russian leadership at many levels."[1]

For Europe, its *Ostpolitik* had no losers. Greater security, greater wealth, hassle-free travel. Everyone would benefit, Russia too. Those who failed to get it were simply "wrong". But it was not a message that got through in Moscow, where Putin continued to analyse the world in terms of rivalries. Ukraine in particular was special to Russia, and Putin could not tolerate the country falling under Western political influence. It was an affront to the strongmen's ethos, the *code duello*. Leaders stayed out of each other's backyards. The West had thrown down the gauntlet. And in contrast to his predecessor Yeltsin, Putin was just the man to pick it up.

The Kremlin responded by revving up its own model for integrating the post-Soviet space, the Eurasian Economic Union. Relations with Brussels grew more irritable. Putin's Eurasian integration ideas were taken with a pinch of salt, however. Stateside, Hillary Clinton found the right words: she brushed off Putin's entire venture as "a move to re-Sovietize the region", to create a Soviet Union-lite.[2] And who would ever want to join that club?

Concern began to creep in when Putin started touting his Eurasian ambitions more forcefully in Ukraine in 2013, after the Ukrainian president, Viktor Yanukovich, signalled he was about to sign up to European plans for a "Deep and Comprehensive Free Trade Area". To nip a crisis in the bud, Putin dispatched a special envoy to Kiev, Sergey Glazyev. Not a man who minces his words, Glazyev delivered lines that seemed to come straight out of the Mafia world of *The Sopranos*. "We don't want to use any kind of blackmail", Glazyev began in Kiev, conceding that the issue was "a question for the Ukrainian people".[3] But, he went on, a whole litany of things might, and probably would, happen to Ukraine if it were to sign the EU deal: separatist insurgencies, state bankruptcy, job losses, higher trade tariffs for exports to Russia and higher gas prices. "Suicidal", he added. "A huge mistake."

Russian trade penalties were introduced as a shot across the bow. It meant that Petro Poroshenko, later Ukraine's president but then still running a confectionary business and known as Ukraine's "Chocolate King", was no longer allowed to supply the Russian market. Hatchet man Glazyev was just the character to make it look like old-fashioned Soviet-style arm twisting. But perhaps that was precisely Putin's idea. At least no one could accuse him of not having made his objections clear.

The strongman's power politics ruthlessly targeted Ukraine's dependency on Russia. And it worked. Suddenly, Ukrainian President Yanukovich seemed less sure about his European ambitions. Putin was using "a nineteenth century mode of operating towards neighbours", responded Polish foreign minister Radek Sikorski, one of the Eastern Partnership's chief architects.[4] European Commissioner Stefan Fuele lamented in turn: "This is not how international relations should function on our continent in the twenty-first century."[5] It became a line the Europeans repeated ad nauseam. "We have to do a better job in communicating with our Russian friends … that the Eastern Partnership is not against them, against their interest", the European Commission insisted.[6] Moscow had turned the Eastern Partnership into a binary "us-or-them" dilemma, Merkel added.[7]

But for Putin, the duellist, international politics had always been about "us" and "them". The notion that this had recently changed he considered hogwash, a ruse to make Russia lower its defences. Unfortunately, however, his projection of strength in Ukraine had not sufficed to deter the Europeans from pressing ahead. If Putin wanted to remain stuck in a time warp, the Europeans found, then he needed to be jolted into the future. Under no circumstances could Moscow be allowed to drag its neighbours in the region along with it. "The time for limited sovereignty is over", Commission President Barroso declared.[8] No new Iron Curtain!

On 28 November 2013, Europe's top leaders flew to Vilnius to sign trade deals with Moldova and Georgia, and following a climactic sit-down with Yanukovich too, or so they planned. Following six years of arduous negotiation over dense pages of legal prose, Europe's leaders were not planning to give up easily. The occasion had long been framed as a milestone event. Champagne corks were meant to pop in the fifteenth-century Palace of the Grand Dukes of Lithuania. Razed to the ground by Russian soldiers some 200 years ago, and since then restored to its former glory, the palace formed the perfect location for a diplomatic triumph.

But Yanukovich refused to buckle. In the tug of war Moscow just pulled harder, he complained, as the Europeans piled on the pressure over supper. Russia offered a $15 billion loan and slashed gas prices, tangible benefits and respite from bankruptcy, the sort of language Ukrainians understood. Europe's terms were less persuasive: IMF-style austerity, structural reforms and only €610 million in immediate support. *Un bonbon dans un joli papier*, Yanukovich called it, a sweetmeat in a nice wrapper.[9]

There was but one way forward, he suggested: a three-way deal in which Ukraine joined both Europe's free trade zone as well as Putin's Eurasian Union. A score draw of sorts. But his proposal was swiftly rejected. "I feel like I am at a wedding where the groom has suddenly issued new, last minute stipulations",

Merkel told Yanukovich.[10] "It would be like inviting China to the table at talks to agree an EU–US free trade deal", an EU diplomat sneered.[11] Brussels was confident and stood firm. The entire idea was wrongheaded. How could Ukraine be member of two trade blocks at the same time? WTO rules would not permit it.[12]

ACCUSED OF INTERFERENCE

Putin, it briefly seemed, had struck the decisive blow. Events, however, proved less predictable, eventually transforming the duel into a no rules cage fight. The image of Ukraine bowing to its master Russia touched a raw nerve in Kiev, driving pro-EU protestors onto the streets. Quickly their numbers swelled into the hundreds of thousands, setting up camps in streets and government buildings. Covered in a blue sea of EU flags, Kiev's Independence Square, simply known as Maidan, became the crucible of the protests. Rock music blared through loudspeakers. As police truncheons battered the crowd and teargas canisters span through the air, it was here that the real battle would be decided. Might the door to Europe yet be prised open?

Five days into the Maidan protests, a familiar face pops up in the crowd. Guido Westerwelle, Merkel's foreign minister, goes on a walkabout, a caravan of German journalists in his wake. Amid protestors clamouring for Yanukovich to resign, it is a tightrope walk. But Westerwelle claims he is not there to pick sides in what is a Ukrainian domestic affair. He wants to pass on a different message, and he wants to shout it through a bullhorn: yes, the door to Europe is still open! "*Hier schlägt das Herz europäisch!*", Westerwelle enthuses to journalists afterwards.[13] Here the heart beats European!

Europe was not planning on sitting out the revolution as a spectator. Maidan became a pilgrimage destination for Western politicians extolling the virtues of a European choice. Catherine Ashton, the EU's high representative for foreign affairs, dropped by for some supportive pats on the back. The firebrand EU-federalist Guy Verhofstadt whipped up the Maidan crowd with visionary and hopeful language, as did US Senator John McCain, never one to miss an opportunity to poke Putin in the eye. Obama's assistant secretary of state Victoria Nuland came armed with cookies, which she demonstratively handed out to protestors. When later she was accused of having picked a side in a domestic debate, she apologetically declared she had handed out cookies to riot police too.

About to host the world in Sochi for the 2014 Winter Olympics, the flurry of foreign visitors infuriated Putin. Western efforts to stir up protests at Maidan transgressed the most basic of diplomatic norms, as he understood them. If Yanukovich decided to clamp down on the protests, he was within his rights, Putin was certain, just as any European state would be. "Why are prominent European politicians actually encouraging the moves in question", Russia's foreign minister Sergey Lavrov demanded to know, "although in their own countries they immediately clamp down on any encroachments on the letter of the law?"[14] Putin waded in too: "I can only imagine what the reaction would be if in the heat of the crisis in Greece or Cyprus, our foreign minister came to an anti-European rally and began urging people to do something."[15]

In February 2014, a recorded phone conversation mysteriously appeared on YouTube in which Victoria Nuland and Geoffrey Pyatt, the US ambassador in Kiev, revealed the degree to which the West was involved in engineering a handover of power behind the scenes. Nuland – referring to Maidan leaders Vitaly Klitschko and Arseniy Yatseniuk, later the country's prime minister – says: "I don't think Klitsch should go into the government ... I think Yats is the guy."[16] Frustrated by the tardy Europeans, she cries "Fuck the EU!" Pyatt, in response, says: "No exactly, I think we have got to do something to make it stick together because you can be pretty sure ... that the Russians will be working behind the scenes to try to torpedo it."

It was a first but tellingly robust salvo in the information war. In Moscow's eyes the facts were clear, and they were damning. The West had been caught red handed plotting regime change, and therefore acting out of the bounds of the permissible. But in Europe the leak caused a stir for other reasons. Nuland's sniping against Brussels laid bare divergences in how Europe and Washington viewed the crisis. But the allies collectively shrugged off the charge of interference. They had not done anything wrong. The West was merely supporting Ukrainians in their wish to freely decide their own future. If Putin wanted to turn this into an "either-them-or-us" decision then let Ukraine choose, but freely.

Putin's idea that Ukraine, by Yanukovich's hand, *had* already chosen never gained much traction in the West. It was Maidan that expressed Ukraine's true choice, not "Kremlin-vassal" Yanukovich. Europe only had eyes for the youthful, modern, liberal Maidan, which demanded the rule of law, freedom and democracy, an honest and European future. Its narrowly contracted lens organized Ukraine's hotchpotch of diverse interests, histories and identities into simple categories. Maidan was "the people". Those who harboured reservations to its goals? They only appeared as the victims of Russia's relentless propaganda or as the tainted beneficiaries of Yanukovich's kleptocracy, foot soldiers paid a handful of coins to wave flags at counter-protests.

Two weeks later, after snipers on rooftops had fired into the Maidan crowd, the pressure cooker was ready to blow. In an attempt to pull the country back from the brink of civil war, the Europeans, with Putin's backing, confronted Yanukovich with an eleventh-hour plan to phase in the end of his tenure by the end of the year, followed by elections.[17] Reluctantly the president assented to their proposal, which further committed him to not introduce martial law. But the very instant he did so, his regime collapsed like a house of cards. Having become a sitting duck for the lynch mob, the same night the president fled to the east and to safety, spinning his ignominious escape from Kiev as a working trip to inspect factories.[18] Maidan leaders understood their moment was now. Within 24 hours they had called for Yanukovich's arrest and for Ukraine's parliament to appoint an interim president.

Did Ukraine witness a people's revolution? Or did it experience a foreign-supported takeover by the mob, an illegal form of regime change? Having been holed up in Olympic Sochi for two weeks (where on top of everything else he also had to witnesses the US ice hockey team beat Russia), Putin did not need long to make up his mind. The war was about to be lost, he surmised. Western victory celebrations were delicately managed. The biggest threat, the West knew, was blowback from Moscow. Phone calls were made. Merkel to Putin, Obama to Putin. Reassurances were given. Europe's win-win discourse was wheeled out once more to offer Moscow solace. "It is not about pulling them away from Russia", British Foreign Secretary William Hague ruminated. "It's about enabling them to make their own choices."[19] Never at any stage, he explained, had this been about "West versus East", a primal grab of territory in the borderlands.

The more perceptive Merkel understood a sacrifice was required from Maidan leaders. "We know that about 15 million people of Russian origin live in Ukraine", she said, "and they have to find themselves in the work of the gov-ernment as much as everyone else."[20] In Crimea, close to 80 per cent of the vote had gone to Yanukovich in 2010. In eastern cities like Donetsk and Luhansk that number had hovered around the 90 per cent.[21] But through its refracted lens, this "other" Ukraine seemed to be the robotically tweeted figment of a Russian propaganda campaign, the remnants of a consciousness that, engulfed by the new European *zeitgeist*, would simply cease to be. They were the losers of a win-win world, who theoretically could not even exist.

However, having watched his strategies go up in smoke, Putin was in no mood to listen. Resuscitating Yanukovich's political corps, Putin knew, was impossible. "He has no political future. I told him that", Russia's president admitted when he had returned to Moscow from Sochi.[22] But Maidan, he also knew, was not the people's revolution the West had made it out to be. Dmitry Medvedev, his prime minster, launched a blistering attack on Western suggestions that Moscow ought to recognize the new Maidan government. "If you consider Kalashnikov-toting people in black masks who are roaming Kiev to be the government, then it will be hard for us to work with that government", he made clear.[23] "Some of our foreign, western partners think otherwise, considering them to be legitimate authorities. I do not know which constitution, which laws they were reading, but it seems to me it is an aberration ... Something that is essentially the result of a mutiny is called legitimate."

GOING FEUDAL

There were still cards Putin could play, illegitimate cards even by the standards of the strongmen. But if the West could stir up a crowd of Kalashnikov-toting hooligans, assuredly so could he. And the strongman's extensive network of fealty and homage gave him the perfect tools for doing so without overtly violating the diplomatic norms the West had so blatantly broken at Maidan.

The operation commenced at dawn on Thursday 27 February, when uniformed gunmen stormed the regional parliament in Simferopol, Crimea. Swiftly the gunmen established a perimeter around the building. They then barricaded the doors and hoisted the Russian tricolour. Not much later, pro-independence politicians from Crimea arrived to convene an emergency session, calling for a referendum to decide whether the future of the peninsula belonged to Russia or Ukraine. It was a new revolution, a counter-Maidan revolt, and one executed at lightning speed.

Alarm bells went off in the West. Who were these gunmen? Their uniforms looked odd and were not identifiable as those of Russian soldiers. A voluntary, pro-Russia self-defence militia said one. Former *Spetsnaz*, Russian special forces who had retired to Crimea, said another. The next day similar "little green men", as they were christened in the West, kept popping up in strategic locations on the peninsula. "Provocateurs are on the march. It is the time for cool heads", the new Maidan government warned.[24] The fear was that clashes would be seized upon by Moscow to launch a full-scale military intervention, as it did in Georgia in 2008. But it turned out the intervention was already in full swing. It was a cloak-and-dagger operation. The more the little green men began to appear, dressed in uniforms without insignia, the clearer it became. They were Russian soldiers in disguise. Two days later, the future of Crimea had been decided.

The West was stunned. "You just don't invade another country on a phony pretext in order to assert your interests", Obama's secretary of state John Kerry fumed.[25] His words were ill-chosen, an open invitation for Moscow to smirk: what again were the reasons for invading Iraq in 2003? More phone calls were made to Putin. But the conversation turned in endless circles. Moscow kept denying its interference, precisely as the West had denied its own interference in Maidan. This, the Kremlin maintained, was a true people's revolution, Crimea's legitimate struggle to determine its own destiny.

Expert at feudal machinations, Putin knew well how to keep up the façade of strongmen propriety. True, he argued without blushing, those little green men may have been Russian citizens, well-trained Russian soldiers even. But they were certainly not acting on official instructions. They were merely volunteers, "patriotic" fighters who for their ideals only, and in their spare time, supported the spontaneous uprising of the Crimean people to determine its own fate, which happened to be to rejoin the Russian Federation. The whole operation had been executed outside the formal structures of the Russian state, by NGOs, so to speak. To be on the safe side, the Kremlin procured a letter from Yanukovich, still claiming to be president, which asked for Russia's intervention. Either way, international law had been religiously observed.

Merkel could not believe her ears. Had he gone bonkers? Comparing notes in a subsequent phone call with President Obama, the chancellor claimed Putin was "in another world".[26] It was a telling remark, and she was not wrong. Putin did live in another world, the world of the strongmen. But the sentiment was no different in the Kremlin, which felt it was Merkel and Obama who lived "in another world".

Obviously, the idea of Russian soldiers filing holiday requests in a spur-of-the-moment surge of patriotism was a smokescreen, as later Putin came close to admitting.[27] But as a scam it was so evidently false and so poorly concealed that for the Kremlin it hardly even counted as a lie. Besides, could the same not be said of the countless NGOs and foreign-funded protest movements through which the West encouraged revolt abroad, including at Maidan? For Putin, revolutions are *never* spontaneous or arranged in the pursuit of freedom or ideals. They are always managed and organized, and always for reasons of power. If only the West were as honest about its own deceptions! Encouraging revolt and secession was never just okay, to be sure, not even for a strongman like Putin. But in this instance Russia's manipulation of the truth felt entirely justifiable and within the bounds of the norms.

No less than Merkel or Obama, Putin was certain that he was on the right side of history, a feeling strengthened by Russia's understanding of how the Cold War had ended, namely in a historic grand bargain with the West. According to this deal, the Soviet Union, then led by Mikhail Gorbachev, would back Germany's unification. In return there would be no further eastern advance of European structures – and NATO above all – beyond what was then the status quo. Not "one inch to the east", as George Herbert Bush's secretary of state, James Baker, emphatically put it.[28]

Much has since been said about this deal, which the West categorically denies ever existed. Whether it existed or not is a moot point. Like so much else in the encounter it depends on perspective, on what language one speaks. If there is such a deal, Westerners point out, where is the paperwork? Where are all the signatures? At the very best, provisional noises of reassurance were made at Moscow's behest, of which faint traces still exist in the minutes of diplomatic meetings. But these verbal gestures, the argument goes, do not add up to a binding and ratified agreement, which means no deal ever existed.

For a strongman, however, legal form is only ancillary in world politics. Treaties are for bureaucrats and lawyers, not for great men and duellists. Like Churchill and Stalin, the strongmen strike deals during the parley, and frequently they do so in secret. If for the West the law decides whether an agreement ultimately exists or not, in the strongmen's fellowship it is personal diplomacy. What is decisive is the handshake: men looking each other in the eye and then deciding to trust each other to behave as agreed. In a world of sovereign power and strength, not reliant on institutions or law, nothing can be more binding than "my word is my bond". Receiving verbal reassurances that the deal "stood" was as valid as any signed piece of paper.

For Putin, Merkel and Obama had joined a long line of Western leaders whose word sadly meant nothing at all. Even if this was done through subterfuge and deceit of its own, Russia seemed entitled to shield itself from hostile encroachment into its space. Push back, after all, was what all great powers would do if others trespassed on their turf. "If you compress the spring all the way to its limit, it will snap back", said Putin, clarifying the mechanics in his address welcoming Crimea into the federation.[29] It was a simple matter of physics, one of power's great iron laws.

A PARLEY AT THE SUMMIT

In the West, Putin's power discourse fell on barren ground. "We believe not in the law of the strongest, but in the strength of the law", Merkel summed up her deepest convictions in the German *Bundestag*.[30] It was a cleverly chosen phrase, one her Putin-friendly predecessor Gerhard Schröder once coined to oppose the US-led invasion of Iraq in 2003 (which Merkel then supported). She now used it to silence his mutterings of protest against the hawkish response that was taking shape in Europe.

Europe's leaders needed to confront what was the biggest security crisis on the continent anyone cared to remember. Putin's gamesmanship reverberated through Eastern Europe. If he was ready to rip up the rules over Crimea, where was he going to stop? Strength was needed, or he would not stop at all. That everyone could agree. But what did strength mean? Two positions crystallized in the debate. One pleaded for the use of diplomacy combined with economic sanctions which could be dialled up in severity depending on Russia's responsiveness. The other advocated a more forceful response, supplying Kiev with state-of-the-art arms so it could crush Russian-backed insurgencies by military means.

When Putin's peoples' rebellion against Maidan spread to the Ukrainian cities of Donetsk and Luhansk in the eastern region of the Donbass, the clamouring for an armed response became noticeably louder. It was a position with powerful backers. Bombarding the public with reports about Russian tank movements on the Ukrainian border, four-star US General Philip Breedlove, NATO's ranking officer in Europe, repeatedly warned that a Russian advance on Kiev was only hours away. His warnings sent shivers down European spines, which was precisely what the general meant to achieve with his statements.[31] In a phone call with Commission President Barroso, Putin inadvertently fuelled those fears himself. Had he wanted to, Putin tried to reassure Barroso, he could easily take Kiev within two weeks. The Europeans took it as a threat. "Putin is effectively at war with Europe", a Baltic leader fretted.[32]

But whereas the operation in Crimea was quick and decisive, the not so spontaneous revolt in Donbass turned into a drawn-out, messy and nasty war. This time Kiev fought back. Russia did just enough to keep the anti-Maidan revolt alive, at times only barely. As in Crimea, it maintained it was not involved in what it described as an internal Ukrainian affair. But while it was clear that Putin would never give up on the peninsula, the Donbass was negotiable.

Europe prevaricated. It allowed Merkel to strategically place herself in the political middle. After Russia-backed separatist fighters in the Donbass mistakenly shot down a passenger jet en route from Amsterdam to Kuala Lumpur in July 2014, new and more damaging economic sanctions were swiftly agreed. The event was a political catastrophe for Putin, another instance of his vassals badly messing up. However, backed by Obama, Merkel fought off the pressure to start a proxy war on the continent. Europe would continue to bet on diplomacy. It would try to cut a deal with the strongman.

It was not an easy or even obvious step to take. Europe had its own ghosts to contend with. At a European summit, David Cameron warned his peers against "repeating the mistakes made in Munich in 1938".[33] Was it possible to negotiate peace with men like Putin who believed only in power? Would Ukraine not suffer the fate of Czechoslovakia in 1939? But doing deals with strongmen, Europe slowly began to realize, would be inevitable, just as later it would come to understand it would be inevitable to make deals with Donald Trump. Europe was far from keen to whip out pen, ruler and map and draw new lines of influence across the continent. But at some level that was precisely what needed to be done. Putin was not going to let go of Ukraine. He demanded his "percentage" of influence, to put it in Churchill's terms, and the question that needed to be settled was how large that percentage was going to be.

Merkel fronted the effort, which from a European view was a soiling business. If anyone could succeed it was the chancellor. She alone possessed the authority to survive the political fallout. Moreover, no one else had dealt with Putin longer. She had learned to weather his negotiating techniques, for example when in 2007 Putin had let his black Labrador Konni sniff at her feet in his Sochi residence, claiming he did not know that she did not like dogs. Merkel was fluent in Russian, just as Putin was fluent in German. There was no shortage of contact. By some accounts, in the first six months of the conflict alone (February–July 2014) Merkel and Putin spoke over 30 times, French President Hollande and Obama acting as her wingmen. That number rose to 40 by year end.[34]

At the Munich Security Conference in February 2015, a hotbed of Atlanticism, angry US senators scolded Merkel for her efforts at a parley, accusing her of being a latter-day Chamberlain. "Stand up to what is clearly a lie and a danger", one of them sermonized, aghast at so much European pusillanimity. "Blankets won't stop Russian tanks", called another.[35] Poroshenko, seated in first row, flashed a glance of approval. It was the betrayal of the Ukrainian people, just as once the Czechs had been betrayed. History reverberated through the small conference hall at the *Bayerischer Hof*.

But a superior Merkel responded by pointing out that someone needed to deal with reality. And Putin's great power *was* reality. Militarily, he could not be defeated. Then, speaking with passion, the chancellor went on to explain how she had been brought up in East Germany. Did anyone at the time consider using military means to save East Germany from bondage, she wanted to know? The West chose patience. And eventually it proved to be the right choice.[36] Ukraine's Chocolate King turned president looked less pleased when Merkel had finished. Barroso, it turned out, had got it wrong. The time of limited sovereignty was not quite over yet.

Days later, on 12 February 2015, the Merkel–Putin parley resulted in the Minsk II protocol, formally agreed between representatives of Ukraine and the "People's Republics" of Donetsk and Luhansk. The fighting in the Donbass raged on until the final moments of the negotiation. While the protocol was never fully implemented, the worst of the fighting could be contained. The deal, moreover, laid out a broad vision of how the conflict could be resolved. Donbass would gain a form of regional autonomy, allowing it to largely run its own affairs, with Moscow keenly looking over its shoulder. But it would remain within Ukraine. It was the construction that Putin needed to secure the percentage of influence he felt entitled to.

THE PERFORMER'S REVENGE

Its encounter with Putin in Ukraine made Europe realize it could not avoid the language of strength and the duel. The premise on which Europe had based its *Ostpolitik* was that this language had fallen into disuse. But it had led Europe to charge blindly into a hornets' nest.[37] It had journeyed into a space that was unmistakably geopolitical and governed by the rules of strength, and it was now required to think in those terms.

In Russia, Putin arrived at a different set of conclusions. Events in Ukraine confirmed that the West, for all its talk about win-win deals, had no respect for the norms the strongman felt underpinned global order. For years he had shown willingness to work with the West, such as in the war on terror in Afghanistan and Iraq. In November 2010, in an article in the *Süddeutsche Zeitung*, he had proposed an ambitious free trade area that stretched from Lisbon to Vladivostok, an idea the Europeans had simply laughed away. The only thing he had asked for, but had never received, was respect. Now it was time for a change of tack. To discourage Western insolence, Putin concluded, he needed to give as good as he got. If the West would foment unrest in Russia's backyard, or even in Russia itself, then from now on Putin would return the favour.

The seeds for this change of heart had been planted two years before the crisis in Ukraine, when in the winter of 2011–12 a generation of disillusioned Russian liberals took to Moscow's streets in what some referred to as Russia's Snow Revolution. They were protesting against fraudulent practices during Russia's parliamentary elections, which coincided with Putin's announcement that he wished to return as president. It was a move that crushed all hope for change. For Putin, it was a testing time. His authority wobbled like it had never done before. Elsewhere, the Arab Spring was forcing strongmen out of power. With Putin's election to follow in March, the Kremlin was on tenterhooks, keeping a watchful eye on how large the crowds of protestors were growing. As a performer, the elaborate show Putin had put on for his audience for years, and that formed his contract with the people, suddenly threatened to go awry.

It was the price Putin needed to pay for a daring but ultimately unconvincing piece of theatre: the infamous *rochade*, the castling move with his double Dmitry Medvedev. The role that Medvedev had faithfully performed for four years, the promise of change he represented, had now come to an abrupt and for the audience entirely unsatisfactory end. Moscow's liberal intelligentsia felt robbed of its future. However, the Kremlin saw something more sinister behind the protests: the hand of the West. When the protests erupted following the Duma elections, Putin immediately blamed Hillary Clinton, secretary of state in the Obama administration. "The first thing that the Secretary of State did", Putin remarked, was say the elections "were not honest and not fair … She set the tone for some actors in our country and gave them a signal."[38]

Clinton, Putin felt, was meddling with the Kojèvian theatre of authority he directed and starred in. She had muscled herself onto his stage, crashed his performance and now incited his audience against him, suggesting he was not the fearless warrior or the impartial judge he had long pretended to be, but really only a thief. As seen from Moscow it was obvious. Many of the protest's leaders had known links with Western governments, think tanks and NGOs, which offered them funding and platforms for publicity. Clinton stood her ground. She did not deny those links existed, but insisted the US merely wanted to promote free and fair elections. It was all part of what was called dual-track diplomacy, which was a perfectly normal and legitimate practice. "Human rights is part of who we are", Clinton explained.[39] But when the protestors in Moscow began chanting "Putin is a thief!", dual-track diplomacy looked a good deal less routine.

What had made a bad situation worse was Obama's decision to dispatch a new ambassador to Moscow, his White House Russia advisor Michael McFaul. On his first day in office, McFaul met with senior Kremlin officials, as was customary. The next day, however, he demonstratively held court with the Putin opposition in Spaso House, the US embassy residence. He wanted to hear directly from Russian civil society. The optics of the meeting were devastating, validating the impression that opposition leaders were merely doing the West's bidding. A throng of Russian television cameras filmed the activists as they passed through the residence security gate. "Receiving instructions from the Embassy of the United States", a caption to footage posted on YouTube said. Afterwards, the participants to the Spaso House meeting stated they had exchanged only generalities. But in paranoid Moscow there was no one who believed them. Did Russian officials ever pop in for a cup of tea with the opposition in the West?

McFaul was a political scientist and intellectual, the author of books on post-communist Europe and its transition to democracy, a science mockingly described as "transitionology". McFaul had never shied away from public controversy. In earlier academic work he had argued that Russia hovered somewhere in the twilight zone between dictatorship and democracy.[40] And under Putin, McFaul maintained, the country was heading towards dictatorship. It fitted perfectly into Russia's narrative of Western interference. Citing the title of his 2001 book, *An Unfinished Revolution in Russia*, a Russian journalist demanded to know: "Has Mr McFaul arrived in Russia to work in the specialty? That is, finish the revolution?"[41]

Persistently harangued by the media, McFaul's reputation in Moscow never recovered. Two years later he was back at Stanford University.[42] Russian society was being mobilized to defend itself against an enemy, one that evidently did not respect the codes of the duel. Tolerance for foreign "influence" was being squeezed out of the system like the air out of a bagpipe.

Meanwhile, inside the Kremlin, minds were ripening to test a more offensive form of mobilization too. If the West continued tinkering with Russian elections, why not tinker, destabilize and sabotage right back? Why not fund and support radical protest movements in Europe and the US: anti-establishment populists, anti-globalists and Europhobes? In the strongman's club of foes, interference in the domestic political drama performed by rivals was taboo. But if a little tit-for-tat could get the West to quit its own interference, would it really be so objectionable? After what had happened at Maidan, it certainly seemed worth a try.

Putin's chief instrument for his brand of dual-track diplomacy was the internet, the Western technology that ironically had helped topple strongmen during the Arab Spring. While the West hid its interference behind its democratic intentions, at least in Putin's eyes, he used the cloak of his feudal network of vassals. The effort was to be spearheaded by a private company, the Internet Research Agency, a troll factory based in the district of Olgino in Saint Petersburg. So-called "Olgino Trolls" would post reader comments to articles in Western media articles and manage Twitter accounts and Facebook pages to spread real and fake news stories. The goal was to found online pro-test communities in the West and to radicalize voters who opposed the EU and globalization, accused the police of racism or felt that politicians had sold out the country to foreigners and Muslims.

There was no ideational superstructure at work behind these efforts. The only goal was disruption: to destabilize Western governments in the same way the West destabilized Putin. Russia's version of dual-track diplomacy was a business shorn of principles, but effective nonetheless. Arguably its greatest achievement was that the West began to copy Putin's own combative mindset. Putin detected foreign influence behind the faintest whiff of domestic protest. Now so did the West. Suddenly, Russian trolls and agents lurked behind every tweet. Russian "influence" hid in every corner, even in the Oval Office. Russia hacking US elections "was a 9/11 scale event", Thomas Friedman of the *New York Times* contended.[43] "They attacked the core of our democracy. This was a Pearl Harbour-scale event."

When Putin welcomed Marine Le Pen in Moscow during the campaign for the French presidency in 2017, no one in Europe viewed her visit as a routine piece of dual-track diplomacy; it was obvious interference. It was the same when Russian money was reported to have found its way into the coffers of Le Pen's political party. Europe too was mobilizing itself against foreign influence, against Russia's "fifth column",[44] as liberal frontman Guy Verhofstadt put it in a tweet, not realizing that he was stirring up the precise same sentiments that Putin had unleashed in Russia.

Trump, Brexit and the rise of populism in Europe were hardly the doing of internet trolls in Saint Petersburg, just as the protests in Moscow and Kiev had not been the doing of Western dual-track diplomacy. But given how many in the West came to *perceive* Moscow's impact, and how some magnified Russia's role for their own political purposes, it hardly mattered. For Putin, the whole experiment seemed a massive accomplishment, crowned by Trump's election victory in November 2016.

Less fortunate, however, was that Trump's unexpected success blew up the Kremlin's image of Westphalian propriety. Media and the FBI were quickly able to link Russia's troll farm to Yevgeny Prigozhin, the entrepreneur whose rise in the restaurant and catering business had strangely coincided with Putin's own story of success. Prigozhin had worked his way up from the humblest of roots, running a hot-dog stand in Saint Petersburg back in the 1990s. What followed in the years after was a fairy tale of conquest in the restaurant business, which included winning sizeable public contracts for supplying meals to schools and official state events. In 2012, Prigozhin won a contract supplying Russia's defence ministry with meals, a most lucrative business, but also most unlikely to have come without certain strings attached. It earned him the moniker "Putin's Chef".

Officially, Prigozhin was still only a businessman. Putin denied they were ever on personal terms.[45] But whatever the truth was, perception began to live a life of its own. Putin's refrain was that, as long as the patriotic bloggers Prigozhin funded stayed within Russian law, it was none of the state's business. "In the US you have a certain Mr Soros, who interferes in all kinds of business the world over", Putin argued in an interview with Austrian television.[46] "My American friends often tell me the United States have nothing to do with this; it only concerns his private business. With us, it is Mr Prigozhin's private business. That is my answer. Are you satisfied with it?"

Evidently the answer was anything but satisfactory, and Putin knew this better than anyone. For it was precisely the answer Western politicians always gave him when he complained about election interference. Was the idea of George Soros merely running a private business any less crazy, Putin demanded to know? Western leaders were never held responsible for the political influence Google or Facebook exerted in the world. Why was he?

But the cover provided by his vassals had been blown, and the idea that Putin conducted part of his foreign diplomacy through private structures of fealty and homage came to be seen as fact. The louder the strongman denied the state's involvement, the more patent that fact only seemed. It came at a political cost. While the use of vassals had needed to persuade the world Kremlin interference did not exist, the world now saw its interference everywhere, even where it was not. Businessman, journalist, pianist, ballerina, student or just Russian citizen, any Russian could be presumed to be an agent acting on Putin's orders. Indeed, anyone could also claim to be an agent of the state. The absence of detectible and formal links to the Russian state, such as institutional job titles or insignias on uniforms, offered no certainty, as Yevgeny Prigozhin had amply demonstrated.

The "fuzziness" of Putin's feudal state allowed the McCarthyite frenzy aimed at Russia to mushroom. Allegations of interference and meddling could be construed on no firmer grounds than that a Russian individual "had ties with the Kremlin", whatever the words "ties" and "Kremlin" still meant. Anyone defending the Russian point of view could be dismissed as a "Kremlin troll" or "Putin poodle". In Western media reporting about malign activities undertaken by Russians on foreign soil, subtle but crucial differences in language, such as between "Russian" and "Russia", began to look hazy. To establish "Russia's" involvement, it sufficed to demonstrate the involvement of someone "Russian". The default assumption became that Putin had a finger in the pie.

This was what landed Siberia-born gun enthusiast Maria Butina in a US jail for spying. The Washington-based student had sought to establish links between the National Rifle Association in the US and the pro-gun lobby at home in Russia. Unquestionably, Butina's goals had been political, an instance of dual-track diplomacy even. But she was no Russian official or in any other knowable capacity acting on behalf of the Russian state. Nevertheless, in 2018 a heavily armed FBI swat-team raided her apartment and charged Butina with having acted as a Russian agent. Why she should have been a state agent rather than an engaged self-starter and gun devotee remained uncertain. "When I heard that something was happening to her", Putin angrily complained, "I started by asking all our secret service chiefs: who is she? Nobody knew anything about her!"[47] But in Putin's Russia, how could one ever be certain? One of Butina's fellow Russian gun enthusiasts happened to be an official at the Central Bank of Russia. It was enough to get her convicted to 18 months in prison under the terms of a plea deal.[48]

THE GENIE AND THE BOTTLE

Moscow regularly accuses the West of Russophobia, and often rightly so. But by obfuscating the boundaries between public and private in foreign diplomacy it is a disease that Putin has partly inflicted upon himself. Getting the genie back into the bottle will be hard, perhaps even impossible. However, when we look at interference and meddling through the prism of the strongman, it becomes possible to see how this might be tried, namely by negotiating a cease and desist agreement that restores the club rules of propriety, specifically its non-compete clause, according to which some spaces should remain forbidden. Unfortunately, of course, it is only when we apply the prism or language of strength that such a deal begins to make sense.

In July 2017, Sergey Ryabkov, Lavrov's deputy in the Ministry of Foreign Affairs, led a senior delegation of Russian diplomats to Washington. In his back pocket he carried the outline of a secret deal, which the Kremlin thought could end the propaganda war.[49] The rumpus caused by Russia's version of dual-track diplomacy had sunk relations with the West to depths uncharted since the end of the Cold War, and it now even threatened Trump's own presidency. Time to start talking peace, or so Moscow judged. Trump had been in office for six months. The political conditions seemed ripe.

The deal seemed simple: an informal ban on interference in the domestic politics and elections of others, in other words, a return to the Westphalian rectitude of sovereign states and the restoration of one of the core elements of the strongmen's club ethos. Russia's bloggers mothball their smartphones, other agents of influence are leashed. The West does the same with its NGOs, think tanks and other forms of dual-track diplomacy. No more McFauls or Clintons. No more Maidans. Mutual disarmament of sorts. Now that Western leaders understood they could be destabilized too, they had a clear incentive to play ball.

The Ryabkov plan, however, had one snag, which was that in its own eyes the West had never done anything wrong. There had never been any meddling or interference. Western governments, the problem was, could not put their bloggers back on the leash, because they did not have one. What they had was a free press, a free internet and a free market. Anyone could publish whatever they wanted about Russia or even Donald Trump. If George Soros used his wealth to fund anti-Putin campaigns, governments could not stop him. The West could wind down its dual-track diplomacy and stop supporting pro-democracy movements abroad, but as Clinton put it, democracy was "part of who we are".

Putin needed the West to recognize that its democracy promotion was on par with his own methods of influence, which served no greater goal than disrupting the opponent. Only an admission of guilt could unlock the door to the quid pro quo deal the strongman was looking for. That admission, however, was not forthcoming, neither from Europe, and in spite of Trump, nor from the US. "Thank you very much, but now is not the time for this", were the icy words with which US diplomats sent Ryabkov bundling off to the airport.

Seen through the lens of the strongman, it also becomes clear why, as long as its peace efforts are rebuffed, Moscow will not let up. Until the West scales back its interference, why should Putin scale back his? Relations, consequently, are at an impasse. A popular view is that Russia and the West find themselves in a new Cold War, in which Russia ought to be "contained", as McFaul's illustrious predecessor in Moscow, George F. Kennan, counselled in the Long Telegram in 1946. But hostile as it is, Putin's Russia is not Soviet Russia, and its interference in foreign elections is not aimed at unleashing an ideological revolution. Putin's language is that of the duel. When the Soviet

Union imploded, Europe and the West thought the world was on the cusp of a global liberal age. The distinction between friend and foe, between winners and losers, would be extinguished forever. In Putin's eyes that distinction changed, but it never disappeared. Rivalry had merely assumed its old appearance of the duel, governed by its norms. He much preferred it that way.

In its ongoing encounter with Putin, Europe needs to decide whether, and if so to what extent, it is prepared to engage in the duel on the duellist's terms. It has refused to do so in the information war, which presumably is in part owing to the fact that, in reality, Russia's disinformation campaigns in the West are a great deal less disruptive than they are sometimes claimed to be. However, Ukraine was another matter. When the EU launched its Eastern Partnership in 2008, the posture Europe instinctively assumed had been that of the educator. It explained its rules, principles and values, and then explained them some more, promising an era of freedom, stability and prosperity for all. After Putin proved an obstinate student, castigation and expulsion followed. But the West's sanctions proved as futile as its lectures and it dawned on Europe that playing the teacher was fundamentally useless.

Europe had entered a world governed by other rules, principles and values. And in this world, the Eastern Partnership had foundered. Instead of stabilizing and securing its neighbourhood, the policy contributed to further instability and war. The EU needed to revise its *Ostpolitik*, taking account of some of Moscow's and other local sensitivities, even if it still regarded those sensitivities as plain wrong. It was the treacherous path Merkel ventured onto in the 2015 Minsk accords, which bracketed the fighting. The deal sketched the contours of what an acceptable settlement would eventually look like, narrowing the future options for both Russia and Europe. Ukraine would clearly not be fully integrated into European and Atlantic structures, but nor would it become Moscow's vassal state. It would need to eke out an existence "in between". Europe tacitly accepted as an inalterable political reality that Crimea had become part of Russia, even if its secession had been illegal. It also quietly recognized that Russia had legitimate interests in Ukraine. The continent assiduously held back from encouraging Ukraine to apply for NATO or EU membership.

Is it ever okay to haggle over principles and values that should be upheld universally? How far does one travel along the slippery path of the strongman's parley? These are hard political and moral questions, which can never be fully settled. However, they are questions that must be faced. Haggling over principles is of course redundant when you hold all the aces. You simply impose your preferred language on the encounter. But when power is divided more equally, compromises may need to be made. Putin did not raise the white flag at the first sign of European disapprobation. Western sanctions hurt. But he shrugged off the pain and turned to China for succour. Then the strongman hit back at the West, using the weapons he had at his disposal. The time for pleasantries, jokes and pretending was over. Like a duellist with wounded feelings, he hit hard and without remorse.

CHAPTER 7

Erdogan: drawing borders

Hey, EU wake up!

Recep Tayyip Erdogan, 10 October 2019

AUDIENCE WITH THE SULTAN

On 5 October 2015, European Council President Donald Tusk hosted Turkey's Recep Tayyip Erdogan for a special dinner in Brussels. It was no occasion for pleasantries, even less for lectures about the rule of law in Turkey. Brussels was in full crisis mode. And to conquer the crisis it needed help, the strongman's help.

A torrent of refugees had been making its way to Europe since the start of the year. On the run from poverty and war in Syria and the Middle East, the human convoy passed through Erdogan's Turkey before embarking on packed dinghies and small boats to Greece and the European Union. It was a perilous journey. Thousands perished at sea. Their bodies washed ashore on some of Europe's most idyllic coastlines.

But the many hundreds of thousands who made it to Europe's shores found nothing to stop them. No walls or fences, no border guards, booths or gates, no police asking for papers. The Union possessed no system for guarding its external borders. And so the caravan just trudged onwards, via Serbia, Hungary and Austria to Germany, where most migrants planned to stay. If the Greeks could not guard the Union's external borders, the only practical solution seemed to resuscitate the continent's internal borders. But this, too, was an unappealing scenario.

By the time Donald Tusk and European Commission President Jean-Claude Juncker broached their plan to their Turkish guest, Europe's options had dramatically shrunk. The pressure cooker needed to vent steam or it would blow. Europe needed Erdogan's support in keeping the refugee stream at bay. Might Turkey provide them with shelter, buy the EU some time at least? Turkey would of course be fairly compensated.

That evening it must have been hard for Erdogan, an intensely proud Turk, to fight back a smile of satisfaction. Was this Europe begging for help, *his* help? As long as he could remember, Turkish leaders had begged for Europe's recognition and acceptance, and the Europeans, infuriatingly, had always withheld it. They had had him, Recep Tayyip Erdogan, jump through hoops like some circus animal. They had instructed and chastised him, confronted him with impossible conditions. In the early years of his rule he had dutifully complied, enacted his role as Europe's suitor. But now, the strongman sensed, history was on the move. A new role was being forged for him and Turkey, a new destiny. This time, *he* could make Europe jump through hoops. An opportunity too good to waste, he thought, as he coolly gestured Tusk and Juncker to take their seats around the dinner table. He did so with the same air of authority that the great Ottoman emperors had once exuded in Europe. He was ready to listen to their petition. "As if at the Sultan's", a European official described the moment later.[1]

Erdogan signalled he would be willing to do a deal. But this time, he made clear, Turkey would be setting the conditions. He was not minded to give Europe an easy ride. He demanded money and critical EU reports on human rights in Turkey shelved. He asked for visa liberalization. It was time for the strongman to adopt a more assertive demeanour, one reflecting the new balance of power.

The strongman spelled it out again in negotiation rounds that followed later. With millions of refugees stranded in Turkish camps, he held the upper hand. "We can open the door to Greece and Bulgaria anytime and put the refugees on buses", Erdogan told Tusk and Juncker in a November meeting in the Turkish resort of Antalya.[2] The strongman only upped his demands. He wanted six instead of three billion euros. "So how will you deal with refugees if you don't get a deal?", he asked sarcastically. "Kill the refugees?"

Name me one "delivery", just one little thing Europe has done for Turkey so far, he angrily shot at Juncker. What progress had been made on membership? For 50 long years, all Europe had done was frustrate Turkey's bid.

When Juncker replied Turkey had not always been a democracy, the strongman scoffed. As if democracy was the reason. Do not compare Turkey to Luxemburg, he teased Juncker. "Luxemburg is just like a town in Turkey."

To help the political haggling forward, Merkel understood the strongman needed courting. He needed Europe's respect and recognition. In late October, days before Turkish parliamentary elections, the chancellor paid a visit to Ankara's Yildiz Palace, once the residence of the Ottoman sultans, and – reluctantly – sat herself down in a gilded throne next to Erdogan. An excellent piece of political theatre for the strongman, but a humbling moment for the chancellor and a political sacrifice. The fallout in Germany was predictably disastrous. For Turkey's strongman, though, it was confirmation. A new era of respect and parity had arrived. In March 2016, with plenty of helter-skelter along the way, the migration agreement was finally agreed, to Europe's great relief.

The continent's headaches, however, were only just beginning. Europe's relationship with Ankara was not going back to what it had been before. Erdogan no longer cared about the EU's approval and its obsession with rules. Other actors were more important, and less bothersome. A deal with Trump in October 2019 had cleared the way for Erdogan to order his military to occupy parts of northern Syria, something he had long wanted to do. With Vladimir Putin, the other big strongman in the Syrian desert, he had built a relationship based on trust and personal respect. They were men who fought for causes often diametrically opposed to his. The US supported the Syrian Kurds, terrorists in Erdogan's eyes, while Putin had propped up Syria's Bashar al-Assad, who Turkey loathed. But he knew they were men he could always do a deal with. They spoke the same language of strength and respect. They were part of the same club of rivals, the fellowship of strength.

Europe's approval Erdogan did not seek, and not just because he would not have received it, but also because he did not need to. When various European countries called for sanctions and arms embargoes in response to his incursion into Syria, Turkey's president knew exactly how to respond. "I say it again: if you try to frame our operation there as an invasion, our task is simple: we will open the doors and send 3.6 million migrants to you."[3] He sounded ruthless and Machiavellian, like a strongman no longer bound by the rules of morality. "We will never accept that refugees are being weaponized and used to blackmail us", the scandalized Donald Tusk responded.[4] But it was not as if those refugees would need to be bussed to Europe at gunpoint. To the contrary, that is where most of them had always wanted to go. More to the point, given that the EU had still not fixed its migration system, it could hardly brush off Erdogan's threat as bluster. Europe still needed the strongman's help. And it needed to learn to live with the consequences.

BORDERS AND FRONTIERS

Europe's encounter with Erdogan was wrought with anguish. The crisis had created a new dependency on the strongman. But that was just part of the reason. The other part was connected to how Europe pictured itself as an ever-expanding civilizational space, to how it drew the vital distinction between "self" and "other" or "friend" and "foe". The EU had never really cared much about its external borders. In fact, it did not even have a concept of borders, not in the modern sense of the term at least.

For the strongmen borders are inescapable facts of life, the necessary pillars of international order. "Borders are fundamental", as the Hungarian Viktor Orbán once put it. "Without borders, existence is impossible. Something which has no borders, no contours, does not exist."[5] What he referred to, of course, were the borders of the modern Westphalian state, borders that clearly delineate space that is *political*, a territory whose inhabitants govern themselves. Such borders are linear, binary and mathematically precise. They can be physically signposted by walls, fences or just by lines on a map. You are either inside or outside a political space. Borders may coincide with dividing lines in nature, as in the case of island states, or with the outer edges of continents, but such natural phenomena are non-essential aspects of borders. The borders of political space are always created by conventions, decisions and deals. They are institutional facts, the "outcome of a fumbling process and a series of clashes", as historian Jacques Le Goff puts it.[6]

However, for the EU things are less straightforward, less political, less linear. "The concept of borders", as EU commissioner for enlargement Olli Rehn once argued, "is restrictive and static. It has a ring of finality, rather than opportunity, and limits our minds."[7] Josep Borrell, currently EU high representative for foreign policy and security, views borders as "scars" which were "made by fire and blood".[8] "I don't like borders", he added. It is an aversion wedged deeply in the EU's design, in which borders tend to appear as barriers to be erased. Freedom of movement forms the EU's sacred goal. The enclosure of space, for Orbán the metaphysical condition of "being", forms Europe's greatest taboo, the negation of its existence.

The Rome Treaty (1957), which forms the basis of the European Union, prescribes no spatial limitations.[9] It determines that a state needs to be "European" to qualify for membership. But what is Europe? A continent, perhaps. But Europe is certainly more. It is democracy, the rule of law and human rights. Europe, it is argued, is a union of values, a *Wertegemeinschaft*.[10] But if so, then where is Europe? Where does it end, if it ends at all? Our values are not rooted to one part of the earth; they are portable. And if values are portable, Europe must be portable too. It was in line with these convictions that the EU grew from the original 6 to 12, to 15, and – once the greatest symbol of enclosure, the Berlin Wall, had been torn down – to 28.

The EU prefers to think of space in terms of "frontiers" rather than borders of a political kind. Frontiers "are innovative and dynamic", Commissioner Rehn argues. "Frontiers denote challenges, borders mere geography."[11] In this conception, frontiers refer not to the perimeters of political spaces or states, but to the outer edges of civilization, to the last outposts beyond which nothing but wilderness lies, no human experience at all. A frontier, as Frederick Jackson Turner described the American West, is "the meeting point between savagery and civilization".[12]

Viewed as civilizational or normative space, Europe's physical contours are determined by the integration of its values in the political-legal practices of its neighbours. The areas where its values thrive, or where they are actively aspired to, lie on our side of the frontier or at least within its grasp. Those areas of the world possess a "European vocation". Places where those values are shunned, or countries that travel in the opposite direction, lie beyond the edge.

Whereas borders are sharp, frontiers are blurry. Normative space does not stop abruptly, nor are its perimeters identifiable with precision. Civilization only gradually makes way for savagery. Where precisely the decisive, identity-altering change to "the other" or "the foe" occurs remains unclear, if such a decisive shift can still be said to occur at all. Whether Europe ends here or there becomes an unanswerable question, a matter of degree, of indeterminate grey zones as opposed to the "in" or "out" of political space defined by borders. In normative space, one easily gets stuck "in between": be neither one nor the other, or be both.

Moreover, just as savagery is meant to be conquered, frontiers are meant to expand. The borders of civilizational space are always on the move; they are organic and open-ended. It is possible for civilization space to contract, but that would be a bad thing, a regression. Europe's neighbours either "make progress" or they succumb to "backsliding". Frontiers often move slowly – they creep, unnoticeably – yet nothing is forever fixed. For aspirant members a European destiny is always possible. Nothing is ever set in stone.

Matching its concept of frontiers, the EU invented a unique language of diplomacy, a novel way of interacting with its neighbours, which essentially amounted to civilizing them. Whereas borders suggest the language of the duel and its egalitarian ethos, frontiers require the encounter to take the hierarchical shape of an exam, which when passed facilitates entry into the civilized world. Europe assumes the role of gatekeeper and examiner in this encounter, while its neighbours are "candidates", to be surveyed and assessed objectively on the basis of performance criteria and progress reports. This assessment is chopped up in stages and modules – "chapters" in Brussels jargon – until finally the candidate secures access to the inner sanctum. The examiner and gatekeeper, in turn, is obliged to faithfully inspect the candidate's progress, and when all tests are met to grant access.

To be sure, Europe's self-image as an ever-expanding civilizational space was much more than self-flattery. At one stage it was a powerful force that changed the course of history. Liberated from the Soviet Union, the post-communist states of Central and Eastern Europe chomped at the bit to pass their tests as candidates, which most of them did in May 2004. EU membership helped to stabilize their new democratic politics. Following the breakup of the Federal Republic of Yugoslavia, the prospect of EU membership contained revanchist sentiments in the Balkans, which was no mean feat.

The principle of frontiers was also enshrined in the EU's so-called Neighbourhood Policy, launched in 2004. With every expansion east or south, the Union acquired new neighbours. And those ever more distant neighbours needed to be piloted into Europe's civilizational space in turn. One branch of the policy protruded east, later renamed as the Eastern Partnership, the policy that would ultimately provoke Putin's wrath, the other south into North Africa and the Middle East. A new "Ring of Friends" was to be created. The phrase was aptly chosen, for at journey's end waited not full membership but a looser form of association. "Everything but membership", as European Commission President Romano Prodi summed up the offer at the time. In practice, it meant things such as preferential access to the Union's single market, participation in EU financial programmes and visa liberalization.

The Ring of Friends concept was brilliant. It rendered the concept of frontiers actionable in still novel ways. Europe, the implication was, would never "end". Instead, it would only "fade out" the further one travelled outward from its centre. Membership ties would gradually change into looser friendships, some close, some less close. But nowhere was it necessary to draw hard or final lines between "us" and "them", "friend" and "foe". There were only degrees of organic, civilizational connectedness and corresponding modes of market access and collaboration, changing in intensity perhaps, but never in kind.

Brilliant as it was, Europe's doctrine of concentric circles suffered from in-built defects, which surfaced as the EU expanded. Domestically, as Europeans began to long more for stable communal identities, the Union's inherent fuzziness became a liability. The obligation to always keep the door ajar, to never slam it shut, lost its appeal. If the "us" was only a matter of degree, a liberal consensus spreading east and south, would there eventually be an "us" left at all?

The second defect was that Europe's neighbours, and Erdogan above all, began to baulk at the idea of gatekeepers and candidates, which flew in the face of his longing for equal respect. This was partly because Erdogan had other political goals than joining the EU, and increasingly took to strong-man methods to achieve them. But it was also because Europe, having grown weary of enlargement, kept raising the bar, pushing membership further away. Expectations, the message from Brussels was, needed to be adjusted downwards. But if Europe struggled with "enlargement fatigue", Turkey suffered from "reform fatigue".

With Erdogan, Europe's frontier diplomacy began to lose its coherence. The countless scuffles that came to define the relationship were no accident. For Turkey, but also for Europe, the obligations of the candidate and the gatekeeper had become a prison. Both sides felt the need to break out of the type of encounter they had imposed on themselves. The candidate increasingly stopped behaving like a candidate. But the gatekeeper also stopped behaving like a gatekeeper, no longer prepared to open the gates to candidates who pass their exams.

EUROPEAN OF THE YEAR

The problem was that Europe could never openly say so, at least not without running foul of the doctrine of spatiality that it had enshrined in its treaties, the idea of frontiers. Definite clarity of the "in-out" kind could only be given in that other type of space: political space with clear-cut borders. But the EU had not been constituted as that type of space. It did not possess the required vocabulary.

The incompatibility might have led to the sacrifice of the one or the other. To govern is to choose. But a choice would have been politically costly and moreover impossible to agree on. A compromise was needed. To all intents and purposes the door to Turkey would be bolted shut. A definitive line would be drawn in the sand, a de facto border. But for reasons of legal dogma and principle, this border still needed to be depicted as a frontier. Materially, the encounter with Erdogan evolved into a duel, an interest-based contest between morally equal states and their leaders and envoys. But the diplomatic form of the exam would be maintained as a façade.

It led to an absurd theatre that was predictable only in its unpredictability. Had the EU been able to openly acknowledge its political borders, Turkey's otherness would have become a tedious, institutional and historical fact. Europe's place in the world would not depend on "evidence" and "arguments", but its borders would simply "be". However, because formally the EU only possessed frontiers, European politicians needed proof of Erdogan's failings as a candidate. Evidence needed to be gathered that Turkey remained beyond the last outpost of civilization.

The masquerading of Europe's border with Turkey might be said to begin in December 2004, when Europe's leaders were still in great haste to open accession talks with Turkey. The political climate in Europe, they could see, was turning. The addition of "new Europe" in the east had led to a hangover in "old Europe" in the west. Wage differentials risked the delocalization of jobs and industries. Turkish membership would "be the end of Europe", former French president Valéry Giscard d'Estaing had cautioned.

Germany's rising political star, Angela Merkel, agreed. But Merkel was not yet in power. In the European Commission, the Union's custodian of legal purity, headed by the Italian Romano Prodi, a more confident mindset prevailed. After cursory debate among the body's commissioners, it recommended the light be switched to green. The Brussels enlargement machine had its hands free for new missions. And those hands needed to be put to work. Gerhard Schröder, Tony Blair and Jacques Chirac concurred.

Turkey had finally managed to get a proper foot in the door. And not a second too soon. For it was the likes of Merkel and Turkey sceptic Nicolas Sarkozy, French president between 2007 and 2012, who were now in the ascendency. However, both leaders faced one major obstacle: Erdogan himself, who at the time enjoyed a reputation as a man of the people who stood up for democracy and freedom. Turkey's new prime minster had himself been jailed for his political and religious convictions. As a candidate it meant he was not someone honest gatekeepers could easily turn back.

Erdogan became prime minster in 2003 and was known as Istanbul's rebellious mayor and the Islamist political reformer who swore to end Turkey's long tradition of military intervention in politics, one of the hallmarks of the fiercely secular Turkish state. The torture practices of Turkey's secret police, he felt, needed to be ended. The death penalty he wanted abolished, another reform Europe had long insisted on. Sadly, there were many things to like about Turkey's new prime minister.

The roots of Erdogan's domestic strength lay in Turkey's stratification in social classes, its division in "white" and "black" Turks, the nation's secular and educated elites in the well-to-do parts of Istanbul, and the conservative, pious and underprivileged Turkey in rural Anatolia on the other side of the Bosphorus. Turkey's elites had always held the important jobs, in particular in the army. They controlled the levers of physical power. But democracy was Erdogan's great friend. As with other strongmen, his power was based on a contract with the people. And the roles he performed to establish and strengthen that bond was that of the leader who promised change, a more prosperous and just future for Turkey's poor and oppressed.

He was also fearless, a warrior. Raised in Anatolia and later in the working-class Istanbul borough of Kasimpaşa, he was a black Turk himself, and proudly so. He had burst on to the local political scene some years earlier as a man of humble origins, the system outsider undaunted by vested power and moneyed interest. He was the streetfighter who dared to go to war with Istanbul's well-heeled elites, who true to Kemalist traditions were staunchly European, secular and modern in their values, but just as staunchly undemocratic in their politics.

Erdogan ran on a populist ticket before the West even knew what populism was. But to his credit, he did not seek to dispense with the republic's secular identity altogether, the statist, modernist heritage forged by Mustafa Kemal Ataturk (1881–1938). Erdogan chose to build on that legacy, to reform the republic rather than burn it to the ground. There would be no return to the Ottoman caliphate, to a premodern regime of padishah's. But in turn, Istanbul's secular elites needed to know one thing: he, Erdogan, the people's not-so-secular champion, would not be removed by a coup d'état. A modus vivendi needed to be found between "white" and "black", between the modern, affluent and European Turkey, and Erdogan's Turkey of the common man. The country's secular elites could keep their wealth and secular lifestyles, but the strongman expected to be courted and mollified, and to run the country without their interference.

The Turkish economy hardly suffered under Erdogan's new concordat, posting record levels of growth. To international acclaim, he managed to secure the support of Turkey's Kurds, who until then had been ruthlessly persecuted. Erdogan emerged as their saviour and as a peacemaker, granting them new political and cultural rights. Even on the intractable issue of the division of Cyprus, the island's northern half claimed by Turkey, the prime minster advanced new and consensual positions. What Erdogan seemed to propagate was an inclusive model of moderate Islamist democracy, proving Huntington's prophesied "clash of civilizations" wrong.

It sufficed for readers of the *European Voice*, a Brussels-based paper for the EU's policy and diplomatic elite, to vote Erdogan "European of the Year 2004". If he really was the Muslim equivalent of a European Christian Democrat, who were Merkel and Sarkozy, Christian Democrats themselves, to deny Turkey a place around Europe's table? Erdogan's passion for reform seemed to have turned Turkey's accession into an open-and-shut case. "Whoever still wants to put forward arguments against Turkey had better hurry up", *Der Spiegel* – approvingly – quoted a European diplomat.[13] Because with Erdogan running the country, those arguments were running out fast.

RATTLING THE CHAINS OF THE LAW

For *The Economist* it all added up to "the impossibility of saying no".[14] But still, ways to say no needed to be found. The challenge lay in the fact that the EU had chained itself to the rules and obligations of its role as educator and gatekeeper, which meant the question on the table was not whether it was *desirable* that Turkey joined, but only whether Turkey was *ready*. And if so, membership would follow automatically. All else was formally beyond the scope of the assessments the Union needed to make until the entire accession process had run its course, until all "chapters" had been closed.[15]

In his 2007 presidential campaign, Sarkozy sought to break free from this self-imposed corset by turning Turkish accession into a key campaigning issue. He left little doubt about his radical, irreverently political vision of a Europe with borders. "I want to say that Europe must give itself borders", he argued at a rally, "that not all countries have a vocation to become members of Europe, beginning with Turkey which has no place inside the European Union."[16] It was a shocking assertion of Turkey's final "otherness" and an effort not just to slam, not just to bolt, but to weld the door shut.

However, as long as Erdogan kept ticking the right boxes, the institutional reality was that the enlargement process would unfold according to its own rules-based logic. Flame-welders did not and still do not exist in Europe's constitutional order. No candidate state can be ruled out on the grounds of size, poverty and religion, or that the gatekeeper happens not to "like" the candidate. There were legal criteria that needed to be respected. Political appraisals above and beyond these criteria formed no part of the EU's operating language. This was why Sarkozy, as a measure of last resort, had an amendment written into the French constitution to the effect that further EU enlargement would need to be ratified by means of a popular referendum, in other words by a sovereign decision.[17]

Merkel shared Sarkozy's concerns. But while she opposed Turkey joining the EU, uprooting Europe's doctrine of frontiers and the EU's status as a *Wertegemeinschaft* would have caused an earthquake in German politics. She preferred to accept in relative silence that Turkish accession had acquired its own momentum. Formally, it was Erdogan who would decide not just Turkey's but also Europe's destiny. Europe could only passively watch. It could only record the candidate's progress, and read out the final verdict.[18]

But this was still only formally true. Increasingly, Europe's impulse was to reclaim the ability to determine who was "in" and "out" for itself, and to do so by sovereign decision alone.[19] If the Union's tests and treaties stood in the way of such a decision, to hell with its tests and criteria! Ways to force the issue needed to be found by going around the rules. As Trump might have put it, "We're Europe, bitch!" Enthusiasm for Turkey waned further in 2005, after referenda on the EU's new Constitutional Treaty in France and the Netherlands had been catastrophically lost. Whether Turkey was "ready" became a political irrelevance.

Borders were never directly observable in EU legal documents or discussed in official Brussels meetings where formal decisions were taken. But their growing reality could be inferred. Institutionally, the shift was expressed in terms of the candidate's "test scores", still the only language available. Initially glowing assessments turned into biting criticism overnight. If the indeterminacy of frontiers worked in Turkey's favour in December 2004, when it was decided to open negotiations, subsequent years showed how this elasticity could also be used against it. Turkey's progress was first assessed as slowing down, and then as going into reverse.[20] The gatekeeper was ever less willing to turn a blind eye to the candidate's shortcomings. "The party is over, and now comes the time of delivery", Olli Rehn sternly lectured late November 2005.[21] Membership criteria, he made clear, needed to be met "to the letter".

The Eastern and Central European countries that joined in 2004 had been given target dates for their membership. For Bulgaria and Romania, joining in 2007, those "graduation dates" had virtually been engraved in stone. But for Turkey no such dates were agreed. Brussels preferred to keep the talks as open-ended as possible. The great urgency that had once turbo-charged enlargement made way for even greater political lethargy. "It is obvious that the EU accession process is no bullet train – no Eurostar, *pas de TGV*", the Commission warned. "It is rather like the Orient Express, a train which takes its time ... Yes, it is a slow, slow train coming, and not precisely up around the bend."[22] This time the Union did not mind a bit of drift.

Of the 35 negotiation chapters one was completed in the summer of 2006. But then the EU scuttled negotiations in the territorial conflict over Cyprus. The disputed status of the Mediterranean island proved a boon for Europe's Turkey sceptics. Parts of the talks were frozen until Erdogan agreed to open Turkey's air and seaports to trade with Cyprus, something he would only do as part of a wider settlement on the island's status. Such a settlement, however, remained far off, and no one in Europe was in particularly great haste to bring it any closer. Meanwhile, the overall tone of the European Commission's Turkey progress reports only grew gloomier.[23]

Suddenly, the novel term "absorption capacity" crept into official EU documents. The idea was that the Union needed to be "ready" itself to accommodate Turkey. The cost of enlargement to the Union needed to be gauged, and if that cost was too high, accession would have to be put off. The new approach chimed well with Europe's longing for spatial finality, with its desire to claw back its sovereignty from the rules it had imposed on itself. But within the EU's logic of frontiers, the notion of absorption capacity was a profanity, a "dangerous tool in the hands of those who want to keep out Turkey and stop enlargement altogether", according to one EU analyst.[24] Others rejected the idea as a "pseudoscientific" and a "vague and politically charged term".[25] If it found its way into official EU texts and papers, the concept "would undermine years of patient attempts to build up a unique European doctrine ... of enlightened soft power".[26]

When the European Commission was asked to flesh out what absorption capacity meant in a policy paper, it relegated its analysis to the paper's annexes, where it assumed less formal weight.[27] The concept could hardly be mentioned, at least not in any official capacity. It tinkered with the Union's political metaphysics.[28] As Cecilia Malmström, later the EU's trade commissioner, put it: "If we fix the European Union's borders today, we will prematurely limit the spreading of democracy."[29] Formally, it would never come to this cataclysmic point. To revise its approach to enlargement the EU required the unanimous consent of its member states. And its orthodoxy of frontiers could still count on some steadfast supporters, not least the UK and Poland, who were rooting for the Union to expand into the Balkans and Ukraine.

As suddenly as it appeared, the language of absorption capacity vanished from EU official language. Materially it made little difference to the outcome. For Europe, the issue of Turkey evolved from *whether* to say yes or no, into *how* to say no. As long as the Union's official doctrine of frontiers could be upheld, even if with a large dose of hypocrisy, everyone seemed quietly content with keeping Turkey firmly outside the door.

BOSS OF THE BOSPHORUS

It could not fool the wily Erdogan, of course. That rules and criteria were only a cloak for strength and power needed no more explaining to the strongman than it did to Putin. It was how his own feudal machinations worked. If for whatever deeper reason Paris and Berlin decided they did not want Turkey in, they would always find "objective" reasons for the candidate to fall short. More importantly, the entire masquerade suited Erdogan. EU membership had never been his own project. Rather, it had been a project that he had inherited from the Kemalist Turkey, whose elites continued to hold most of the key jobs inside the bureaucracy and still controlled the economy.

For Erdogan, the EU had a more mundane value. Accession talks would keep Turkey's generals in their barracks, just as they would keep in check what Erdogan called the "deep state", an invisible network of plotters intent on restoring Kemalist rectitude. When in 2007 Turkey's General Staff warned the country's parliament not to elect Erdogan's fellow Islamist, Abdullah Gül, to the office of president, Brussels wasted no time in making known its great displeasure.[30] The examiner did precisely what Erdogan hoped he would do. He firmly rapped the candidate over the knuckles. There was no need for Erdogan to either see through EU accession to its end or to kill off the process. He was neither possessed by Ataturk's messianic belief in progress, nor had he fallen under the spell of reactionary piousness. As long as the EU kept dangling the carrot of accession in front of Turkey's vindictive elites, his purposes were well served.

It bought Erdogan time to consolidate his power, to grow his own feudal networks inside the Turkish state, which for black Turks such as himself had always been inaccessible. For this, he relied on his ally the Islamist preacher Fethullah Gülen, who commanded the loyalty of a large flock of loyal and well-schooled followers. These followers were now to be placed into positions of influence. The goal was to create a network of loyal clients, a "state in a state" as Erdogan later called it, which owed fealty and homage to him instead of the old values of Kemalism.

As Erdogan's hold over Turkey grew more secure, Europe's value as an insurance policy against coups dwindled. Erdogan could fight his own battles, relying on the system of vassalage he had created with brother-in-arms Gülen. In 2007 and 2010, state prosecutors, many loyal Gülenists, opened investigations against a large number of plotters and saboteurs accused of being part of Turkey's scheming "deep state". It was, of course, a classic purge. The allegations were mostly fake, but hundreds – senior army officers, opposition politicians, journalists – were convicted and jailed.[31]

If in the early years Erdogan needed to fear a backlash by the republic's wealthy elites, by the start of the next decade those elites had been largely neutralized as a threat. Erdogan's hunt for power, boosted by an unbroken string of victories in elections and referenda, had been a rousing success. So successful, in fact, that his presence in the republic began assuming the same ubiquitous shape of its legendary founder, Kemal Ataturk. Erdogan, it seemed, had traversed the full distance from being the state's perennial outsider, imprisoned for reciting an Islamic poem, to being the state's ultimate insider, locking up politicians and poets himself.

For Europe, Erdogan's metamorphosis from "European of the Year" into the "Boss of the Bosphorus" was lamentable. But in one regard it made life noticeably more comfortable. In contrast to Erdogan the democrat, Erdogan the strongman obviously flunked all his exams. And he could not have cared less. In spring 2013, Erdogan ordered police to crack down on young, urban and mostly secular protestors around Istanbul's Gezi Park, "looters" in his words. When he was done, 12 protestors lay dead in the streets. The result: a freeze of EU accession talks, at least of the parts of the talks that had not been frozen before. When in 2014 Erdogan won popular elections for Turkey's presidency – he had reached the term limitations of the premiership – *The Economist*, which earlier had described Erdogan as "impossible to say no to", crowned him as "The Next Sultan".[32]

Erdogan's fallout with Gülen in December 2013 cemented his reputation. Accusing Gülen of orchestrating a smear campaign against him, he now began purging the preacher's Islamist followers. They had been instrumental to him once, but now they needed to go. "We will root out the bad apples or whatever is necessary", he announced.[33] Erdogan's problem was that his Islamist vassals were ultimately more loyal to Gülen than to him, and therefore could not be trusted. It had made Gülen far too powerful for Erdogan's liking, and a potential pretender to the throne he occupied.

It was brother against brother, black on black, and very quickly it became an all-out witch-hunt. The Gülen-loyal newspaper *Zaman* was raided by police, its editors replaced, and then placed under state supervision. Dozens of other media outlets were shut down. The parallel structure of vassalage that Gülen had built needed to be dismantled again. Erdogan instantly recognized the preacher's hand in the coup d'état of 15 July 2016, a last-ditch, pre-emptive effort to get rid of Turkey's president. Declaring a state of emergency, the onslaught against the preacher's movement went into overdrive. Civil servants, magistrates, police officers or schoolteachers; the merest whiff of Gülen patronage now sufficed. The fortunate were fired. Those less fortunate were imprisoned.

Journalists seemed to be a favoured target.[34] Turkey's prospects as a candidate for EU membership were falling to pieces. What made things worse was that Europeans of Turkish descent could find themselves in jail too. "Turkey has been taking giant strides away from the European Union for some time", Commission President Jean-Claude Juncker summed up his verdict in 2017.[35] Erdogan was indifferent. "To tell the truth, we don't need membership anymore", he reflected.[36] He could afford an approach no less opportunistic than Europe's, blowing hot or cold depending on whatever suited him best politically. For European politicians harshly disciplining Erdogan only had upsides. But for the strongman too, a brawl with "hypocritical" Europeans worked wonders. It perfectly matched his act as daredevil and streetfighter. Nothing mobilized the support of his support base more.

On Saturday 11 March 2017, Dutch Prime Minster Mark Rutte knew the moment for a good punch-up had arrived. Both men faced important elections, Rutte to secure re-election in the face of a populist anti-EU revolt in his country, Erdogan to win a referendum that would transfer executive power to the office of president, which he now held.

To canvass votes among the sizeable Turkish diaspora in Western Europe, Erdogan had ordered his minsters abroad. But when his foreign minister, Mevlüt Çavusoglu, announced his intention to address a political rally in Rotterdam, Rutte did not dither. No stranger to electioneering himself, he warned that the Turks had better stay away, the further the better. When Çavusoglu said he would come all the same, Rutte upped the ante, stating that his plane would be denied landing rights. End of story.

But this was only the beginning. Never one to give up lightly, Erdogan resolved to instead send his minister for family, Fatma Kaya, already campaigning in Germany. It was a shrewd plan, a streetfighter's plan. The Dutch could deny Turkish planes landing rights for all they cared, but on the Saturday of the rally Kaya would simply take her ministerial car, sneak across the non-existent German/Dutch border, and address the crowd.

The stand-off that followed played itself out as darkness fell over the city's streets.[37] Excitement had reached fever pitch, as rumours swelled that Kaya was making her way to Rotterdam, snubbing Rutte's injunction. A large crowd of enthusiastic Erdogan supporters had gathered to welcome her, chanting "Allahu Akbar" and waving Turkish flags. Also growing quickly in number were the riot police and Dutch and Turkish news cameras.

When Kaya arrived in her armoured Mercedes, protected by Turkish security guards, a tense, hours long stand-off followed. Police ordered her to drive back to Germany, but the minster, phoning for instructions, refused. Police dogs growled, straining on their leash, while the crowd was getting restless. But neither Erdogan nor Rutte blinked. They had no incentive to. It was Rutte who finally decided that if the minister did not return voluntarily, her car would be towed back to Germany with the minister still in it. "Hands off my country", he warned Erdogan the next day.

The strongman responded by calling Rutte a fascist and a Nazi. Diplomatic ties were suspended, economic sanctions threatened. Memes of Rutte with a Hitler moustache flooded Turkish social media. None of it did him any harm. To the contrary, as a performance it had worked flawlessly. At home and in Europe, politicians and media praised Rutte's cold-bloodedness and hardnosed stance. He comfortably triumphed at the polls four days later. Some weeks later, Erdogan won his referendum too. Among Turks living in the Netherlands, angered by Dutch insolence, the yes vote had been strong.[38] Sanctions never materialized, and it was not long before Erdogan again called Rutte his "old friend".[39]

SCHOOL'S OVER

The duel between Rutte and Erdogan – and, if anything, it was a duel – was as good a sign as any that Europe's encounter with the strongman had morphed into something else. The hierarchy between examiner and candidate had made way for an egalitarian relation between rivals and contestants. A similar transformation, of course, had already occurred in the EU–Turkey migration pact of 2015–16. Viewed through the prism of the exam, the pact was an anomaly. Examiners cannot enter into side deals with candidates for special favours. It opens the door to blackmail, in particular if the candidate is a bully like Erdogan.

Only weeks after the migration deal had been signed, a German satirist, Jan Böhmermann, read out a poem on public television channel ZDF in which he called Erdogan a "goat fucker" and a "watcher of child pornography". Erdogan was livid. He demanded prosecution under German defamation laws. Böhmermann belonged behind bars, he felt, where assuredly he would have ended up in Turkey. The outcry that followed in Germany was predictable. However, the expected avowal of freedom of speech by Merkel did not come. In "Erdogate", as the affair came to be called, the chancellor first assented to Erdogan pursuing his interests through the German courts. Only after her position drew massive flak at home did she toughen her line.

Had the chancellor become hostage to her own migration deal? She had certainly invited that suspicion. One thing became clear: the migration pact had fundamentally altered the nature of their relationship. In the context of that deal, both leaders had been equals, players, negotiators and envoys of their countries and its interests. Europe's civilizational language of frontiers, of "progress reports" and "criteria", lost its meaning. It was replaced with the political language of borders, and the diplomatic ethos belonging to that language was that of the duel and the duellist.

More painfully than any other episode, the EU's migration deal demonstrates how it is caught between its established identity as a civilizational space and the nascent reality of a Europe that is a finite, stationary political space, and that must deal with other such spaces towards its east: Turkey, Russia and China. What it shows is that Europe engages in two types of encounter, which it finds hard to reconcile: the officially sanctioned encounter between civilization and savagery (the frontier); and the political encounter between equals in the duel (the border), the reality of which it can never fully acknowledge.

The tension between the sanctioned and concealed encounter is problematic. As long as quid pro quo deals with strongmen like Erdogan are necessary, making such deals will always appear profane, illicit and hence politically costly for those who make them, putting Europe at a disadvantage. Those deals will either be shunned, or they will be masqueraded as something more noble, a tactic that renders European foreign policy opaque, unaccountable and duplicitous. Erdogan had already made the point in 2007: "If the EU doesn't want us, they should say it now and clearly ... If we are not wanted, then both sides don't need to waste their time with negotiations."[40] More importantly, Europe's desire to take charge of its destiny as a sovereign agent will be harder to realize if efforts to do so must be articulated in an official language unsuitable for the job. The EU will not develop a mature strategic culture if the language of power can only ever be whispered.

To gain access to the language of power, Europe's taboo on borders will have to be broken first. A formal decision to end accession talks with Turkey would be a step in that direction. Such a decision would not strictly require the Union to abandon its doctrine of frontiers or its identity as a civilizational space. Given how deep Erdogan has strayed into the wilderness, it might be argued, the candidate can no longer be considered a candidate, and consequently the examiner no longer an examiner. It would be one last act of mendacity, but also an act that would pave the way for recognizing what Europe's encounter with Erdogan has already become: a duel. We would all know the frontier would be final, that is to say a border, the outer edge of a Europe that to all intents and purposes is political.

CHAPTER 8

Xi: defying the celestial empire

This world is not tranquil, and a storm – the wind and rain – are coming. And at the approach of the rain and wind the swallows are busy.

> Mao Zedong, in conversation with Henry Kissinger[1]

THE HOME STRAIGHT

On 17 January 2017, days before Donald Trump would stride into the White House, Xi Jinping rose to the Davos lectern to address a dejected audience of global business leaders at the annual gathering of the World Economic Forum. Globalization would continue, Xi argued determinedly, if not under US stewardship then under that of his own. "The global economy is the big ocean that you cannot escape from", China's strongman said, picking his words carefully. "Any attempt to cut off the flow of capital, technologies, products, industries and people between economies, and channel the waters in the ocean back into isolated lakes and creeks is simply not possible."[2]

The conference hall packed with the great and the good of global capitalism found itself in violent agreement with the Marxist leader. And when he had finished, it broke into applause worthy of a Communist Party clapping frenzy.

Xi was no liberal, but globalization had powered China's rise for 40 years, and its demise would spell disaster. For Trump, globalization seemed a dead end, but for Xi it was the path to regaining China's strength. Smashing the world's architecture would be destructive. What was needed was a new global order, one that would supplant the old structures of the West. There was much to be said for Trump's new politics of strength. But he needed to make sure this brand of politics did not spell the end of globalization.

It turned Xi into the unlikeliest of Davos's heroes. Since his elevation to general secretary in 2012, he had only acted in the best of strongmen traditions, solidifying his personal hold on power by jailing rivals under the guise of anti-corruption campaigns. He had unleashed a brutal policy of cultural assimilation on China's Uighur population in the western province of Xinjiang. To strengthen his authority, he studiously aligned his image with that of China's "Great Helmsman" Mao Zedong, the founder of communist China, assuming his title of "Paramount Leader" and launching an app dedicated to "Xi Jinping Thought", which quickly became known as Xi's Little Red App. The goal was not to revive Maoist doctrine. Rather, it was to establish his authority and legitimacy as a ruler. Xi's word was law, as Mao's had been. They shared a lineage.

In 2018, Xi abolished presidential term limitations, to the dismay of the Western world. It paved the way for Xi to monopolize power in China for years to come. As nearly always, the concentration of power in the hands of one man was linked to how the nation experienced its history, more precisely the risk of the country's ruin, a Machiavellian doomsday event that could be avoided only by the exceptional powers of an exceptional man. However, in the case of China that event had already taken place some 175 years ago, when superior European power had prised open China to Western trade, influence and science. And Xi was merely the latest in a line of strongmen tasked with avenging China's great humiliation.

Shared by all its modern leaders in some form, Xi's "China Dream" was to rejuvenate his country's fortunes, to catch up with Western science and technology, and eventually to surpass it. By the time Xi grabbed the reins of the party, the long and hard journey to rehabilitation had reached a new and decisive phase. Mao had founded the state, his successor Deng Xiaoping had made it rich, and now Xi would make it strong. "All of us can feel that we are closer … than at any other time in history", Xi prophetically noted in a speech.[3] One more heave, his message to the people was, declaring that at the centennial of communist China in 2049, the dream would finally come true.

This last push required international ambitions that Xi's predecessors had always scrupulously avoided. Deng's China had taken the path of economic modernization. It sought access to the West, to its markets and technology. But it did not seek to change the world. Deng and his successors realized that to win the access it sought, China needed to appear poor and unassuming. "Pretend inferiority and encourage his arrogance", as Sun Tzu explained in *The Art of War* regarding how to defeat the enemy.[4]

Deng's strategy worked and radically transformed the country. Growing at an average rate of 10 per cent a year according to World Bank data, China set a pace no other country has ever been able to match. When Xi took control of the country in 2012, Chinese gross domestic product (GDP) had already surpassed that of France, the UK, Germany and Japan, and it was fast closing in on the United States. Hundreds of million people had found their way out of poverty. State-of-the-art infrastructure and huge government-controlled corporations had sprouted out of the ground like mushrooms. However, Deng's stratagem of lying low was falling victim to its own success. Western businesses and politicians increasingly complained about Chinese over-capacity, state subsidies and the lack of reciprocity in market access. The West's willingness to grant unfettered entry to its markets and technology was eroding.

For Xi it meant the time had come for a less self-effacing approach. In its next and final phase, China needed to rebuild and reshape Western order in its own image. The stronger China grew, the greater the risk Western powers would try to contain it. Global finance was still built around the US dollar's status as the world's reserve currency. International trade and bank reserves were dominated by the dollar. It meant no one could fully escape the jurisdiction of US sanction laws. Technological platforms like SWIFT, which provides the financial plumbing of global markets, were controlled by Washington. The White House could freeze its rivals out of the global trade system at the mere flip of a switch.

It was an awe-inspiring political weapon and one that the US had begun to use with growing gusto. But it was also a state of affairs inconsistent with Xi's China Dream. That dream's realization required a globalized economy that did not depend on Western-controlled plumbing. Xi believed he had precisely the right vision to achieve it. His world would not be a Trumpian place of "isolated lakes", which the Davos community so dreaded. But neither would it be the global order the West had created. This would be China's big ocean, an integrated world based on its own philosophy of strength. As its designer and creator, the power to grant or deny access to this world would belong entirely to Xi, putting China back at its centre.

CONNECTED BY FEUDAL POWER

In September 2013, Xi set out his vision for a globalized world in a speech at Nazarbayev University in what was then still called Astana, Kazakhstan.[5] "This land", he began, "has borne witness to a steady stream of envoys, caravans, travellers, scholars and artisans travelling between the East and the West." In the Kazakh capital, once at the geographic centre of the ancient Silk Road, he "could almost hear the camel bells echoing in the mountains and see the wisp of smoke rising from the desert".

What the world now needed, Xi went on, was a Silk Road for the twenty-first century, a vast Eurasian belt of economic connectivity, new corridors bustling with trade, entrepreneurialism and cultural conversation, linking China in the far east with Europe in the far west. It was a beautiful vision and no stillborn piece of political rhetoric. China, it became clear soon enough, was ready to throw its full weight behind its new Silk Road, offering $1 trillion in credit and engineering muscle to actually build it.

What Xi notably failed to offer was a clear definition of the goals and operational scope of his Belt and Road, as the initiative is known today in the West. The idea's geographic reach has remained open-ended and ever expanding. Eurasia and Africa lie at its core, but there is no single road; there are many. For now, "Belt" refers to six land corridors traversing numerous countries towards China's north and west: Russia, Central Asia, Turkey and Eastern Europe. "Road" refers to various sea corridors and the many countries and ports along them: Malaysia, Pakistan, Djibouti, Greece, the Arctic maritime route in the north, which global warming is making accessible.

As nearly all Western analysts of the Belt and Road remark, its guiding principles seem no less wide ranging than its geographic scope. In February 2019, the effort was reported to encompass no fewer than 1,700 infrastructure projects, while partnerships had been concluded with 125 countries across the globe.[6] There is no official doctrine that neatly lays out what kind of "connectivity" the Belt and Road proposes to build and how. The plan does not confine itself to constructing roads, or railways and ports, although these clearly form an important part of the initiative. It incorporates energy infrastructure for gas and electricity as well as digital, telecoms and 5G data networks, which Chinese technology giant Huawei has already begun rolling out across the globe. It includes people-to-people relations, travel and cultural exchange.[7] The Belt and Road, moreover, does not just connect east and west; it also aims to fill the vast space in the middle, with industrial parks, economic hubs and productive capacity that adds to the value chain.

The Belt and Road's nebulous and sweeping ambitions meant the project was met with uncertainty in the West and elsewhere. People did not know whether to applaud or jeer, a feeling that never went away. Connecting Eurasia and the world was a goal the Europeans endorsed and shared, the vision of a true Davos internationalist. If China was ready to pay for it, so much the better. On the other hand, Xi's ambitions seemed so vast that no one could pin down exactly what the Belt and Road was or what it was meant to achieve. Where did the Belt and Road begin, and where did it end? How did the project relate to the existing global order?

The answers to these questions start to become clearer when we try to make sense of Xi's Belt and Road vision through the lens of the politics of strength. In essence, I argue, the Belt and Road is nothing but the strongman's way of organizing and controlling globalization. It is a global vision of a world connected not by rules but by strength, and that therefore clashes with and also supplants how Europe pictures the world. As Siemens CEO Joe Kaeser once put it, the Belt and Road "is going to be the new WTO – like it or not".[8]

As an alternative theory of globalization, the Belt and Road's modus operandi is based on the principles of feudal power, and more precisely the power of the renminbi: Chinese purchasing power. The Belt and Road is project led and unashamedly transactional. Its constituent part is the bilateral business deal, while the totality of the Belt and Road, and ultimately the glue that keeps the world together, is formed by the sum of all such bilateral deals. In Xi's philosophy of world order, there is no place for supranational institutions, charters or communities that connect the parties involved in such deals. Partnership only requires a memorandum of understanding directly signed with Beijing. There are only two contracting parties: a country that needs funding for investment in roads, airports, electricity plants, port terminals, digital or other connectivity infrastructure, and cash-rich China, which makes those funds available and leads the project's implementation.

It makes the Belt and Road a direct, efficient and malleable form of organization. Formal procedures that stipulate constraints and obligations are superfluous. The EU imposes standards of governance on those who want its funding, as does the IMF. Those standards must be scrupulously applied if money is to ever change hands, as current and aspiring EU members such as Greece, Serbia and Albania can attest. The Belt and Road circumvents all such obligations, promising instant and no-questions-asked gratification instead. Nothing, Beijing has found, opens doors quite as fast as the promise of cold hard cash. By contrast, the benefits of European-style integration can take years to materialize. "The French are late, very late. And they have no money", a Djibouti government official complained when Macron visited the former French colony in 2019 and was received in its Chinese-built presidential palace.

That said, it would be naïve to think the Belt and Road partnership creates no obligations of its own, beyond the servicing of financial debt. As in all feudal arrangements, the hierarchical implications of the Belt and Road are always palpable. As creditor and investor, Xi sits at the top of the chain. It is to him that the recipients of funding owe fidelity, just as vassals owe an obligation of fidelity to their lord. It is an expectation often too delicate to acknowledge in public. But in a relationship of great inequality and dependency its reality is hard to avoid.

It is possible to recognize in the Belt and Road, as others have done, certain features of China's imperial tributary system of diplomacy, also known as "All under Heaven" or *Tianxia*, which allowed Beijing to rule over vast parts of Central, East and South East Asia right until the nineteenth century.[9] It was a feudal system made possible by inequality, by China's civilizational, economic and technological superiority, which placed it at the centre of Asia and the world as a matter of course for centuries.

Imperial China viewed the earth as one civilizational space, with itself in the middle and without political borders or states. Less civilized, less well-off peoples circled in Beijing's outer orbits, growing ever less civilized the further they were from the centre of power. However, those barbarian peoples could gain access to the spoils of its civilization, on the condition that they bowed to the emperor's authority. Foreign envoys and merchants were welcome to obtain trade privileges, protection, political recognition and other coveted goods from Beijing. All they needed to do in return was to pledge their fealty, pay tribute to the "Son of Heaven" as the world's highest authority, the contract the emperor's strength was based on.

China's Celestial Empire was harmonious and theoretically in perfect balance, emanating organically from its natural and civilizational supremacy. Barbarians could be "managed" without compulsion, conquest or violence. There was no desire or even need to forcibly thrust Chinese civilization onto others. Its order rested solely on voluntary submission, a two-way deal as in the Belt and Road, which for both parties in the relationship was attractive. Faraway people who saw no profit in engaging with China did not have to, as long as they minded their own business. There was no need for multilateral institutions. *Tianxia* posited its own consensual hierarchy, based on virtue and merit alone.

Similarly, Xi hails the voluntary and peaceful nature of the Belt and Road as its core strength, which he contrasts with a Western model of globalization based historically on colonial conquest and the imposition of its values and customs on a heterogeneous world. The Belt and Road offers what he calls a "win-win", a truly mutually beneficial deal that leads to a more "inclusive" form of globalization. The Western idea of win-win, which also exists, is predicated on the prior acceptance of its rules and liberal values, a proviso that, if not met, triggers sanctions and intervention. China's win-win order, on the other hand, has no entry criteria. The Belt and Road is open to all states, without prior vetting based on moral criteria.

The ancient Silk Road, used by traders and adventure seekers from all over Eurasia, nicely sums up the kind of connectivity that Xi appears to want to forge. Enabling one of the first waves of globalization, the Silk Road was never built for one side to impose its values, duly certified as universal, on the other. It merely enabled trade and discovery in the spirit of equality and mutual respect. It facilitated cultural conversation and learning, the exchange of ideas, practices and knowledge, not the interference in foreign cultures or the imposition of values upon one's neighbours. For the same reason, the term "connectivity" captures Xi's idea of globalization better than the word "integration", which posits an end state in which disparate parts meld into one unified whole. Connectivity, instead, merely connects what is meant to stay separate. Xi's point is that one can connect Eurasia without turning China into Europe, or Europe into China.

In language that effortlessly blends Confucianist with Marxist ideas, Chinese intellectuals close to this vision, like Wang Yiwei, the author of *China Connects the World*, argue that the Belt and Road gives birth to a whole "new human civilization", heralding the triumph over Western "dualism", which is mired in a cycle of "estrangement and confrontation".[10] Humanity, Wang argues, expects something better than "the curse of US hegemony". Not Chinese hegemony, to be sure, but a world without hegemony, just the place the Belt and Road philosophy would deliver. The world envisaged is one made of different states and equal cultures, but rewired and connected according to Belt and Road principles it will be a world of harmony, peace and order.

But, of course, that world is only based on a different type of inequality, which official Belt and Road rhetoric likes to skip over. In Xi's "big ocean", order, harmony and peace are always premised on China's superiority in wealth and technology. Just as *Tianxia* always requires a centre and a periphery, a lord and vassal, so does the Belt and Road. One state must always be elevated above the others, a "Middle Kingdom" wealthier, more virtuous and more advanced. Only in the presence of a Son of Heaven who is strong do lesser sons have someone to kneel to. Only then, in other words, is there someone who possesses the means to structure, connect and steer the world from above, which in a world not connected by rules and institutions is a necessity.[11]

This hierarchy may be implicit rather than explicit, but what we get in the Belt and Road is international order based on a protection contract between the strong and the weak. No one needs to subscribe to Chinese values, norms and customs. But recipient countries do have to accept Beijing's suzerainty. The defenders of *Tianxia*-based order are not wrong to point at the win-win logic that lies at the system's core. Theoretically, such contracts are stable and spontaneous equilibria based on the rational consent of the parties concerned. No one is forcing anyone to take the deal. Yet, there is an obvious hierarchy in the system without which it falls apart.

It explains why the reality of the Belt and Road, and globalization based on strength, is not always as harmonious as Beijing makes it out to be.[12] Xi consistently denies the Belt and Road is a political trap and he goes out of his way to stress its collaborative nature. But dependency and fealty are engrained in the system's DNA, and some day that fealty might be called in. Malaysian Prime Minister Mahathir Mohamad has warned against "a new version of colonialism".[13] Equally, Cambodian politicians have warned against their country becoming "a de facto Chinese colony".[14] The Belt and Road may be a consensual deal between interdependent parties, but this interdependency mostly tilts in one direction, as it always does in creditor–debtor relationships.

US officials accuse China of using "predatory economics".[15] If debts grow too large to be serviced, creditors can make their power count, which Beijing did when it forced Sri Lanka, unable to repay its loans, to lease China its port of Hambantota for 99 years. Other Belt and Road countries groan under their debt to Chinese lenders. Seen as a Belt and Road cornerstone, Pakistan owes as much as half of its debt to China, according to estimates.[16] Philippine officials, in turn, are concerned Beijing possesses remote operating technology that enables it to turn off their country's national power grid.[17]

To counter the criticism of "debt-trap diplomacy", Beijing has promised to step up its game, pledging to meet governance and sustainability standards.[18] Xi seems to argue that the Belt and Road is only dealing with teething problems. He may be right. New recipient countries continue to sign up to the Belt and Road. However, there are other and more fundamental reasons why Xi's "win-win" philosophy does not provide the universal and inclusive form of globalization it purports to offer.

To begin with, the Belt and Road's modus operandi manoeuvres China into a zero-sum relationship with Europe and its vision of globalization and integration based on rules. Since their philosophies of connectivity are fundamentally at odds, neither China nor Europe can logically fit under the other's "celestial" umbrella. The Belt and Road may be open to countries with diverse cultural and moral traditions, but it cannot be open to those who reject its model of globalization based on hierarchy, even if this is a hierarchy of the virtuous.

Furthermore, because Xi's logic of global inclusivity is based on hierarchy, it excludes strongmen who are equal in wealth and power, or who for whatever reason refuse to kowtow to Xi as their "overlord". There is Donald Trump, of course, but also Vladimir Putin, who is less strong than Xi but no less determined to resist vassal status. Trump, Putin and Xi subscribe to the same philosophy of globalization based on strength. But in that philosophy the problem is that one of them must take the top seat, while the others are relegated to vassal status. It is no coincidence that Indian Prime Minister Modi has consistently rebuffed the Belt and Road and considers China's growing involvement in its neighbourhood, including Pakistan, as a significant strategic threat.[19]

Consequently, we end up not with one "big ocean", as Xi pledged, but with a world that is divided, not in "isolated lakes" perhaps, but in several isolated oceans. In other words, what we get is what Carl Schmitt in his spatial theory of politics called *Großraumordnung*, order that is neither universal nor based on sovereign states but that hovers "in between", organized around "great spaces" or spheres of influence integrated around a dominant power such as China, the US or indeed the EU.[20]

Xi's Belt and Road, then, is easier to conceptualize as a large Sinocentric space, a Greater China that connects large parts of Eurasia and Africa based on its strength, but that still has to recognize that it begins and ends somewhere, in a spatial sense. Precisely where this space will end, nobody of course quite knows. But no matter how inclusive or universal in intent, Xi's feudal empire will exist in parallel to other great spaces, such as the feudal empires led by Trump, Erdogan and Putin and Europe's rules-based order. And how to connect those empires in turn, other than through the duel and its egalitarian codes, is a question that Xi has yet to answer.

CHAINS OF DEPENDENCY

It took time for Europe to fathom the geopolitical challenge it was dealing with in the Belt and Road. "It has been two, three years now ... and we are still figuring out what it actually means and what we can do about it", a European diplomat (based in Beijing) told the *South China Morning Post* in May 2017. "It's just a show", said a colleague, shrugging off a question about the flagship Belt and Road summit Xi was hosting that year.[21] In Europe roads are roads, trade is trade and geopolitics is geopolitics. But for Xi, as for all strongmen, roads, money and power are one and the same. Economic supply chains are never just supply chains; they are chains of dependency.

The West had long been frustrated with China. But it framed the challenge China posed in terms of its own principles of order. In 2009, US President Obama compared the situation to a basketball game: "For years, we used to trounce them. So if they threw around a few elbows in the lane, it did not matter, we could ignore it."[22] But now the game had become much closer and still "the referee wasn't calling any fouls". Perhaps, the president concluded, we need "to start throwing around some elbows ourselves".

This allegory was shared in Europe, where the language of reciprocity formed the staple of trade diplomacy. Levelling the playing field in trade, in Europe's analysis, was what the whole China problem was about. European companies just needed to get the same access to China as Chinese companies got to the West. Intellectual property needed to be respected. China needed to stop flooding the world market with subsidized goods, a practice that drove European industries to bankruptcy. In short, the rules needed to be the same for everybody.

However, in Xi's Belt and Road, Europe encountered a very different beast, harder to capture in these terms and images. The Silk Road needs more "reciprocity", French President Macron tried during a visit to Xian in January 2018, the Chinese city where the ancient trade route started. "If they are roads, they cannot be one-way."[23] The Frenchman's logic, of course, was faultless. However, Xi's roads were not about trade surpluses and market access; they were about shifting the balance of global power. The real questions posed by the Belt and Road were: who owns the road or controls access to it? Who polices the road? Who writes its traffic code? In politics, metaphors and images are rarely as innocent as they look. This was not another case of China breaking the rules of the game; it was Xi tempting the world to quit basketball, an American game, and to take up a different sport, with different rules, and – let's not forget – a different referee.

In 2015, Chinese construction workers started arriving in Montenegro, the small but insulated mountain state on Europe's Adriatic coast, not too distant from the Croatian island where, according to some historians, Marco Polo was born 750 years ago. They were coming to build the first stretch of a motorway linking the southern port of Bar to neighbouring Serbia in the north,

connecting the country onwards to Hungary and EU soil. Our "pathway to
the modern world", Montenegrin officials beamed, claiming the road would
unlock a golden age of development.[24]

Cutting through Montenegro's undulating terrain, the road needed to be an
engineering marvel, boasting state-of-the-art tunnels and spectacular bridges.
Western investors had repeatedly turned down the project, unable to make
the numbers add up. European Union funding was mired in red tape for the
Montenegrins. But the Chinese hardly blinked at the road's cost of €20 million per kilometre. Beijing seemed to care little about constraints and rules.
Agreeing up to €1 billion in loans, it just wanted to get things done.

Everywhere in south-eastern Europe Belt and Road projects were springing
up. In 2016, the state-owned China Ocean Shipping Company snapped up the
ailing Greek port of Piraeus for €280.5 million, an asset the Greek state had put
up for sale, ironically, under Brussels pressure. Gratefully, Beijing pounced.
Piraeus, China's ambassador said, was destined to become the Belt's "dragon's
head", China's new sea gateway to Europe.[25] In Europe, appetite to put in a
rival bid for the Greek port had been predictably scant. Greek authorities had
first floated the idea of a European sale to the port of Rotterdam, which they
preferred to a Chinese bid. But the Dutch were not interested.[26] As it turned
out, Greek workers did not rue the decision. China promptly and energetically
set about modernizing the port. Now able to secure a fat slice of Chinese
imported goods, Piraeus rocketed up the ranks as the fastest-growing con-
tainer port in the world.[27]

To connect Piraeus to its hinterland, China made funds available for building a new €3 billion high-speed rail link between Belgrade and Budapest, to
the great pleasure of Hungarian prime minister Viktor Orbán, who although
not known for his love of things foreign, is a staunch Beijing ally. In Belgrade,
Chinese engineers built a new bridge across the Danube, dramatically slashing
commuting times for city dwellers. "We have enjoyed an increasingly warm
relationship with China in recent years", said Aleksandar Vucic, currently
Serbia's president, "one that is destined to become even stronger."[28]

Transport and other forms of connectivity in the Balkans were crying
out for investment. However, it was Beijing, not Europe, that seemed more
eager to step into the breach. In Bosnia, China agreed billions in loans for the
upgrading of the country's energy infrastructure. Locals saw little reason to
protest. "Brussels has spent 20 years telling us what to do, and we have nothing to show for it", a journalist pointed out.[29] What was the country to do?
Compared to doing business with EU apparatchiks in Brussels, the Belt and
Road was a straightforward transaction. Beijing came armed with cash, not

with vows and values. Explaining the difference, a satisfied Balkan state official said that working with China is "not a marriage, it's a one-night stand".[30]

To structure its economic diplomacy towards Central and Eastern Europe, China used its "16+1" diplomatic format, which became the "17+1" when Greece officially signed up in 2019. This loose grouping of countries brings together states, both inside as well as outside the EU, that roughly straddle Europe's eastern borders, facing China on the distant horizon, countries such as Poland, Hungary and the Baltic states. The grouping's name already gives away its most important *Tianxia* feature: its members are not equal. To be sure, the 17 in the pack are equal. But the "+1" visibly stands apart from the rest. It occupies the centre and elevated ground. There is good reason why Europeans never call the EU the "25+2" (Germany and France being the two) or NATO the "28+1", even if for Trump that flag covers its load much better. The European Union is "the 27". Only as a supranational whole does the Union form a "+1".

By contrast, the "17+1" is held together only by the discrete, one-to-one relations that link its individual parts to the group's centre, its Son of Heaven. "17+1" leader summits, observers have noted, are a rapid succession of bilateral meetings between Xi and the group's other 17 leaders, not a platform for gathering leaders around the same table. Usually, moreover, these bilateral meetings take no longer than an hour.[31] Then Xi receives another supplicant. The grouping has a small but permanent secretariat, based in Beijing and staffed by foreign ministry officials from China. Like barbarian peoples centuries ago, the 17 are permitted to send envoys – "national coordinators" in modern parlance – to Beijing to convey their wishes. But the practice, of course, merely confirms the grouping is not based on equality, but on strength and feudal hierarchy.

Obviously, Xi's Balkan spending spree did not go unnoticed in Paris, Berlin and Brussels, where officials began scratching their heads at so much largesse. Watching the Belt and Road spread across Asia and Africa was one thing; seeing it push into European territory was a slightly different matter. Concern was growing, particularly over Chinese state-run companies taking majority stakes in strategic port facilities in places like Valencia, Bilbao and Zeebrugge in addition to Piraeus. Ports had played a long and mostly unhappy role in the history of Europe's relations with China. The ability to control and block access to China's trading ports had been at the heart of British gunboat diplomacy in the nineteenth century, which was partly responsible for forcing Beijing to cede Hong Kong to Britain. Losing control over its ports was what had started China's "century of humiliation". Could there be similar consequences if China took control of Europe's ports?

European reservations to the Belt and Road arose for two reasons. First, its projects flouted Europe's governance standards, which would lead to a range of practical problems later on. In Montenegro, European Investment Bank studies showed the planned motorway would attract little traffic. The project ignored environmental impact assessments and most of the construction jobs created would be filled by Chinese firms.[32] "Their fiscal space has shrunk enormously", one European official fretted. "They have strangled themselves. And for the time being this is a highway to nowhere."[33] The Belt and Road was perhaps quick, the argument was, but it was also dirty, and eventually it would all end in tears. Like wedlock, European connectivity did come attached with certain strings and stipulations, but in the long run it promised greater security and stability.

More importantly, perhaps, Europeans began to understand how Beijing's cheque-book diplomacy might not just be buying it a new Silk Road, but also levers of influence. If the Montenegrins defaulted on their loans, for example, contracts specified that China would get access to parts of its land put up as collateral. More generally, disputes involving Belt and Road projects would not necessarily be decided by independent international courts in London, Paris or other places in the West, but potentially also in China, where Beijing announced two purpose-built international courts of its own, one in the city of Xian for the land-based Belt and the other in Shenzhen for the maritime Road.[34] Additionally, in order to keep the money flowing or to secure debt relief, European Belt and Road countries might be called upon by Beijing for political favours.

The wake-up call arrived on 18 June 2017, when Athens' leftist firebrand prime minster Alexis Tsipras took a last minute decision to block an EU-statement at the United Nations criticizing China's human rights record. Tsipras rejected the statement as "unconstructive" and "selective". African recipients of Chinese investment, sensing perfectly what was expected of them, had long backed Beijing whenever such matters arose in the UN. With Greece invoking its blocking powers in Brussels, the entire European Union had been forced to join their ranks. In a press statement, Beijing promptly thanked Athens for "upholding the correct position".[35]

The incident showed that China had won a direct lever of influence in the EU, speaking through the voice of its backers. It did not need its partners to leave the Union. Much better that they were inside the club. It allowed Beijing to be there with them, and throw sand in the EU's wheels whenever this suited its interest. Above all Viktor Orbán, whose Hungary was the first EU country to sign a Belt and Road memorandum with Beijing, proved a loyal and useful client, consistently sabotaging critical EU foreign policy declarations on China.[36]

In September 2017, Germany's foreign minister, Sigmar Gabriel, alert to the risk of EU members being picked off, demanded Beijing treat the continent as "One Europe", just as Europe follows a "One China policy", officially dealing only with Beijing, not with the breakaway "Republic of China" in Taiwan. Rather than speaking to Athens, Budapest and then Warsaw, Gabriel implied, Beijing should speak directly to Brussels. Chinese officials, however, responded with scorn. China was a sovereign state. But what was Europe? The EU, a spokeswoman rubbed it in, was only "a regional organization composed of sovereign states, not a sovereign country itself … We hope that he can clarify what he means by 'one Europe' and whether there is a consensus on 'one Europe' among EU members."[37]

China was perfectly within its rights to seek bilateral investment ties with EU states, the argument went, be it in the 17+1 or any other form. It was those states, moreover, who wanted their own direct ties with China, without having to go through Brussels and assuredly never Gabriel's Berlin. If Germany wanted Europe to act as "One Europe", it needed to get its own house in order. And yet, the comments confirmed what seemed increasingly obvious. Xi, like Trump, was scheming to splinter the EU. Sliced and diced, he could enrol Europe in his own feudal empire.

Europe began looking at China and its Belt and Road through the prism of power and geopolitics, even in Germany, which had avoided that prism like the plague. What stirred Berlin into action was the Chinese takeover of robotics firm Kuka in the Bavarian town of Augsburg. German politicians had long hailed the company as one of Europe's great success stories in artificial intelligence. In 2016, touring the Hannover Messe, the world's largest industrial fair, Merkel and her guest Barack Obama had marvelled at the tricks its robots could perform. Yet Kuka was about to be bought by a Chinese rival. German politicians had urged other European investors to take over the firm, but they did so in vain. "Lots of names were floated", the Kuka CEO commented, "but were they prepared to do something? We had one offer on the table."[38]

Germany's relationship with China had been strong and focused on trade and investment opportunities. However, for China, it dawned on Berlin, trade and investment was also about geopolitical strategy, a greater design for a new world order. Its behemoth state-owned companies were not only profit-making businesses; they were taking their marching orders from Xi. It made politicians wary of China hoovering up European assets of strategic industrial and technological value. "The question is, are the economic relations being linked with political questions?", Angela Merkel openly wondered after meeting the prime minster of Macedonia in 2018.[39]

Western claims that the Belt and Road forms China's "Trojan horse" continue to get short shrift in Beijing, which angrily denies the Belt and Road has untoward motives. Official Belt and Road rhetoric is always soothing. It stresses that the project serves the goals of mankind in its entirety, not just China's. In his address to the 19th Communist Party congress, Xi himself did his best to reassure the world of his intentions. "China will never pursue hegemony or seek expansionist policies", he said.[40] But viewed through the prism of strength, such statements sound hollow.

Is such rhetoric a deliberate and cynical lie? Is Xi Jinping the world's new evil mastermind, deceiving and plotting to enslave it? Reality, of course, tends to be less premeditated, planned and morally clear cut. A more plausible explanation may be that when Xi decided Deng's era of modesty was over, and began to project China's power outwards onto the world, he fell back on the country's imperial modus operandi not as a naked bid for power, but as a philosophy of world order. What alternative models were there? A modernized version of "All under Heaven" was simply China's way, and as long as its emperor was virtuous and wise, it would be the best and only right way. The West does not promote democratic institutions and human rights to secure its global hegemony, although this is typically what strongmen like Xi and Putin believe drives the West. It believes the liberal model to be "who it is" and that it offers the best system of order for the world. Listening to Xi, his motivations and intentions seem no less honourable and sincere.

CONTROLLED RIVALRY

Whether such honourable objectives make the spread of Xi's empire any easier to curtail is, of course, another matter entirely. On 12 March 2019 the European Commission took the bold step of formally branding China a "systemic rival", much in the way the US had done in its national security strategy.[41] In the same breath, the EU body made clear it still considered China to be a "cooperation partner" with "closely aligned objectives", for example in combating global warming. However, it strongly urged its member states to deal with China "in full unity", implying Beijing was deliberately setting EU states at odds with each other, much in the same way as its imperial diplomatic strategists had tried to manage foreign "barbarians" in the past.

It was a watershed moment for the EU, which had not used language with such geopolitical undertones before. As always, a balance needed to be struck. Yet something had shifted. Brussels was claiming a space of its own and telling Xi not to interfere. Calling Europe and China rivals was not remarkable in itself, but by adding the word "systemic" the Commission made clear that it saw this rivalry as political. Europe finally acknowledged what the Belt and Road was: a system of global governance and integration that was radically at odds with its own.

How to halt that system's expansion would be a new question for Europe, if it were not too late. By declaring a massive trade war against China in 2018, Trump had already given his answer. America's strongman, of course, was not gravely troubled by the built-in feudal propensities of Xi's internationalist philosophy, viewing the world in much the same vein. Trump's problem was more prosaic: Xi's power might soon overshadow his. Xi was a duellist for whom Trump felt great respect. But the time had come to clip his wings, before he might beat him in the duel and claim the fealty of states that were currently still beholden to the US. Trump keenly understood that China's rise, as well as America's relative decline, depended on China's integration into the trade system and its global value and supply chains. The solution was easy. Having plugged China into that system, it now needed to be unplugged, for example by imposing new and higher tariffs on Chinese goods. In a nutshell, China's economy needed to be "decoupled" from that of the US and also from Europe's, in the same way that, during the Cold War, the Soviet economy had been cut off from Western markets.

This was not a strategy the Europeans would entertain, however. Europe's economy had become entwined with China's to such an extent that decoupling would have been suicide. The continent realized it needed a new strategy to protect itself from Chinese influence and statecraft. But what it did not need was the economic equivalent of a Wild West shootout of the kind that Trump proposed. "Do we in Germany and Europe want to dismantle all interconnected global supply chains … because of this economic competition?", Merkel wondered in an interview, adding that "complete isolation from China cannot be the answer".[42] China was never going to return to its pre-Deng status in the world, no matter how hard Trump might try. "We may agree that China is a strategic threat", said a European diplomat, "but you can't just put them in a corner."[43]

Whereas Trump favoured a "maximum pressure" stratagem, the Europeans favoured a "controlled" rivalry, more appropriate for an interdependent world, or so they felt. The position the EU converged on was that its rivalry with

China should be curtailed to selected areas, to markets of strategic importance such as network infrastructures and artificial intelligence. Elsewhere, Europe would seek to collaborate with Xi and advocate trade liberalization, as it had always done, as long as China played by the rules. At least Xi did not deny global warming, unlike Trump.

Moreover, Europe did not think of itself as locked in an existential race with Xi for global supremacy, the world's top seat. Europe, obviously, would never again be the world's number one. It was going to have to learn to live with China's new global strength, just as Xi was going to have to live with Europe and the US. It meant assuming a more vigilant and political posture to Beijing's economic strategies. At the same time, it entailed recognizing that Xi had legitimate demands of his own, which needed to be accommodated.

Hosting Xi at a bilateral meeting in Paris in April 2019, Emmanuel Macron did much to embody the EU's new and more political posture. "The period of European naivety is over", he warned Beijing in the days before the meeting, adding that Europe's relationship with China was not "first and foremost a trading one, but a geopolitical and strategic relationship".[44] Europe, Macron made clear, would not follow Trump's sabre rattling, but it would stand up for its political values and interests. In a demonstration of unity, he had invited Angela Merkel and Jean-Claude Juncker to join the "bilateral" meeting with Europe's rival from Beijing. He would not be roped into the Belt and Road or be tempted by its lure of cash like the states that had joined the 17+1 group. Whenever Xi wanted to deal with Macron, he would have to deal with Europe, *One* Europe.

It was also an important signal to other EU members, who rejected suggestions that they should not benefit from bilateral business deals with Xi. If France and Germany were to have their own bilateral dealings with Beijing, would they not be entitled to the same? However, Macron showed that he was prepared to do what others should also contemplate: build a united front and confront Xi together. Obviously, the matter was not settled so easily. But it was a start, a sign of the EU's growing maturity as a global player.

To slow down the spread of China's influence along its borders, Europe faces an array of hard political choices, which force it to break with the past. European states such as Germany, France and the UK have begun shoring up their structures to screen foreign investment on national security grounds. For decades, this had been a practice that many in Europe ridiculed. David Cameron, prime minister between 2010–16, unswervingly positioned the UK as China's gateway to the continent and the West. His government spoke of "a golden decade" in Sino-British relations and aggressively courted inward investment from China, including in a new nuclear power station at Hinkley Point.[45] Everyone was spying on everyone anyway, the consensus was. More awake to sovereignty issues, Theresa May and Boris Johnson took a less cavalier approach, imposing stricter security conditions on foreign investment.[46] Ownership of strategic assets like ports, power plants and airports became a political issue rather than a purely financial one.

"Digital sovereignty" has become another European goal. A consensus is emerging that Europe needs to build its own enabling technologies, ending its reliance on others. Chinese-built digital networks and technology, the view has become, risk being armed with "Manchurian chips" or "kill switches" that allow Beijing to impair or cut off access to vital digital networks. For the roll-out of 5G mobile internet networks, Europe faces an important choice. Chinese company Huawei is widely recognized to offer the best networks against the most competitive price. Moreover, Huawei technology is already present in parts of Europe's data infrastructure and this technology cannot just be ripped out. However, is it wise to entrust the building of such networks to a Chinese company that, in the final analysis, is controlled by the state?

The solution that has been mooted in Brussels and several European countries such as the UK and Germany is not to impose any outright bans on Huawei or Chinese operators, but to allow them to bid only for the parts of the 5G network that are "non-core" and pose no security risks. The approach is in line with the general idea of "controlled" strategic competition, of ensuring that certain vital economic sectors and supply chains remain in European hands, while keeping the rest of the economy open to global trade and investment, including from China.

Controlled rivalry may be a sensible approach, and if Europe unites around it, it may be a policy that China can eventually agree to disagree on. However, whether Xi can live with such a balanced approach is only one concern this policy raises. The other, and for Europe arguably more decisive question is whether Trump can do so as well. Europe "going soft" on Xi hardly fits his maximum pressure strategy. What would the world look like if not the US but China controlled the global internet, possibly the most important form of connectivity in the future?

Trump's loyal secretary of state, Mike Pompeo, hammered home the point in a speech on 5G in London in May 2019. Huawei building the UK's 5G networks, Pompeo cautioned, would leave the door open to "Beijing's spymasters". Would Margaret Thatcher, the Iron Lady, "allow China to control the internet of the future?"[47] It was more than just a piece of friendly advice from Europe's big brother. If the UK gave its green light to Huawei, Pompeo went on, there would be consequences. No longer would the US be able to offer access to its intelligence networks. There was no need to be particularly subtle about it. The UK was a sovereign country and free to make up its own mind, Pompeo said. But it had better do so "with the broader strategic context in mind".[48] When in February 2020, after much toing and froing, Boris Johnson allowed Huawei to bid for a role in the UK's 5G networks, it was not long before the prime minister received a call from an "apoplectic" Donald, venting fury at his decision, according to officials briefed on the conversation.[49] For a nation that was no longer in the EU and needed to negotiate new trade terms with the US, it did not bode well.

Trump, the episode made clear, viewed his relations with Europe in terms no different than Xi's, that is to say, as the sum total of "+1" bilateral deals that formed his own feudal empire. Assuredly he did not inject cash into European ports and infrastructure like Xi, but he did something far more important: he guaranteed the continent's physical security. And far more explicitly than Xi, from those who benefited he demanded fealty and homage, dues that in his mind could include just about anything he wanted, from buying US liquefied gas rather than Russian gas, to Denmark selling Greenland to the United States, and apparently also to adopting his economic "decoupling" strategy towards his rival Xi.

How far the strongman would go to force Europe into line with his China strategy remained unclear, but he certainly possessed plenty of tools for twisting a few arms on the other side of the Atlantic. Managing the rivalry with Xi in a controlled manner was perhaps the best approach for Europe, but would such a policy be possible if the continent did not first get a better handle on the power instincts of Donald Trump? Indeed, how did one deal with Trump?

While Europe wished to avoid being sucked into economic warfare with China, the cold facts pointed to the possibility that Trump might not let it, viewing Europe as a crucial pawn in his duel with Xi. The continent relied on US military and naval protection, and in the final analysis on its nuclear umbrella. If Europe refused to help curb his great rival Xi, could it still benefit from America's protective shield? "We cannot ensure the defence of the West if our allies grow dependent on the East", said Trump's vice president, Mike Pence, icily answering the question at the Munich Security Conference in February 2019.[50] It was a form of power the US had possessed over Europe since 1945 but that its presidents had always been coy to use, or perhaps had never needed to. But for Trump, who seemed unlike any US president before, nothing seemed more normal. What else was power for?

CHAPTER 9

Trump: cracking the strongman code

I think the European Union is a foe, what they do to us in trade. Now, you wouldn't think of the European Union, but they're a foe.   Donald Trump, interview with CBS, 14 July 2018

FROM FRIEND TO FOE

The need for a new European demeanour was never greater, nor may it ever be greater, than when, in the small hours of 9 November 2016, Donald J. Trump ascended from the gilded catacombs of his Manhattan tower to claim the presidency of the United States.

It was a moment that defied the odds. When, deep into the night, ashen-faced pundits of the US cable networks called the election for the construction tycoon and television star, they looked as if they had seen pigs fly. Something of tectonic significance had changed. Something that theoretically could not have happened just had. What had shifted was history itself. For if history was supposed to bend towards anything, it sure as hell was not Donald Trump.

It was the start of a new "Machiavellian moment" for Europe, a true confrontation with its temporal finitude, one which would force the continent, as the Florentine *consigliere* might have predicted, to reassess the metaphysical core of its politics and assert its own sovereign strength. Europe's assumption had always been that the threat to its liberal order would come from the marauding strongman Putin, from China's new economic might or from religious fanaticism in the Middle East. In fighting it off, it would stand shoulder to shoulder with its more muscular sibling across the Atlantic.

But it now appeared that the greatest danger hailed from the United States. The continent's mortal enemy resided not in the red-brick Kremlin but in the White House. And from this lair, right at the heart of the Western world, Trump could hurt Europe in ways that Putin or Xi or Erdogan could not even begin to imagine. The US had been chief guarantor of the rules-based international order and the awesome sovereign power that underwrote Europe's security after saving it from itself. If Trump wanted to obliterate that order and feed Europe to the lions, who was going to stop him?

All was not lost. Trump's agenda was no more than the rantings of a madman imprisoned in a bubble of fake news, of that the Europeans were confident. And sooner or later that bubble was going to be perforated by the facts. Ensconced in the White House, the responsible people, the "adults in the room", would restore sanity. Europe's leaders were going to play their part. They were going to make the president, described as a "moron" by his first secretary of state and as a "dope" by one of his many national security advisors, come to his senses. They were going to massage and manage him, seduce, educate and nudge the US back onto history's true path.

Europe's effort to edify Trump, however, faced big and unsuspected hurdles. The continent needed to quell a populist revolt of its own, one closely entwined with Trump's rejection of the liberal order. The UK had voted to leave the European Union only months before, while a series of pivotal elections loomed in the Netherlands, France, Germany and Italy. More fundamentally, Europe misjudged the coherence of Trump's discourse and consequently the uphill battle it faced. Trump had an intuitive grasp of the mood that had catapulted him into the White House, of the *zeitgeist* that guided his daily volley of incendiary tweets. Gluing Trump's politics together was a rational plan of sorts. And this plan, which put "America First" in a world of sovereign states, ensured that Trump's bubble of fake news proved more resilient than Europe had held possible.

Describing himself as "a genius", the president was the most vociferous strongman the modern world had yet seen, driven by the unwavering conviction that *he* was on the right side of history, that the world of sovereign states he was going to fashion was how things were always "meant to be". Behind the stream of Trumpian consciousness hid a steely determination to consign Europe's rules-based order to the ash heap of history, to end all pretence of Western exceptionalism and to recover a simpler and more honest world in which America would be number one. Trump did not merely wish to continue the slow strategic withdrawal that Obama had begun; his plan was to rip the liberal order away and to live by the ethos of strength. And no one was stronger than the United States.

It was this plan that Trump began executing with unswerving resolve, as his verbal assaults on the EU, the North American Free Trade Agreement, NATO, the WTO and the Paris climate change agreement showed. Friction with Europe was inevitable, as it was with Washington's foreign policy establishment, which had been bred and raised on a diet of American exceptionalism. The EU he described as "a brutal trade partner" and "worse than China, just smaller".[1] "Europe has been treating us really badly", Trump said in February 2020. "The European Union was really formed so they could treat us badly", he explained, adding that once he had "done" China he would also put a halt to European abuse.[2]

Putin, Xi and the world's other strongmen were, in a deeper sense, much more closely aligned with Trump. They spoke the same language of power. The strongmen agreed on how world order was fundamentally supposed to function, as well as on what they represented to each other. They were never friends or even allies, but they agreed on how to interact, talk and make deals. They were all just battling for the interests of their state. Trump spelled it out: "Russia is a foe in certain respects ... China is a foe economically, certainly they are a foe. But that doesn't mean they are bad."[3] Trump never thought anything less of America's foes. To the contrary, he respected them for their agility, strength and toughness. They were duellists, in other words, but linked through the codes of conduct of the fellowship of strength.

Relations were less evident with the Europeans, who wanted to persuade Trump that the Atlantic world was not a club of rivals, but a fellowship based on values and principles. While Trump and his fellow strongmen got on with the game of global politics as they saw it, the Europeans could not agree there was a game to get on with, not that kind of game anyway. They rejected the premise that Europe and the United States were rivals. But it was precisely the status of foe that Trump set out to forcibly impose on the continent. Free from feelings of guilt or remorse, he tore into old ties of friendship. No exceptions were made, not even for America's oldest friends. Never had a US president more openly and consistently avowed the national interest as the basis of American foreign policy. Even arch-realist Richard Nixon, as his secretary of state Henry Kissinger once sighed in disbelief, felt compelled to put up a picture of the internationalist Woodrow Wilson in the White House.[4] But not so Trump.

For Europe, it proved hard to make peace with its new status as America's foe and rival. Challenging Trump's repeated declarations of enmity, European Council President Donald Tusk, a former Polish prime minster and convinced Atlanticist, tweeted: "America and the EU are best friends. Whoever says we are foes is spreading fake news."[5] But in this dispute Trump held the upper hand. Trump spoke for America. And America was no longer interested in friendship with Europe. Rarely had a piece of news been less fake.

LIAISONS DANGEREUSES

On 20 January 2017, Donald Trump was sworn in as the 45th president of the United States. As Europe began preparing for its diplomatic overtures, it quickly realized the extent of the trouble it was in. It needed to talk sense into the man. But how? For Trump the solutions the continent offered were always the problem, never the answer. The president seemed radically disconnected from the world of high-level diplomacy Europe was familiar with. He operated according to a different code, a code it struggled to make sense of.

As they set about looking for the key, the continent's pre-eminent leaders at the time, Prime Minster May, Chancellor Merkel and President Macron, each employed their own tactics. Theresa May realized Brexit Britain badly needed a friend in the White House, not a foe, and chose the art of flattery, seduction and submission. Merkel, meanwhile, opted for Europe's conventional demeanour of moral superiority, reminding the president of the importance of international rules and treaties. Macron, finally, decided to project an image of strength, sensing correctly that this was the only language Trump understood, the only way to crack the code.

Courtesan

In the week following Trump's inauguration, Europe battled with one of its worst cold snaps in years. Temperatures on the mainland had plummeted far below freezing. But Theresa May was on a plane to warmer places: to Washington DC, where the entire world was thronging at the White House gates, waiting for the audience that she had been granted.

It was a diplomatic coup for Britain, and it could not have come at a better time. Negotiations with Europe were stuck. Among the Brexit faithful, impatience was growing. In a speech at Lancaster House, days before her trip, the prime minister had shored up her Leave credentials. She confidently stated her principles: "No deal for Britain is better than a bad deal for Britain." It was exactly the sort of message that would strengthen her authority at home. But without America's friendship, the prime minster also knew, it would prove a hollow phrase. A place at the "back of the queue", which Obama had threatened with in 2016, would not suffice.

There had been worrying signs of tension with the Trump camp already. Some weeks earlier the president-elect had tweeted that his good friend Nigel Farage would "do a great job" as UK ambassador to the US. It was an opinion the UK Independence Party politician had been all too willing to endorse, leaving Downing Street to scramble for a response. "There is no vacancy", a spokesman had eventually commented.[6] But if May managed to gain the president's trust, her Brexit predicaments might be solved in one fell swoop.

May styled herself as the new Margaret Thatcher, the strong-willed prime minster who in the 1980s railroaded Britain's trade unions into submission. The Iron Lady's exacting authority, resembling that of a strongwoman, seemed the right fit. Steely willpower and fearlessness were required. As an added bonus, Thatcher's aura allowed her to remodel her relationship with Trump on the friendship between the former prime minister and Ronald Reagan. Trump, for his part, loved the idea. "She'll be my Maggie", he confided to aides.[7]

May's flirtatious overtures were not without peril. In fact, the entire rendezvous in the White House was exceedingly dangerous. The uncouth Trump was hardly the sociable Reagan. Trump believed NATO was "obsolete", and he was no less dismissive of the WTO, the rules-based trade system that Britain now depended on more than ever. May had to embrace the president with as much gusto as she could muster. But she also needed to talk him out of his America First agenda. It was a manoeuvre that required the suppleness of an Olympic gymnast, a level of flexibility that May, who was described by a cabinet colleague as operating "on tramlines", did not possess.[8] In the position Britain found itself in, Trump's outstretched hand seemed the greater prize. It offered the lifeline she needed, so she grabbed it.

May's main weapon of seduction was an invitation from Buckingham Palace for a full state visit, all honorific trappings and trimmings included. It was the perfect bait, an irresistible piece of theatre for Trump. The vestige of British imperial power offered exactly the sort of recognition the strongman craved. The Queen herself was to act as the Trumps' host. Seasoned diplomats warned the visit would damage the monarchy.[9] It would not make for a pretty sight, everyone agreed. But Her Majesty was going to have to take this one for the country. And besides, had she not welcomed Xi Jinping before?

If there was some effort to distance herself from the strongman, a bid to talk sense into Trump, May did everything to hide it. "It was an hour of the president holding court and the PM being very diplomatic and not many other people saying anything", described an attending British official after the meeting.[10] A flirtatious May was filmed briefly holding hands with Trump walking along the White House colonnade, playing the infatuated lover. It was teeth-grindingly awkward, for May more than anyone else.

But her silent acquiescence got the job done, or so it seemed. The president confirmed his benevolent intentions towards Brexit, dissing the EU as a meddling "consortium".[11] Brexit "is going to be a brilliant thing", he hoarsely said, pledging to get a trade deal with the UK done as quickly as possible. They were precisely the words she needed him to say, to softly whisper – but to her, not to Nigel Farage, her rival courtesan.

Back in London the visit seemed a triumph. May had salvaged the special relationship. However, the day-to-day business of dealing with Trump proved to have a sobering effect. Holding hands with the president had made for nice images on the evening news, but as the strongman's behaviour over the next weeks and months made clear, it was not going to change his politics. Brexiteers such as Boris Johnson, then May's foreign secretary, maintained that "Global Britain" would flourish in a "post-geography trading world".[12] But that world was hardly going to come about if the president of the United States, not exactly "post-geography" himself, decided to pull the plug on globalization.

Quiet submission, as it turned out, was not the solution. Even outside the EU, Britain's interests were better served by Europe's rules-based philosophy of order than by the policies of an unrepentant nationalist. In the worst of all worlds, Brexiteers had always assumed, Britain would still be able to trade on WTO terms. But they had not reckoned with Donald Trump, whose world did not have a WTO. In the first years of his presidency, on most of the big issues that set the US and the EU apart (global warming, the Iran nuclear deal, tariffs on steel and aluminium) Britain aligned itself with its old partners.[13] In fact, the more violently Trump lashed out against the liberal order and free trade, the more preposterous was the idea of May finding in him the friend she needed, the more preposterous the whole idea of Brexit itself became.

The romance could not last. May was not Farage, the full-throated anti-establishment rebel Trump really fell for. The breakup became official when later that year Trump retweeted Islamophobic videos posted by a British fringe party. It left May no choice. It was "the wrong thing to do", she finally said, already fearing the worst. The counterpunching Trump did not need long to hit back, accusing May of going soft on terrorism: "@Theresa_May, don't focus on me, focus on the destructive Radical Islamic Terrorism that is taking place within the United Kingdom."[14]

By then the invitation for a visit to Buckingham Palace had already been put on ice, to the annoyance of Trump. May did not want the visit to interfere with the snap election she had called, and which nearly lost her the premiership. More fundamentally, it had become clear that she and Trump were not made for each other. When the president's state visit finally went ahead, two years later in June 2019, Theresa May had already announced her resignation, having failed to negotiate Britain's exit from the EU. "What a mess she and her representatives have created", Trump reflected in the weeks following his visit.[15] "I told her how it should be done, but she decided to go another way." May's departure caused Trump no heartache. "While I thoroughly enjoyed the magnificent state visit last month", Trump added, "it was the Queen who I was most impressed with!"[16]

Fears of Trump trampling over palace protocol had been proven unfounded. Moments before Air Force One touched down on UK soil, the president had still lambasted London's progressive mayor, Sadiq Kahn, whom he found to be "a stone cold loser".[17] But in the presence of the monarch he oozed nothing but respect. Respect was precisely what he craved, and what state banquets and royal pageantry were designed for. Having savoured every instant, Trump later praised Queen Elizabeth to the skies. "We had automatic chemistry", he recounted. "She's a spectacular woman."[18] On photographs it had briefly seemed as if Trump had fist-bumped the sovereign. But it emerged the pictures had only been taken from an unfortunate angle, or so the official explanation went. Protocol had been fully honoured.

Relations with Boris Johnson, who took over as prime minister that summer, looked certain to be much smoother than with May. "He will be great!", Trump tweeted, looking forward to the reshuffle.[19] As London's mayor in 2015, Johnson had still accused then-candidate Trump of "stupefying ignorance".[20] But it all seemed forgiven. The attraction between both men seemed immediate and magnetic, as it had been between Trump and Farage. At times, it even looked as if Johnson might effortlessly fit into the strongmen's fellowship, speaking its language of sovereignty and borders.

But the dilemma that May had needed to confront, and that Johnson now needed to face too, had not gone away. As it was about to leave the EU, Britain needed a friend in Washington. But what it got was Donald Trump and his idea of a world based on strength instead of rules. Dissonance was inevitable, as became apparent when Trump scolded Johnson on the phone for not banning China from the UK's 5G network, in early February 2020. For some years, British prime ministers had revelled in the idea of playing "Athens to America's Rome". But with Trump's rise that role had become untenable. As one commentator described the nation's predicament: "the Emperor Nero has now taken power in Washington – and the British are having to smile and clap as he sets fires and reaches for his fiddle."[21]

Governess

If May led the pilgrimage of world leaders to the White House, Merkel made up the rearguard, starting with a phone call in the last days of January 2017. Trump's plans for an entry ban for Muslims were causing a stir. But whereas May looked the other way, Merkel, the Lutheran pastor's daughter, used her phone call to "explain" the Geneva Convention, as her spokesman Steffen Seibert informed the press.[22] It was her attempt to clarify how the rules-based order worked, and why it was better for all to abide by its norms, including the United States.

Trump was unimpressed. Already in November, Merkel made her principles clear. In her congratulatory message to the president-elect she had offered Germany's close cooperation. But not without adding that her offer was conditional on the values of "democracy, freedom, as well as respect for the rule of law and the dignity of each and every person, regardless of their origin, skin colour, creed, gender, sexual orientation, or political views". It was a diplomatic slap down wrapped into the language of the UN Declaration of Human Rights.

The statement did no harm to Merkel's global standing. In liberal circles, it was hailed as a stroke of genius. Already, the chancellor had been the darling of progressives, a status Merkel acquired in the summer of 2015 by offering refuge to Syrians fleeing the war in their country. "*Wir schaffen das!*" Merkel had spurred on her fellow countrymen, in her own version of Barrack Obama's "Yes, we can!"

It was Merkel's golden moment. When the outgoing Obama flew to Berlin for his farewell trip in late 2016, he eulogized the chancellor as America's closest ally, warning her for rocky times ahead, but also advising her to remain true to her convictions, to keep occupying the high ground.[23] Suggestions were made that Merkel was about to take over his role as "Leader of the Free World", a notion the chancellor ridiculed herself. But her international star was rising high and fast. Whether she wanted it or not, and with Trump's election and Britain in Brexit paralysis, the job was hers. Who else would fit the crown?

It made for a frosty start. The portents for her first meeting with Trump in March 2017 were not hopeful. A late winter blizzard on the north-east Atlantic seaboard required her to delay her travel plans. At least it gave her more time to familiarize herself with the president's views on global trade, which reportedly she did by reading a 1990 Trump interview in *Playboy Magazine*.[24] Already had he thumped Germany for freeriding on American largesse. When her plane eventually landed at Dulles Airport, the mood was tense. "The Leader of the Free World meets Donald Trump", some journalists quipped.[25] Others framed the two leaders as the "odd couple". If Theresa May had worked her charm to establish a personal connection, that avenue seemed closed for the chancellor, who once described her younger self as "the girl who eats peanuts and does not dance".[26] She was not one for waltzing hand in hand with Trump through the West Wing. "I'm not going to sit on a golden chair", she revealed her intentions to close confidants.[27]

If an amorous holding of hands was ruled out, what options were left? In earlier meetings with world leaders, Trump had made much of his virile hand-shakes, the "Trumpshake", his habit of clenching leaders' hands so firmly they almost squealed with pain. Cultured Europeans, who preferred to casually kiss each other on the cheek, had poked fun at his alpha male bravado. For Trump, however, the significance of the ritual could scarcely be greater. The Trumpshake was the duel in a nutshell, its perfect visual representation. It was a projection of strength, a piece of theatre that impressed on Americans how fearless he was, how like Kojève's master-warrior he was unafraid of being killed or hurt, and therefore legitimate as their ruler. It was also the moment the duellists demonstrated their gallantry and worthiness, a rite of passage that confirmed their standing as moral equals.

But how could the chancellor ever perform the same ritual? She was a woman and Trump would merely grind her hand to pulp. The forms, demeanours and holy sacraments of the strongmen's club, as he saw them, were unsuitable for women. One could caress or hold a woman's hand, but one could not prop-erly clench it like a man's, one could never project real strength and fearless-ness, nor the sort of respect and worthiness the duel demanded. In the event, Merkel showed no detectable desire to deviate from the demeanour she cus-tomarily assumed in her encounters with strongmen: that of the patient and reasonable governess explaining the rules, the facts, the truth.

It added up to an overburdened event, intensely scrutinized by the global media. The faintest twitch of a facial muscle was likely to be reported as the tell-tale sign of mutual loathing. When Trump's putdown finally came, it was all far less subtle. Posing before an army of hungry press photographers in the

White House Oval Office, both leaders had been asked to shake hands for the cameras. Shake hands please, the press shouted! But sitting in an armchair next to Merkel, Trump continued to icily stare at the floor. Eventually turning to his side, she asked: "Do you want to have a handshake?" But the president had decided there was not going to be any more handshaking or handholding than was absolutely necessary. There was no respect between them, and he was not going to hide it.

Merkel shrugged off the president's behaviour with an assured smile. As a piece of political theatre, it proved far more deadly, turning his adolescent's tantrums into the perfect foil to her wisdom. She stood above such petty insults. Predictably, the chancellor's superiority only fuelled the president's anger about the profusion of Mercedes on American roads, Berlin's refusal to live up to NATO spending commitments, Merkel's saintly status as saviour of refugees. With foes like Xi, Kim and Putin deals could be done. But the chancellor seemed interested only in explaining the status quo, not in changing it. For Trump that was a problem. The US had become "the piggy bank that everybody is robbing", as he explained a year later. "[A] lot of these countries actually smile at me when I'm talking ... And the smile is: we couldn't believe we got away with it."[28] For Trump, Merkel was merely proposing to keep robbing the piggy bank.

The chancellor's open-door policy towards refugees was one area that left her vulnerable to the president's vengeance. The policy had eventually caused Merkel's domestic popularity to plummet and in German elections in autumn 2017 she only barely managed to cling on to power. Germany's political landscape, anchored in the dominance of its centrist parties, had come adrift, an excellent opportunity for Trump to put in the knife and stir up trouble for the chancellor.

Trump's newly appointed ambassador to Berlin, Richard Grenell, was more than willing to do the stabbing. Already on his first day in the job, in May 2018, Grenell managed to cause offence. Following Trump's decision to pull out of the Iran nuclear deal, he tweeted: "German companies doing business in Iran should wind down operations immediately."[29] It felt he was issuing orders to an underling. Grenell explained that his wider mission was to export the Trump revolution to Europe.[30] We "are experiencing an awakening from a silent majority – those who reject the elites and their bubble", he explained. "I absolutely want to empower other conservatives throughout Europe." Evidently he was not thinking of Merkel. "Look, I think Sebastian Kurz is a Rockstar. I'm a big fan", he confessed about Austria's chancellor, a critic of Merkel's migration policies.

Grenell proved to be a self-styled political guerrilla, an agent provocateur of Trumpism parachuted behind enemy lines to incite the masses to rise up against Europe's progressive vanguard, to cement a pan-European anti-liberal coalition around Hungarian populist Viktor Orbán. It was dual-track diplomacy of a sovereign bent, not unlike the Kremlin's influence campaigns in the West, although Grenell conducted the campaign with genuine zeal and passion. From far away in the White House, Trump tweeted his presidential blessings: "The people of Germany are turning against their leadership as migration is rocking the already tenuous Berlin coalition. Crime in Germany is way up. Big mistake made all over Europe in allowing millions of people in who have so strongly and violently changed their culture!"[31]

Liberal Europe's reaction was outraged. Crime was not "way up", it was actually way down! Another instance of Trump ignoring the facts. However, one fact that Europe could no longer ignore was that Merkel's efforts to explain how the rules worked had been a complete failure. She might have been correct. But the president had shown no sign of moderating his views. To the contrary, his views were only becoming more radical.

Confrère

Elected French president in May 2017, Emmanuel Macron had one big advantage over May and Merkel. He was a man. If Merkel used her hands to educate, and May used hers to seduce and flatter, Macron understood how to use his hands to better effect: to project power and respect. In their first meeting in Brussels, a jaw-clenching Macron clasped Trump's right hand so firmly that according to news reporters in the room it caused each man's knuckles to go white. Not for a moment did he wince. Macron positioned himself as neither inferior (May) nor superior (Merkel) to Trump, but as his equal, and therefore capable of giving Trump the respect he yearned for. For once, Europe's demeanour had been right. The *mise en scène* of the encounter, crucial in the strongman's performance, had taken the form of the duel.

Macron himself explained why the handshake was important. It was "a moment of truth", he confided to the *Journal du Dimanche* afterwards.[32] He needed to show that "we are not making little concessions, even symbolically". Trump, Erdogan and Putin "view things according to the logic of power", he went on. And it is by projecting strength, by not letting anything pass at all, that you earn their recognition. Trump's handshake was not some silly game; it was the foundational act of diplomacy itself.

Annoyed Trump aides briefed media that their boss did not expect "smack-talk from a Frenchman 31 years his junior".[33] But Macron's analysis of his own performance was on the mark. Before something could be discussed or negotiated with Trump, respect and equality needed to be established. And this was done by projecting strength, power and worthiness, as Xi, Erdogan and Putin knew. The strongman act chimed nicely with the man "made for storms" that Macron wanted to be in France, the Saviour of the Republic that de Gaulle had once been, and in a more distant past Napoleon.

Macron's other major advantage was that he was French. In a stroke of genius, Macron invited Trump to the celebration of Bastille Day on 14 July. It proved another feat of political choreography. The setting in Paris was perfect: the plushest of red carpets, the dearest displays of camaraderie, dinner at the Eiffel Tower. With Macron's wife, Brigitte, Trump got along splendidly. Even the weather played along. It was the state visit with the royal grandeur that, ironically, May had at that point been unable to deliver, the unashamedly patriotic celebration of national vigour that in Germany for obvious reasons remained unthinkable. Witnessing the customary military parade on the Champs-Elysées, and the spectacle of war planes leaving a blue, white and red trail of the tricolour, Trump promptly decided he wanted a military parade of his own. "You have a tough president", he said, summing up his impressions to journalists as he prepared to fly home.[34]

He had done it, cracked the code, deciphered how Trump and his fellowship of strength worked, or so it appeared. On his official return visit to the United States, in April 2018, Macron enjoyed a three-day state visit with all honours, including a rare address to a joint session of Congress. Aside from the by now traditional power handshakes, Trump even took to exchanging kisses with Macron on the cheek. Were Europe's persuasive tactics finally paying off?

By contrast, Merkel, in Washington days later, had to make do with a three-hour working session. It was a reminder of how unproductive their relations had become. For five months, from September 2017 to February 2018, the two leaders did not even speak at all.[35] Merkel aides still believed their "main challenge" was getting through to Trump. The central problem, their diagnosis implied, was the president's apparent inability to understand the benefits of rules-based order. If Merkel wanted to change Trump's thinking, "it has to happen in relatively simple language".[36] In other words, ways needed to be found of explaining how the world worked to a 12 year old. And if that still did not work, to an eight year old.

Macron grasped the utter futility of Berlin's effort. Europe's language of diplomacy needed to be changed, not dumbed down. Hosting the annual G7 summit in the French seaside town of Biarritz in 2019, Macron showed again what this meant. Knowing that the G7's system of summit declarations had led to acrimony with Trump the year before, he decided to jettison it, adopting the personal diplomacy the strongman preferred. The system "is a perversity because it bureaucratizes the thing", Macron explained.[37] "The communiqués reflect the deep positions of the French bureaucracy up against the American bureaucracy ... And the role of leaders is to veer away from their historic positions, to take liberties, to decide, and to give instructions to their administrations." Trump could hardly have described the art of the deal better.

Macron's flair as a political choreographer allowed him to take over from Merkel as Europe's pre-eminent leader in the world. It was not all a matter of dramatic talent, of course. If the projection of strength became the language of diplomacy, Germany seemed destined to stay marooned on the sidelines, eating peanuts at the dance. The projection of German strength remained hard to stomach for the world, not least for Germany itself.

But diplomatic success also meant that Macron became responsible for getting Trump to change his ways. Sooner or later, he was going to have to do what May and Merkel had failed to do: talk him out of something big, with big gestures of respect, whatever got the job done. And it certainly was not for want of trying. Feverishly he pleaded with Trump not to pull the US out of the Iran nuclear accord. Angrily he opposed US trade tariffs on steel and aluminium. Macron urged Trump to keep the US in the Paris climate change agreement. However, handshakes notwithstanding, making Trump move proved more difficult.

The problem was that while Macron understood and perhaps even relished the codes, demeanours and rituals of the duel, he shunned fighting the duel. Like Merkel, Macron still believed he could edify Trump. When Trump said: "Let's make America great again", Macron countered with: "Let's make *the planet* great again!" In the end, he made clear, France's identity, or Europe's identity, was only its morality, its humanity. "By pursuing our own interests first, with no regard to others", he explained on the centenary of the end of the First World War, "we erase the very thing that a nation holds most precious, that which gives it life and makes it great: its moral values."[38]

Macron was the duellist who never entered the arena, who honoured and respected enemy combatants but who never unsheathed his sword himself, who avoided the power parley, preferring instead to rely on the protection of institutions, courts and rules. In June 2018, the *Washington Post* reported that Trump had proposed that France abandon the EU for a bilateral trade deal with the United States, which would offer France superior trading terms.[39]

When asked by journalists to confirm Trump's offer, Macron honourably refused. "What is said in the room, stays in that room", he answered, cognisant of the club rules.⁴⁰ But what Trump wanted was someone who, aside from behaving honourably, also played the game. In Macron, he had found a leader he *could* do business with, who he respected and perhaps even liked. But Macron never *did* business. The duel was not just made of Trumpshakes, fist bumps and military parades. It also needed to be fought. A new deal needed to be negotiated.

SEVERANCE

In the spring of 2018, it was clear that Europe's efforts to seduce, educate and impress the president had come to nothing. The harder its leaders pressed, the more abrasive he became. Trump looked at the world, as he put it, "from a real-estate perspective", and because he was entirely unapologetic about who he was, he could neither be reasoned with nor shamed into becoming someone else.

Two Atlantic summits made clear the rupture was definitive. First, the infamous G7 summit on 8–9 June 2018 in Québec, at which Trump threw his Starburst candies at Merkel, walked out of the meeting and later withdrew his signature from the communiqué. It had seemed as if Trump had come to the summit, which was meant to be about trade, for an entirely different reason: to raise a stink and pull the United States out of the G7 altogether. The Europeans decided to put a brave face on the debacle. If Trump wanted out, they said, then the G7 could simply go on as the G6. "Maybe the American president doesn't care about being isolated today", Macron cautioned, "but we don't mind being six."⁴¹

The second Atlantic summit took place at NATO's HQ in Brussels on 11–12 July 2018, and it proved that the bottom had still not been reached. If there was a certain parity in size on trade between Europe and the US, in the area of security and hard power it was a different story. For years, most European countries had fallen well short of their commitment under NATO agreements to earmark at least 2 per cent of GDP in their budget towards defence expenditure. Moreover, since in contrast to their trade policies EU member states had always kept control over their own national defence structures, Europe's military capabilities remained fragmented and weak. It formed a perfect whipping tool in the hands of Trump.

When Europe's leaders arrived in Brussels, they looked like supplicants summoned for a dressing down by their biggest and most indispensable benefactor. Realizing they had failed to make good on their promises, their fate seemed uncertain. Confronted by such moments, clever feudatories know what is expected of them. They send in courtiers to appease their lord ahead of their meeting. They sooth their master by steering the conversation towards the future. Let bygones be bygones, they say. What matters is what happens next. Finally, they know never to correct their patron, not even on facts and numbers. No matter how wrong he is, they "suck it up". They all look at their shoes. They attentively listen. Then, they promise betterment, praying their performance – for it is a performance – offers sufficient cathartic release to start afresh.

NATO Secretary General Jens Stoltenberg, former Norwegian prime minister and Europe's go-between with Trump in the organization, made sure all those elements were in place. He had compiled glowing statistics and charts that showed how the Europeans were now catching up on their NATO spending targets. He had prepared an action-packed, forward-looking plan for discussion. He had schmoozed with Trump, working his ego, as had been expected of him as a courtier. Perhaps it sufficed to avoid the spectacle of humiliation after all?

Within minutes of the summit kicking off in the morning of 11 July it became clear there would be no escape. It began with a bilateral working breakfast between Trump and Stoltenberg. Television cameras were present to record the initial exchange of pleasantries between the men. But there was nothing pleasant about Trump that morning, who instantly lashed out at Nord Stream 2, the German-Russian gas pipeline under the Baltic Sea. "I think it's very sad when Germany makes a massive oil and gas deal with Russia, where you're supposed to be guarding against Russia", the president said, leaving Stoltenberg to stare blankly at his toast and orange juice. "So, we're supposed to protect Germany when they're getting their energy from Russia? Explain that."[42]

It was the start the Europeans had hoped to avoid, but which was inevitable. Trump continued his assault later that day: "The US is paying for Europe's protection, then loses billions on trade."[43] "Must pay 2% of GDP IMMEDIATELY, not by 2025", he tweeted.[44] By that evening, Europe's leaders thought they had managed to shift their discussions to future plans, to making a fresh start. But Trump laid into them the next day with even greater venom. The president seemed to be steering the US towards a NATO exit, or at least he was using that threat to put Europe in its place. There was nothing much left to do than suck it up and hope for the best. The G7 could perhaps continue as the G6, but it was hard to see how NATO could continue without the US. Europe depended on Washington for its protection. And with a president in the White House who regarded diplomacy as a real estate deal, it meant America would be exacting a price, on trade, gas deals and much more.

THE DEBUTANT

Even before his European road trip, the president had made no secret which leg he looked forward to most (other than a round of golf in Scotland). "I have NATO, I have the UK, which is in somewhat turmoil, and I have Putin", the president said in press remarks. "Frankly, Putin may be the easiest of them all. Who would think? Who would think?"[45] Humiliation had the virtue of bringing reality into focus. Europe needed a change of plan, to rethink its political calculations. It would need to deal with Trump as he was and would always remain, a rival and foe.

Two impulses fought to prevail on the continent. First, the idea of keeping one's head down, of "riding it out", in the hope that Trump would be impeached by Congress or voted out of office in 2020 or at the latest in 2024. Short term, however, there would be no choice. If a fee needed to be paid for America's protection, in terms of homage, humility and fealty, then it just needed to be paid. Eventually, relations with the US would return to what they had always been, ties of friendship.

The second impulse was that if Europe could not protect itself now, it needed to get ready to do so in the future. It needed to end its dependency, and begin to act like a sovereign power itself, to "take its destiny in its own hands", as Merkel argued in speeches and rallies. While Trump was the immediate catalyst, the impulse found support in the analysis that European and US interests had begun to drift apart earlier and more structurally. After the Soviet empire had collapsed in the 1990s, US and European interests no longer aligned as neatly. Europe would not always be able to count on the US riding to the rescue, something Obama had made clear with his hands-off approach to Syria. The Pax Americana, in other words, had been over for some time, a burden too costly for the US to carry. Trump accelerated its demise, but he had not caused it, nor would future presidents bring it back to life. The latter might not actively try to blow up the EU, but they could not be expected to bail out Europe at the expense of America's own interests.

However, the idea of a "sovereign" or "strong" Europe, as Macron had shown in his encounter with Trump, required a fundamental change to how the continent projected itself in the world, a change of language also. It was the sort of change that could hardly be grasped, let alone achieved, in one electric jolt of conceptual clarity. Europe's sovereignty and strength needed to be achieved in response to concrete events, moments and encounters, in the political back and forth between action and reaction.

Trump's decision in May 2018 to pull out of the Iran nuclear deal, the so-called Joint Comprehensive Plan of Action, was one such moment. The Europeans had tirelessly lobbied Trump to uphold the deal. For some time, the decision seemed balanced on a knife's edge. But when the US announced harsh new economic sanctions against Iran, the EU responded with defiance, announcing plans to shield its trading relations with Iran from US sanctions. *Pacta sunt servanda*, it argued, hoping it would suffice for Teheran to continue to hold up its part of the nuclear bargain. It proved an uphill battle. Would European firms and banks continue to do business with Iran if they risked getting caught in the net of US sanction law? As one by one its companies chose to play it safe, the EU seemed powerless to stop them.

What was new, however, and historically remarkable, was Europe's decision to strike out on its own: to not just politely disagree with the US, but to expressly and vocally set out to undermine its foreign policy. There was readiness, shared by the UK, to enter into a contest with the US that had not existed before. When EU foreign policy chief Federica Mogherini was asked about Washington's power to block European businesses from trading with Iran, she answered with resolve: "[N]o sovereign country or organization can accept that somebody else decides with whom you are allowed to do trade with."[46] The US should not be allowed to become "the trade policeman of the world", agreed Macron's finance minister, Bruno Le Mair.[47]

Trump's ambassador in Brussels poked fun at the EU's rebellion, describing its efforts to insulate its firms against US sanctions as "a paper tiger".[48] John Bolton called the EU "strong on rhetoric and weak on follow-through".[49] They were not wrong, but they glossed over the politically important point, which was that the EU had turned to such hostile language at all. On Iran, Europe now toed a common line with Russia and China, agitating against US foreign policy. The decision acknowledged the growing distance and enmity between former friends. The significance of Europe's longing for sovereignty was not lost on Vladimir Putin, who only had warm words for Europe's cause. It was only "natural for Europe to want to be independent", he said.[50]

Europe's trade diplomacy with Trump was moving in novel directions too, taking the crucial step that Macron had not been willing or able to take. On 25 July 2018, just weeks after the calamitous NATO summit, European

Commission President Jean-Claude Juncker travelled to Washington for the continent's next encounter with Trump. Still on the agenda: how to avoid a US–EU trade war. This time the meeting was bilateral with the EU *qua Union*, as opposed to one of its member states. The difference was important. Neither Merkel nor Macron were vested with the institutional power to make international trade deals on behalf of the Union as a whole. They could seduce, educate and woo the president, as they had tried to. But on matters of trade policy only Juncker, in his role as Commission president, could *play*, that is to say, make deals.

Like Macron, Juncker grasped what the handshake meant, the demeanours and rites of equality and respect that gave the duel its civilizing form. But he realized the duel needed substance too. And the substance of the duel was a contest, a bilateral test of nerves and strength without institutional safety nets. Moreover, Juncker possessed the weapons that permitted him to enter into the arena. If Trump hit out at German cars or French wine, there were plenty of US industries he could strike back at, from Harley-Davidson motorbikes to bourbon whisky. Blows could be exchanged, until eventually it would end in a deal. In other words, Merkel's role in the encounter with Trump was effectively over. Neither in form nor substance could she take part in a duel. However, whereas Macron depicted the duel in form, Juncker fought the duel in substance.

The former prime minster of Luxemburg had so far played a backseat role in Europe's encounter with Trump, leaving Merkel, Macron and May to do most of the heavy lifting. During the NATO summit in Brussels, Juncker attracted attention to himself only once, when fellow leaders needed to prop him up by the shoulders to keep him from tumbling over during an outdoor ceremony. An intolerable bout of back pain, Junker insisted afterwards. One glass too many, was the interpretation media ran with. The president's drinking habits had been the talk of the town for many years. But when Juncker arrived in Washington, his gait had visibly straightened. His mind was clear and focused. He had not travelled that far just to give the president another lecture in international trade law. He had come to *negotiate* something. He was Europe's designated player, and he had come for one reason: to cut a deal.

This shift from form to substance was important. Rightly, it was controversial. Europe agreed to negotiate in Trump's language of strength, abandoning its language of rules. Until then, the EU had refused to make deals on trade with Trump for reasons of principle. Before any deals could be made, the EU's position had been, the US needed to withdraw its WTO-noncompliant punitive tariffs on steel and aluminium. It needed to stop threatening Europe with illegal penalties on imported cars. No negotiations with guns on the table, Macron had been adamant. Trump first needed to acknowledge the world's trade rules.

But in Washington Juncker abandoned the high ground. "I came for a deal – we made a deal", he said after a three-and-a-half-hour meeting. It is "a very big day for free and fair trade, a very big day indeed", Trump stated for his part.[51] Mutterings of protest arose from circles close to Macron, which still favoured a more principled and purist stance. But they quickly disappeared. Berlin, in the meantime, was quietly pleased. Its car manufacturers, already in the dock for flouting EU emission rules, were off the hook for the time being thanks to Juncker's power gambit.

Off the record, EU officials did their best to downplay Juncker's achievement. The deal hardly had substance, they clarified. The talks had just been "talks about talks". But the great significance of the deal was that finally Europe had done what Trump had insisted on: it had traded the language of rules with that of raw sovereign power, of pure market size. The continent had patently failed to convince Trump to stick to the rules. It now saw no alternative but to resort to the president's so-called art of the deal, as well as its concordant status as America's rival and foe. In the Trumpian idea of the deal, negotiating with proverbial guns on the table – and occasionally with real guns, too – was just how one negotiated, and how Europe had to negotiate too if it wanted to protect its interests.

Juncker's deal with Trump had all the hallmarks of the personal diplomacy that strongmen prefer. Its terms were elusive. Detailed commitments were lacking, just as they had been lacking after Trump's nuclear parley with North Korea's Kim, one month earlier. Had anything been agreed at all, Europeans wondered? Normal EU trade deals involved tireless wordsmithing and binding assurances. But this was the parley, and how Trump conceived of political deals between sovereign powers. The US president retracted his threat of punitive tariffs on cars, while Juncker committed Europe to buying more US soya beans. The only glue that held the agreement together were Trump's and Juncker's words. As one EU diplomat candidly conceded: "the [US] bazooka of tariffs on cars is just in the cupboard and could come back any time".[52] But still, for now that threat had gone. And if ever it came back out of the cupboard, on trade the EU possessed plenty of bazookas of its own.

In contrast to the treatment the Europeans had received earlier that month, Trump gave Juncker the respect opponents were due. "Jean-Claude – you're a brutal killer", Trump had told the Commission chief some weeks before their Washington talks, or so Juncker reported with what must have been feelings of pride. "I think he meant it as a compliment, but I am not sure", he added.[53] It was high praise, words Trump normally reserved only for men such as Kim, Putin and Duterte, established members of the fellowship of foes.

European Commission media handlers were unsure what to make of so much recognition. "There is, to a certain extent, good chemistry between president Juncker and president Trump", they contritely admitted.[54] It could change any minute, they added, as if they needed to protect their boss from the dubious honour that had unexpectedly befallen him. There was still a long way to go before Europe could call itself sovereign, a global power. Acquiring the language of strength would take time, as would acquiring independent means of power. Yet it was in the affable guise of Jean-Claude Juncker that Europe had finally cracked the club's entry code, and set foot in Trump's world of the strongmen.

CHAPTER 10

Epilogue: initiations into power

Europe, if it can't think of itself as a global power, will disappear.
Emmanuel Macron, 7 November 2019

EUROPE'S COMING OF AGE

History is about epochal change, and with hindsight we may be able to say
what the change was, what our "age" was about and when it started. In the
storm of time this is a difficult and often impossible task. The historian is able
to connect effect to cause because he already knows the outcome. The politician still has to feel his way at the intersection of past and future, not knowing
what great change is being forged. Bit by bit, this is how he discovers, and
defines, what his age is, and where he can and cannot tread.

Politics is improvisation, Niccolò Machiavelli taught, and improvisation
involves going forward without knowing exactly where you are going, or even
what you are doing.[1] In its encounter with the strongman this is precisely what
Europe is doing. It is feeling its way forward in unfamiliar surroundings, and
it does so by taking small but concrete steps.

This process of improvisation is not random. Events and encounters are
pushing the continent into one particular direction. Europe is discovering *a
certain* path, delineating the outlines of a new era. The more of the path it
travels, the clearer it becomes where it is leading, and what needs to be done
to complete the journey. Minerva's owl only takes flight at dusk, said Hegel.

191

"The vision thing", as US President George H. Bush once called it, becomes easier the further we advance.

Can we already see where Europe is headed? The answer, I believe, is that we can, although not with the precision that may be demanded from us. Europe is discovering the allure of strength. It is looking for ways to find a place for strength in the world of rules it has crafted. What Europe is feeling its way towards, in other words, is the status of a sovereign power, acting independently on the global stage.

That transformation is driven by events and encounters, and by the realization that unfortunately the world is dominated less by rules than by strength. In such a world what alternatives are there for Europe's disparate nations? Throwing one's fate into the hands of one master, the United States, to escape the claws of others, most obviously China, remains one alternative, and not one to be immediately dismissed. But is it really the most attractive option?

The choice between American and Chinese spaces of vassalage or *Großräume*, which European states – and even Russia – today face, is not the choice we faced during the Cold War, when what separated West from East was ideology. In a world dominated by the strong, the weak may of course nevertheless have to make a choice. But the more alluring vision, which has been in the bloodstream of European politics since de Gaulle, is for Europe to become strong itself, for the continent to carve out a free space for itself in the world, to not be "managed" by superior foreign powers, but to become an equal, self-governing and free republic itself.

For this, European states, small and large, need to pool their sovereignty and power. "What is the point of Europe?", de Gaulle asked in 1962. "The point is that one is not dominated by either the Russians or the Americans", he answered. "As Six, we ought to be able to do as well as either of the superpowers."[2] For the general, of course, the allure of strength was the greater glory of France, more than that of Europe. Europe, he argued, was "a lever of Archimedes" for France "to become again what she has ceased to be since Waterloo. First in the world." The concern that de Gaulle's "Six" in fact meant "5+1" was why other leaders put their faith in the institutions of Brussels and its supranational rules.[3]

Nearly 60 years later, the allure of a sovereign Europe, of its potential strength, is felt again. Now that the EU has become "the 27", the idea of a Europe built for the glory of France is no longer in the offing. However, the image of the EU as an Archimedean lever remains a powerful one. It resonates in capitals other than Paris, in Berlin and notably also in Brussels. The world today is structured less around ideological lines than around geographic centres of power, a fact that inevitably leads to the question whether Europe should be a centre of power too. And increasingly the answer is affirmative. Upon assuming office in December 2019, the EU's foreign policy chief, the Spaniard Josep Borrell, pithily summed up the mood in Brussels as well as in many other European capitals: "The European Union", he declared in the European Parliament, "has to learn to use the language of power."[4]

As teachers know, the only way to learn a foreign language is by using it. And in Europe's encounter with the strongmen we can witness how the continent is beginning to do so. We can see how Europe is feeling its way forward, slowly discovering the grammar of strength, how to deal with men for whom power is the only language. Things do not always go well. Mistakes are made. But they are also corrected.

In its confrontation with Vladimir Putin, Europe transgressed the boundaries of influence and was reprimanded. Putin felt he adhered to the rules of the game, the duellist's code, while he blamed the West for meddling in spaces where it was not supposed to interfere. After war broke out in Ukraine, Europe's leaders realized that Moscow's power was inescapable, and that Putin would not be stopped from securing a percentage of influence. The EU responded with sanctions, but it also put a damper on its eastern ambitions, as well as on Ukrainian plans for EU and NATO membership. Implicitly, it recognized one of the core norms of strongmen diplomacy, namely that spaces or spheres exist where one is not allowed to interfere.

In the encounter with Recep Erdogan, Europe began to define itself in terms of borders, politics and geography, instead of frontiers, values and civilizations. Its relationship with Turkey had long been framed by the country's bid to join the EU. Erdogan's power instincts, however, made a mockery of Turkey's accession. The role of "candidate" was incompatible with the respect he craved as an equal. From its side, Europe could no longer recognize itself in the image of a civilizational space with inherently fuzzy, open and ever-expanding frontiers. That image proved incompatible with the political choices it made, or needed to make, for example by striking its migration deal with Erdogan in 2016. The relationship was inevitably derailed and finally recast in novel terms of power, strength and borders.

In its confrontation with Xi Jinping, we saw how Europe discovered that instead of the world's great advocate for global trade and "connectivity", it was only a contestant in a battle between different modes of globalization, one based on rules, the other on strength. Xi was acutely aware that globalization had made China rich. But to regain its global strength, China needed to reconnect the world economy in less Western-centred ways, building trade routes, technology platforms and business hubs that it could control itself. As China rolled out its own model of global integration, the Europeans began seeing Xi no longer as a partner for globalization, but as a "systemic rival" whose close presence entailed political risks that needed to be curtailed.

In Donald Trump, finally, Europe encountered a US president who not only refused to guarantee the rules-based order, but who desired to destroy it, who presented himself not as Europe's friend but as its vengeful foe. Facing the prospect of a catastrophic trade war, European leaders tried to befriend, edify and cajole the president, until they realized that such efforts were futile. They needed to play the game as Trump preferred to play it, as a duel between combatants equal in moral standing. Strength, respect and rivalry were the only languages Trump understood. And more than in any other encounter, it was a language Europe needed to use too.

THE POWER OF BEGINNINGS

Becoming proficient in the language of power is not easy for Europe. It involves a slow struggle, above all with itself. Progress is not as linear as some may wish. It is driven by necessity, by events and encounters. Strength is not a language Europe finds poetic. It often slides back into its mother tongue. Assuredly, like most polyglots, it frequently mixes languages.

Power, moreover, is not necessarily a language that constituents, commentators and media appreciate, as Merkel noticed when she concluded her migration pact with Erdogan. Using the language of power comes at a political cost. For a strongman like Putin, these costs are less high, not because he is not held accountable by an audience – all performers are – but because his audience appreciates an act of princely virtuosity, such as the seizure of Crimea, even if that act carries an economic and legal price tag. On the other hand, it does not tolerate weakness and passivity.

Where does Europe finds itself currently? How do we gauge and assess its forward advance, its coming of age? What is to be done? The four guises of strength described in the first part of this book can serve as a compass.

For Machiavelli, to begin with, strength was linked with the ability to act, with taking the initiative rather than allowing oneself to become fortune's hapless plaything. If princely virtue is the destination, then there is plenty of road to travel for Europe. The war in Syria, and the refugee crisis that drove the EU to the brink, is an example that shows just how much. What Europe lacks in the Syrian conflict is the ability to act. There is no reason why anyone should heed what the continent demands. Consequently, it must suffer the consequences of what others decide. Europe undergoes history, hoping it can contain the fallout through crisis management.

In October 2019, after Erdogan ordered Turkish soldiers into Syria, German Defence Minister Annegret Kramp-Karrenbauer, then still considered Merkel's heir apparent, proposed creating an international security zone in northern Syria. There was nothing wrong with the plan, other than one thing: it was completely out of tune with how the powers on the ground viewed things. "Completely unnecessary", said Russian diplomats, shrugging off the idea, before they moved ahead with their own agenda.[5] The episode laid bare Europe's powerlessness. The future was being decided not in Berlin or Brussels, but in the Russian town of Sochi, on the shores of the Black Sea, where with Donald Trump's blessing Putin and Erdogan were striking a deal that carved up northern Syria between themselves.

It is not hard to identify the missing pieces of Europe's puzzle. Overseeing a huge market, Brussels has global power in the area of trade and business regulation, but it has no military strength.[6] Before the EU can decide anything in foreign policy, it needs its members to be unanimous, which in practice means it does nothing meaningful or does it too late. Financially, the euro remains vulnerable to shocks, a weakness that prevents it from competing with the dollar as a global reserve currency.

It forms a political environment in which bold ideas and disillusionment thrive in equal measure. In November 2018, Macron called for a "true European army", a call that was repeated by Angela Merkel some days later, although more guardedly.[7] Germany itself launched the idea of a European Security Council, which should ease foreign policy decision-making and strengthen the EU's crisis capacity. Jean-Claude Juncker, meanwhile, proposed to shore up the euro with a stability mechanism, whereas Macron launched an elaborate plan for the eurozone to acquire its own budget and finance minister.

Not surprisingly, these ideas rarely survive impact with political reality, and if they do, then only as the precursor of the things they may or may not become in time. The political questions those plans prompt are mind-boggling, as are the compromises and deals that are needed to make them happen. Reluctant EU members always seem plentiful. If, for once, domestic politics is not gridlocked in Berlin, then assuredly it will be gridlocked in Paris, meaning that little happens, to the great frustration of those who clamour for more.

Then again, things move slowly for a reason, not least the democratic nature of European politics. And while the pace may be sluggish, things do change.

Politics is not just about proposing the best solutions, it is also about setting expectations and about conquering the many obstacles that stand in the way. Leaping straight to the end of the journey is impossible. There is little point, for example, in the EU acquiring the ability to act and intervene in a military sense, if it does not first acquire the capacity to talk and think in Machiavelli's language of action and strategy, if it does not first recognize those terms as legitimate.

Politics is art, not science. More important than designs and blueprints is to begin somewhere, even if it is not always possible to say where precisely we will end up. In the area of defence that "somewhere" appears to involve an agreement for European states to pool relatively modest sums of money to develop military equipment such as fighter planes and drones. What this defence fund will eventually grow into is unknown. It could stay small, but it could also develop into something more meaningful. However, what is important, for now, is that it offers a beginning.

Appreciating the power of beginnings is difficult. "The light that illuminates processes of action", as Hannah Arendt once put it, "appears only at their end, frequently when all participants are dead."[8] Beginnings often fall short of expectations. They are easily lampooned. They feel like innocent tremors among thousands of other innocent tremors. But while most stay tremors, some do turn into earthquakes. About Macron's eurozone budget, Dutch finance minister Wopke Hoekstra, arch sceptic of the proposal, once triumphantly said: "The proposal started as an elephant, turned into a mouse and now that mouse is in a cage."[9] The last laugh was his, Hoekstra was sure. French ambitions to create a new financial instrument at the heart of the eurozone had been thwarted. He may, of course, turn out to be right. But he may also be wrong. Lots of things start out as mice in a cage. Until history – or pandemics – conspire to set them loose. After that they are rarely caged back in.

THE POWER OF CONNECTEDNESS

Strength and power, we saw, derives from connectivity, from networks and structures of dependence, from being at the centre of "great space". What does and can Europe do to halt the advance of the Belt and Road and the feudal power it confers on Beijing? What can it do to extend its own connectivity in the world?

In 2018, the EU launched its own Eurasian strategy, occasionally billed as its answer to the Belt and Road.[10] The differences between the two connectivity strategies are stark. China's approach is based on cash, on investing in infrastructure. Xi's goal is global strength and power. Profits are less important. European connectivity, on the other hand, is based on rules. And for political motives those rules leave little room. Investment, the EU's strategy argues, must ensure "market efficiency and be fiscally viable". From the standpoint of business, it is the only sound investment policy. But seen through the prism of power, it is a policy that allows China to gobble up strategic infrastructure such as the Greek port of Piraeus, an omission that Macron has labelled as a "strategic error".[11]

In Europe's philosophy of connectivity, money appears as an afterthought, if it appears at all. Connectivity is "not purely an investment challenge", the EU document stipulates. The greater task is to develop "consistent and aligned rules, standards or practices". Essentially, what Europe offers is a diluted form of EU membership. It offers access to its market and to other benefits, based on a common framework of law (its own laws, of course) that allows people, goods, services and capital to move freely across borders. Once these rules and sufficient fiscal rigour are in place, private capital will follow by itself, as it did in the EU.

Again, this may make for good business sense. And if partner countries and neighbours do take up the EU's offer, it also grows its global strength. However, as long as Europe tries to beat Chinese cash with proposals for new and often onerous regulation, which frequently offend local sensitivities, it is not surprising that many countries put their faith in the Belt and Road. Power stations need to be built, cables put in the ground, tracks laid, roads paved. Rules, standards and values, on the other hand, are an invasive nuisance.

Strength and power do not come for free. Hard choices have to be made. Principles may need to be sacrificed. This is equally true in the area of digital connectedness. An industry observer once summed up Europe's challenge: "If Mr Macron gets grumpy about the internet in Paris, he can call Mountain View ... There are only three people in the world who can make a local phone call – Mr Xi, Mr Trump, and Mr Putin."[12] If digital sovereignty is to be measured by the ability to make "a local phone call", what does it take for Europe to get there? According to Angela Merkel, "Europe, as a general rule, needs to be able to do everything itself".[13] To compete with China and the US on digital and AI technology, size is essential. However, EU restrictions on mergers make achieving size difficult, a constraint that its Chinese competitors do not face. Trade-offs are impossible to escape.

Likewise, he who wants a seat at the table in Syria will need to make the right choices. Trump's complaints about Europe's disinclination to commit resources to the war on ISIS are correct. Money as such is not Europe's problem. With an economy only modestly larger than that of the Benelux, Russia shows that geopolitical influence is not just an issue of having money, but also of spending it. One way for Europe to get influence in Syria would be to help with the eventual reconstruction of the country, a task the World Bank estimates would take 15 years and cost $250 billion.[14] Financial assistance always comes with political influence, and the ability to set conditions, prevent a further exodus of migrants and enable the return of war refugees to Syria. But such influence would come at a moral cost. Europe would have to do business with Basher al-Assad, which EU leaders, bar Viktor Orbán, refuse to do.[15] This is a cost one can choose not to pay. But it would also be a choice to remain a spectator, to jeer from the sidelines while Putin and Erdogan decide the future.

He who wills the end also wills the means, the philosopher Kant said. But so far Berlin mostly likes to keep its hand on its wallet, while Paris prevaricates in other areas. Thinking strategically, few things make more sense than for Balkan states like Albania and North Macedonia to eventually join the EU, lodging the region more firmly in Europe's rather than China's or Russia's orbit. However, here it is Paris that has its foot on the brake, at least for the moment, facing a public that remains sceptical of enlarging the EU.

Kicking the can down the road can be a wise thing to do. But if Europe is to embrace the language of power, hard choices cannot be avoided. Like all politicians, those in the EU have the habit of selling their policies as a win-win game, an approach that since Brexit we know as "cakeism". "Ethical AI is a win-win proposition", Brussels claims for example, while its plastics strategy is "a true win-win" for cutting pollution and boosting growth.[16] The impression is that we can get things for free, that tragic decisions need not be made because there are no downsides, be they moral or economic. In a world based on strength and connectedness, however, that is rarely the case.

THE POWER OF PROJECTION

Power must be projected. Who does this for Europe? Russia has Putin. Turkey has Erdogan. Who is "Europe's strongman"? If global politics is based on one-to-one relationships, on respect and bilateral deals made between men or women who represent sovereign powers, who represents sovereign Europe?

For de Gaulle, who pictured the EU as a great space led by France, the answer was self-evident. Neither Trump nor Putin would have scared the general. He would have been as comfortable making deals with Recep Erdogan as with Xi Jinping. But the problem that frustrated de Gaulle 60 years ago was that the Union's other members could not picture themselves as vassals to Paris, or any other state. Europe's language of rules emerged precisely because this language allowed the continent to sidestep the question of who was in charge. If power was anchored in treaties and in rules-based institutions like the European Commission, then no single leader needed to be in charge. The rules were in charge.

In a world based on strength and its diplomatic ethos, two forces pull Europe in opposite directions. Europe needs a man or a woman to perform the role of strongman in the encounter, to project strength and respect and to cut deals in the parley. On the other hand, for internal reasons the Union has been constructed in ways that leave no space for such a role. As the Union's rule-applier in chief, the European Commission and its president can and do speak for the Union in the world, in trade negotiations for example. But given that they are designed as a bureaucratic and technocratic escape pod from the world of geopolitics and power, the EU's institutions are not fitted out to project strength.

In its encounter with men such as Trump, Xi and Putin, we see how Europe finds stopgap solutions to the problem. Often these solutions are entirely informal and issue specific, involving not one but several European leaders playing complementary roles, so-called double acts. And as for all leaders with strongman ambitions, securing personal authority holds the key.

No EU leader has greater authority among her European peers than Angela Merkel, which in her case is above all the authority of impartiality and fairness, of what the philosopher Alexandre Kojève called the authority of "the judge". The chancellor led Europe's diplomacy with Putin on Ukraine, flanked by French President Hollande and Macron, a constellation known as the Normandy format because it was first used at the commemoration of D-Day in 2014. Merkel was able to speak for Europe in the talks with Putin because, as on various other issues, she occupied the middle ground between different ideas in Europe of how Russia's strongman needed to be handled, a position of neutrality that still holds today. Between the Poles, who demanded harsh retaliation, and the Italians, who never stopped fretting about the economic fallout of sanctions, who else could negotiate with Putin for Europe?

However, in Europe's effort to argue Trump out of the trade war he threatened, Merkel's authority among her EU peers was weak. Here, the chancellor proved unsuitable for the job of Europe's strongman. For dealing with Trump, Europe had no use for neutral judges. The continent needed a leader who was fearless and who relished the duel, whose authority was that of the master and warrior, as Kojève described it. With Trump, Europe needed a man "made for storms", and when Emmanuel Macron arrived on the scene in 2017, he immediately made the role his, supported by Commission President Jean-Claude Juncker.

Both leaders devised – or improvised – an effective partition of roles between themselves. As president of the Fifth Republic, the job created by and for de Gaulle, Macron possessed all the necessary means to project strength and respect. He gave Trump the recognition that was so important to him: the red carpets, the military parades, a national history, in short, the form and appearance of sovereignty. But to make deals, to actually contest the duel, Macron needed Juncker, who alone was empowered to represent the EU on foreign trade. Juncker, in turn, could not survive without Macron's powers of projection. "I don't think that President Trump knew ... who Jean-Claude Juncker was", the Commission president's chief aide confessed at the end of his mandate, something that changed only because Macron and Europe's other leaders told Trump that on trade he should "speak to Jean-Claude".[17]

In the encounter with Xi, Macron tried to enhance his European authority as a leader by inviting Merkel and Juncker to a bilateral meeting with China's leader in Paris in April 2019. On a trip to China later that year, Macron did not just bring French businessmen along, as was customary, but also a European commissioner and a German government minister. His projection of unity was not just aimed at Beijing; it was also a clever appeal to his EU peers to alter the relationship with Xi from "27+1" into "1+1", a relationship of equals. Macron was showing Europe's leaders the way forward, he was making a bid to be recognized as their leader and their voice in the world.

Not surprisingly, the leaders of Europe's largest and most powerful states, Germany, France and until recently the UK, play important roles in projecting European strength in the world, along with the leaders of the EU institutions in Brussels. However, they need to earn the authority among other EU leaders to do so, and as this authority can be won, it can also be lost, sometimes very easily.

Keeping the confidence of fellow EU leaders is vital, something that Merkel's centrist politics may be more likely to succeed at than Macron's impatient intellectualism. Whereas Merkel, "the judge", always moves slowly, and sometimes not at all, Macron is in a great hurry, shaking up the status quo, taking risks. It is an act that can boost a leader's authority, in the right circumstances. But it can also boomerang, which is what happened when, in an interview with *The Economist* in November 2019, Macron announced the "brain death" of NATO.[18] What authority he had built up among his EU colleagues evaporated in an instant, in particular in Europe's east, which had never fully trusted Macron's instincts on Russia. Placing herself above Europe's fray, Merkel responded by publicly dissing her French colleague, a move that again propped up her own brand of authority. Ironically, the episode even made Trump reach for higher ground, calling Macron's comments "very, very nasty" and "very dangerous". "You just can't go around making statements like that about NATO", the man who once described NATO as "obsolete" remarked.[19]

THE POWER OF THE DUEL

The language of power, finally, amounts to more than coercion or enforcement. It is better described as a morality, an ethos or habitus, an alternative way of thinking about order, diplomacy and what Europe fundamentally is. A popular but misleading way of conceiving of a sovereign Europe is to picture its strength as a mere "add-on", as a new annex to an old building. On this account, sovereign Europe is everything that Europe already is today, plus a new element that renders it strong: an army, robust economic sanctions, intelligence capacity, a stronger euro, majority-based decision-making in foreign policy. What we get, in a nutshell, is "values plus power", Europe's traditional rules-based and multilateral politics plus effective coercive tools to defend and enforce those rules.

In the summer of 2019, Macron called on Brazilian President Jair Bolsonaro to urgently put out rampaging wildfires in the Amazon rainforest. Angered by the strongman's intransigence, Macron threatened that unless Brazil did more to combat the fires, France would block an important EU trade deal with Brazil and South America's Mercosur countries. It was a move straight out of the Trump playbook, a power play that used market access as a tool to get what he wanted. But Macron used it to promote a universal rather than national interest. He was saving not just France, not just Europe; he was saving the entire planet.[20] In short, it was values plus power.

In this example, power merely seems a neutral instrument of coercion. However, as an organizing principle of global politics, the language of power amounts to more than law enforcement on a grand scale. Strength is a set of values in itself, a way of doing things, captured in the norms and behavioural codes that govern the duel. "The Amazon is Brazil's – not yours", responded

Bolsonaro, summing up one of those codes.[21] Plant more trees yourself, within your own borders. The language of power, in other words, includes its own dos and don'ts, the so-called *code duello* and its norms of respect and equality. Thinking of the world in terms of strength and power alters the nature of arguably the most basic distinction in international politics, that between "us" and "them", "self" and "other", "friend" and "foe". Diplomacy based on strength, moreover, is detached from institutions, rules and laws. It regards formal treaties as mere footnotes to personal deals made between leaders.

Using the language of power, then, has normative consequences. For example, quid pro quo deals with Erdogan on migration appear as normal rather than corrupt. What is more, size is allowed to matter. In a world based on strength there are spheres of influence and other great spaces in which foreign powers ought not to interfere. It is no longer per se wrong for Putin to claim the West has no business, or should at least tread with care, in countries such as Ukraine, Georgia and Belarus. In the language of power, promoting the rule of law and democracy is only permissible if this helps stabilize countries and regions. Power can indeed mean bombing Basher al-Assad or other depraved dictators, but it can just as much mean doing deals with them.

The "values plus power" formula appeals to EU politicians because it makes a strong Europe look like more of a good thing. Sovereign Europe simply means a Europe that stands up for its values, for its way of life. But in reality, strength is a competing set of values, a different way of life. It cannot be screwed onto the EU, like the single currency could be attached to the single market. The new and the old are not complementary. If we want the new, the old needs to budge. Using the language of power more means using the language of rules less. It is not rules *plus* power, but rules *or* power.

For Europe this is a momentous choice. Rules have always formed the bedrock of the story that Europe tells the world about itself. They form its narrative of legitimacy. There are good reasons why this narrative emerged, along with its codes of conduct, taboos and prescribed ways of thinking, speaking and acting. Europe's long history of internecine warfare, and Germany's more recent role in it, meant power was to be feared. The EU was only conceivable *without* power, in the form of common frameworks of law, and by expanding these frameworks inch by inch.

So deep-rooted has the language of rules become that the EU uses it even when the decisions it takes have plainly nothing to do with applying rules. This is what happened when in 2015 Brussels cited consumer protection laws to impose labels on goods and produce from Israeli settlements in occupied territory. Often the EU does so because it possesses no other language in which to act. In 2014, Victor Orbán agreed a €10 billion deal with Putin to build a nuclear power plant in Hungary. It was a provocative and political move for many reasons. However, when Brussels waded into the debate it did so on the basis that EU procurement rules might have been breached. The political dimensions of the Orbán–Putin deal had not escaped anyone's attention.[22] But there was no other way the Commission could question the plans.

Equally, whenever Europe asserted its interests in the world, in foreign policy or international trade, it did so through the WTO, the UN and other global institutions. Outside this rules-based habitat, Europe remained at a loss and relied on NATO, which, of course, was really the US. The EU did not have the words, the aptitude or inclination to define its global interests in terms of strategy. Individual officials may have entertained strategic considerations, but there could never be an effort to do so systematically. Strategy was inconsistent with its self-image. Europe dealt in rules, the US dealt in power, until eventually the entire world would use its language of rules.

But if we now introduce the language of power because the world did not work out that way, we are not merely adding another layer of policies, structures and instruments on top of what the EU possesses already, what in Brussels phraseology is called "competences". What we propose alters every single layer of the structure, all the way down to Europe's narrative of legitimacy, its self-image. If politicians or observers encourage the view that coming of age just means acquiring tanks, aircraft carriers and other tools of coercion, they sow only disillusionment. More importantly, they misrepresent what needs to be done and what coming of age fundamentally means, namely a change of habitus, a *moral* transformation. Lifelong habits and political norms need to evolve, and only then does it make sense to expect new "competences".

Europe's coming of age, in this sense, is measurable above all in words, demeanours and actions, for example in how the continent approaches its encounters with the strongmen. It is not change that is immediately cashed out in new structures, political jobs or treaties. Nor are we like Saul on the road to Damascus, struck down by blinding light and converted. When Trump was elected president in November 2016, it briefly seemed that such an epiphany might occur. But Europe has since learned that coming of age takes place gradually and through an inward struggle, which is unlikely to ever be resolved.

CHOOSING STRENGTH

Given what this transition entails, can we be confident Europe will advance at all? The answer is that there is no guarantee it will. Psychologically, clinging on to the status quo is often the easiest option, until it is no longer an option. Different historical experiences moreover divide Europeans. The UK has now left the EU. Germany remains reluctant to embrace the language of power, which is reminiscent of its dark past. The EU and its rules-based order have served the country well. Why rock the boat? In Poland and the Baltic countries, the wounds struck by Russian aggression in the past are fresh. The security guarantees Europe obtains from the US remain sacrosanct. Why risk change?

Such conservative sentiments are powerful in Europe. However, that does not mean nothing can or will change. Learning a new language, to begin with, does not mean other languages must be forgotten. Europe's liberal order of rules is not an illusion of youth to be shed with advancing years. Instead, growing up means being comfortable with *different* languages. It means learning to view the world through the prism of rules *and* through the prism of power. Europe should be fluent in its liberal values, but it should also be strong. It must become aware that it is but one community in a pluralistic world that is potentially hostile, and that may destroy it. Acting politically, as Machiavelli pointed out, means confronting the friction between what is ideal and what is possible, between what is right and what is necessary. Adulthood is not the period when the hard questions in life get answered; it is the period when those questions get asked, when we need to deal with the moral dilemmas that our parents or protectors handled for us.

In the end, it boils down to the question we started out with: why choose strength? What is its allure? The answer is assuredly not that the politics of strength is universally superior to the politics of rules. If we weigh the benefits of living in democratic states like Denmark or Canada, where the rule of law is robust, against the benefits of living in states where the rule of law is weak, the verdict is easy. But such like-for-like comparisons are trivial. In politics the choices we face, unfortunately, are never as clear cut. The attraction of strength is not that it is what we would pick if we can have it all. It is what we pick because we cannot.

Machiavelli believed the best form of government was that of a free and law-based republic, like his own Florence and the other city states of Renaissance Italy that inspired the tradition of free government in the West. However, determining what is best was just the easy part. The difficult part of politics was bringing the republic about, as well as defending it against the calamities and events that inevitably befall all states. Freedom, then, was never just a choice; it was a conquest, an ongoing battle in which the strong prevail. The conditions for peace, prosperity and freedom were rare, Machiavelli noted, and where they did occur, they were fragile and perishable. Foreign kings and pandemics threaten destruction. Financial crises corrode social harmony. Insipid corruption turns the people against their elites. It is because order is so fragile that the need for strength arises, for ways to stabilize the environment allowing free republics to thrive.

The fickleness of history is increasingly felt today. The West may still believe its civilization and way of life are the best, a shining example to the world. But its relative wealth and power are shrinking. The world that was once organized around it is increasingly organized around others. Historically, there is nothing extraordinary about this. The West was not always at the centre of the world. Civilizations expand, but they also contract. The question, however, is how to respond when they do.

In the nineteenth century, the era of China's decline, its ruling class responded with arrogance.[23] Believing its ancient culture to be superior to any other culture, and certainly to Europe's, the presumption was that China would always remain at the centre of the world, and in charge. When the Europeans, who had already colonized much of East Asia, eventually demanded influence in China, Beijing responded as overbearingly as it had always responded to foreigners. It viewed and treated the Europeans as barbarians, as supplicants from far-flung outposts who had come to offer tribute and to study and emulate its wise customs and traditions, something that because of European boorishness would probably be futile.

Even after having been routed by superior European military force, China kept seeking shelter in its old Confucian habits and demeanours, imagining itself at the top of a civilizational hierarchy, while the West languished somewhere near its bottom. But when China's emperor thanked his foreign guests for their tribute and ordered them to go home, the Europeans simply chose to stay. Progressive Chinese thinkers proposed studying Europe's ways, at least its modern technology and weaponry. But such proposals seemed nonsensical to traditionalists, a form of profanity and treason even. Nothing could be learned from barbarians. Only after suffering humiliation after humiliation did China conclude that its cultural sophistication would not protect its freedom.

Today, if Europe clings to the notion that the world just wishes to emulate its model, be taught by it, it risks making the same mistake. It will tell strongmen like Putin and Erdogan to behave or go home, and they will only laugh and go about their business as before. Indeed, if Europe's position is that the truthfulness of its liberal values suffices to secure its sovereignty, it may need its own century of humiliation to discover that only the strong can be free.

There are two further arguments for keeping things as they are. The first is that history is not as dangerous and boundless as Machiavelli believed, and is instead guided by a rational plan that culminates in universal peace and harmony around liberal principles and values. This progressive view of history, which has underpinned Europe's self-image at least since the end of the Cold War, is losing its currency, however. Who still bets on peace in the Middle East, or on China converting to liberal democracy?

The second and more forceful argument for the status quo is that Europe can count on others to use their strength on its behalf because they share the same liberal values of freedom. This has been the continent's assumption since the Second World War, and while in his first presidential term Trump has knocked severe dents in that assumption, he has so far not left it completely demolished.

For Europe, short- and long-term considerations play a role in its strategic relationship with its great protector, and they need to be carefully balanced against each other. As Merkel has said, "currently" there is no alternative to relying on US firepower, and rather than disparaging NATO we need to keep it alive.[24] While the fee Europe needs to pay the United States for its protection is undoubtedly going up, the continent has no choice but to pay it, for example in the forms of buying F-35 fighter planes and other US-made military hardware, or by aligning its trade policies towards China more closely with those of the US.

But whether it is smart to wager Europe's security on US power for the next 10 or 15 years is a different question. How certain are we that the US will remain a reliable partner? How far will dealmaker Trump or his successors go in driving up the protection fees Europe needs to pay? If the US imposes punitive tariffs on German cars or other European goods, in theory the EU could retaliate by imposing equally painful tariffs on US goods. But would such retaliatory measures be possible if the US threatened to withdraw its protective shield?

In December 2019, the United States Congress – and not, it is worth emphasizing, Donald Trump – decided to impose devastating sanctions on companies working to complete the Nord Stream gas pipeline, the German-Russian project that links both countries under the Baltic Sea, and which along with Europe's China policy forms a major US bugbear. In a letter to one of these companies, the US made clear its unequivocal intent. "There is no discretion", it specified. "You face a binary choice: stop NOW, and leave the pipeline unfinished ... or risk putting your company out of business forever."[25] America was acting in the interest of Europe's energy security, the letter further explained. Berlin's gas deal with Putin needed to be thwarted, not for its sake, but for Europe's.

German politicians felt bitter, perhaps even humiliated. The US just wants to sell more of its own liquefied gas, some fired back. "European energy policy is decided in Europe, not the US", Heiko Maas, the German foreign minister responded defiantly, as Western construction companies readied to pull out of the pipeline project.[26] But was he right? Those who farm out their protection to the strong, also farm out their freedom. They can never eliminate the possibility of extortion. For a long time, European politicians believed this could not happen. But who believes it still? As Joschka Fischer, former German foreign minister, puts it: "For Europeans, it would be the height of folly to sit back and wait for the fateful tweet to arrive."[27]

Having prospered for 75 years under America's shield, some argue that Trump barks worse than he bites. Eventually, he will be gone. In the meantime, annoying the strongman only sows doubt about America's commitment to Europe's security. It invites the barbarians who prowl Europe's borders in the east to try their luck. Europe must be humble and pliant, they warn. The point of view is not without merit. There is nothing wrong with keeping one's head down, if you are weak. However, there is a difference between keeping one's head down and sticking one's head in the sand. Neither arrogance nor docility will keep foreign kings and barbarians away. In the end, there is only one thing that will: choosing strength. Is it a vassal or sovereign? This is the question Europe faces. In a world dominated by power, no question is more important.

Notes

PREFACE

1 *The Times of Israel*, 11 November 2015.
2 Michael Oakeshott, "Political Discourse", in *Rationalism in Politics* (London: Liberty Press, 1991). This is not to say, of course, that falsifiable claims are never made in politics ("There are no Russian soldiers in Ukraine", "It was Ukraine that shot down the plane"), or that we are in a post-truth era. But such testable claims are clearly not exhaustive of a political discourse.
3 *The Fog of War: Eleven Lessons from the Life of Robert S. McNamara*, directed by Errol Morris, Sony Pictures Classics, 2003.
4 Quoted in the *Washington Post*, 27 April 2008.

CHAPTER 1

1 "The European Witch-craze of the Sixteenth and Seventeenth Centuries", in Hugh Trevor-Roper, *The Crisis of the Seventeenth Century* (Indianapolis, IN: Liberty Fund, 1967).
2 *Newsweek*, 20 June 2018, reporting an account of the event given by eyewitnesses to Eurasia Group president Ian Bremmer.
3 Tweet, @realDonaldTrump, 9 June 2018.
4 Interview with *The Guardian*, 17 November 2018.
5 *The Times*, 15 January 2017.
6 Ted Malloch interviewed by the BBC, 25 January 2017.
7 Ted Malloch quoted in *Der Spiegel*, 6 February 2017.
8 Quoted in *Politico*, 28 June 2018.
9 Interview with *The Times*, 15 January 2017.
10 Robert Cooper, *The Breaking of Nations: Order and Chaos in the Twenty-first Century* (London: Atlantic, 2003).
11 In January 2017, Francis Fukuyama wrote in *Prospect Magazine*: "We cannot preclude the possibility that we are living through a political disruption that will in time bear

comparison with the collapse of Communism a generation ago." See also Robert Kagan, "The Strongmen Strike Back", *Washington Post*, 14 March 2019.

12 Leonid Bershidsky, *Bloomberg*, 9 November 2017.

13 Martin Wolf, *Financial Times*, 27 February 2017.

14 Two other world leaders could be mentioned as part of the strongman revival. In 2018, the former army captain Jair Bolsonaro was elected Brazil's president. Known as "Tropical Trump", Bolsonaro bills himself as the restorer of laws and discipline in the continent's best tradition of the *caudillo*. Second, Indian prime minister, Narendra Modi, re-elected in 2019, is often accused of encouraging a personality cult, fanning Hindu nationalism and of applying strongmen tactics in managing the Indian economy. See for example the *New Yorker*, "The Strongman Problem, from Modi to Trump", 18 January 2017; Adam Roberts in the *New York Times*, "Modi's Strongman Economics"; and Gideon Rachman, "India's Narendra Modi Has Had a Free Pass from the West for Too Long", *Financial Times*, 11 November 2019.

15 Quoted by *CNN*, 14 April 2020.

16 Tweet, @JoeBiden, 14 April 2020.

17 Ivan Krastev, *After Europe* (Philadelphia, PA: University of Pennsylvania Press, 2017).

18 *The Concept of the Political* [1932] (Chicago, IL: University of Chicago Press, 2007). Schmitt's ideas are surrounded by controversy, not least because he joined the Nazi party in 1933 and quite blatantly sympathized with its causes, even if he later fell out of the regime's favour, in part because his ideas were never *völkisch* enough. While his ideas are certainly critical of liberalism, they have, in my view, far less in common with Nazi ideology than with the idea of strength explored in this book.

19 Comments made to ZDF's Brussels correspondent Markus Preiss, @markuspreiss, 24 February 2019.

20 Dutch Prime Minster Mark Rutte in his "Churchill Lecture" at the University of Zurich, 13 February 2019.

21 Books that serve this need include Michael Wolff's *Fire and Fury: Inside the Trump White House* (London: Little, Brown, 2018); Bob Woodward's *Fear: Trump in the White House* (New York: Simon & Schuster, 2018); and David Frum's *Trumpocracy: The Corruption of the American Republic* (New York: HarperCollins, 2018), the front cover of which has Robert de Niro hailing the book as the "essential guide to the malevolent tragedy that is Trumpocracy".

22 See Steven Levitsky & Daniel Ziblatt, *How Democracies Die* (New York: Crown, 2018); Timothy Snyder, *The Road to Unfreedom* (New York: Tim Duggan Books, 2018); Yascha Mounk, *The People vs Democracy: Why Our Freedom is in Danger and How to Save it* (Cambridge, MA: Harvard University Press, 2018); David Runciman, *How Democracy Ends* (New York: Basic Books, 2018).

23 Madeleine Albright, with Bill Woodward, *Fascism: A Warning* (New York: HarperCollins, 2018), 4–5.

24 For a useful overview of the different conceptual distinctions made, see Erica Frantz, *Authoritarianism: What Everyone Needs to Know* (Oxford: Oxford University Press, 2018), in particular chapter 5.

25 See Frantz, *Authoritarianism*, in particular its concluding chapter.

26 Carl Schmitt, *Political Theology* [1922] (Chicago, IL: University of Chicago Press, 1985).

27 For the idea of rules as *constitutive* of power and the institutional nature of power, see H. L. A. Hart, *The Concept of Law* (Oxford: Oxford University Press, 1994), which refers to such rules as "second-order rules" or the rules of recognition. These types of rules confer

authority and the power to make law ("first-order rules"), take public decisions and so on, to bodies, offices and ultimately their incumbents.

28 For example, Francis Fukuyama, *State Building: Governance and World Order in the Twenty-First Century* (Ithaca, NY: Cornell University Press, 2005), as well as his *Political Order and Decay* (London: Profile, 2015).

29 For a critical discussion of the failed states approach and the idea of state building, see Susan Woodward, *The Ideology of Failed States: Why Intervention Fails* (Cambridge: Cambridge University Press, 2017).

30 Fukuyama, *Political Order and Decay*, 25.

31 Quoted in the *Financial Times*, 23 December 2019.

32 For the essential element of time in transitions to democracy, see Sheri Berman, *Democracy and Dictatorship in Europe: From the Ancien Régime to the Present Day* (Oxford: Oxford University Press, 2019).

33 "The popular belief in a 'strong man' who, isolated against others, owes his strength to his being alone is … sheer superstition, based on the delusion that we can 'make' something in the realms of human affairs – 'make' institutions or laws, for instance, as we make tables or chairs", Arendt points out. The strongman acts alone only at the point of initiating action, but "the strength of the beginner and leader shows itself only in his initiative and the risk he takes, not in the actual achievement". To achieve something, the strongman needs to get others to join in or be able to represent them, to act for them. See Hannah Arendt, *The Human Condition* (Chicago, IL: University of Chicago Press, 1989), 188–9, and more generally Hannah Arendt, *On Violence* (Orlando, FL: Harcourt, 1970).

34 For the concept of improvisations in European politics, see Luuk van Middelaar's excellent *Alarums and Excursions: Improvising Politics on the European Stage* (Newcastle upon Tyne: Agenda Publishing, 2019).

35 Interview with *Der Spiegel*, 5 January 2018.

CHAPTER 2

1 Quoted by the Press Association, 31 March 2014.

2 Interview with NBC's Matt Lauer, quoted in the *Washington Post*, 8 September 2016.

3 Interview with Fox News' Bill O'Reilly, quoted in the *New York Times*, 10 August 2017.

4 Quoted in the *Daily Mail*, 20 May 2014.

5 J. G. A. Pocock, *The Machiavellian Moment* (Princeton, NJ: Princeton University Press, 1975).

6 Pocock, *The Machiavellian Moment*, viii.

7 Pocock, *The Machiavellian Moment*, 8.

8 Jacques Le Goff, *The Birth of Purgatory* (Chicago, IL: University of Chicago Press, 1984).

9 Pocock, *The Machiavellian Moment*, 160.

10 Interview with Bob Woodward, in *Fear: Trump in the White House*.

11 Paul Kagame, "2010 Oppenheimer Lecture: The Challenges of Nation Building in Africa", at http://roganfoundation.org/blog/the-challenges-of-nation-building-in-africa-by-pres-paul-kagame/.

12 Former aides and loyalists who have since fallen out with Kagame have reported on his "rage", citing the tendency to personally "thrash" staff with sticks. See Jeffrey Gettleman, "The Global Elite's Favorite Strongman", *New York Times*, 4 September 2013, which quotes a former Kagame driver saying: "If I was to diagnose him, I'd say he has a personality disorder."

13 *The Prince*, chapter 18.

14 Quoted in Anjan Sundaram, "Rwanda: The Darling Tyrant", *Politico Magazine*, March/April 2014.

15 "The reason for this", Machiavelli writes, "is that, where the material is so corrupt, laws do not suffice to keep it in hand; it is necessary to have, besides laws, a superior force, such as appertains to a monarch, who has such absolute and overwhelming power that he can restrain excesses due to ambition and the corrupt practices of the powerful." In *The Discourses* (1532), book 1, chapter 55 (London: Penguin Classics, 1983).

16 In his classic study *Making Democracy Work: Civic Traditions in Modern Italy* (Princeton, NJ: Princeton University Press, 1993), Robert Putnam argues (177) "that there may be at least two broad equilibria toward which all societies … tend to evolve and which, once attained, tend to be self-reinforcing". Where social capital and civic traditions are poorly developed, rather than democratic government, "we should expect the Hobbesian, hierarchical solution to dilemmas of collective action – coercion, exploitation, and dependence – to predominate". While this is a suboptimal state of affairs, "minimal security, no matter how exploitative and ineffective, is not a contemptible objective for the powerless".

17 Quoted in Ali Gheissari & Vali Nasr, *Democracy in Iran: History and the Quest for Liberty* (Oxford: Oxford University Press, 2009), 56.

18 *The Guardian*, 28 June 2017.

19 Putin's comment referred to plans to topple Libyan ruler Gaddafi in 2011, which he rejected as ill-thought through. Quoted in the *Financial Times*, 25 February 2011.

20 *The Discourses*, book 1, chapter 9.

21 However, François Mitterrand, who opposed de Gaulle at that time, argued: "He was no more involved directly in the plot than God in the creation." Quoted in Julian Jackson, *De Gaulle* (Cambridge, MA: Harvard University Press, 2018).

22 Quoted in Jackson, *De Gaulle*, 470.

23 Quoted in *The Guardian*, 1 June 1958.

24 In *Le Monde*, 13 September 1958. "*Je ne crois pas en Dieu, mais si dans ce plébiscite je devais choisir entre Lui et le prétendant actuel, je voterais plutôt pour Dieu: il est plus modeste.*"

25 Emmanuel Macron in *The Guardian*, 20 October 2017: "I believe our country is on a cliff edge, I even think it's in danger of falling. If we weren't at a tragic moment in our history, I would never have been elected. I'm not made to lead in calm weather. My predecessor was, but I'm made for storms."

26 Interview with *Le Un*, No. 64, 8 July 2015. The execution of King Louis XVI in 1793, Macron argues, left France with a profound sense of emptiness and a deep psycho-political yearning to see that void filled. The president's job, as de Gaulle understood, is to fulfil that need and become a "surrogate-King", a liberal strongman of sorts.

27 *The Discourses*, book 1, chapter 16.

28 Political scientists Jonathan Powell and Clayton Thyne count 475 coup attempts since 1950, 236 of which were successful. See "Coups in the World, 1950–Present", at https://www.jonathanmpowell.com/coup-detat-dataset.html.

29 "I Toppled Saddam's Statue – Now I Want Him Back", BBC News, 5 July 2016.

30 Cited in *The Guardian*, 19 May 2013.

31 Quoted in the *Financial Times*, 31 May 2017.

32 See Fukuyama, *Political Order and Political Decay*, which argues that liberal democracy consists of three kinds of institutions that best develop consecutively: the state, the rule of law and finally democratic accountability. If we were to borrow Fukuyama's conceptual distinction, the strongman aims to achieve the first stage, that of securing effective government and, if successful, the second stage of the rule of law.

33 Quoted in Graham Allison, Robert D. Blackwill & Ali Wyne, *Lee Kuan Yew: The Grand Master's Insight on China, the United States, and the World* (Cambridge, MA: MIT Press, 2013), 27.

34 Quoted in the *New York Times*, 18 May 2000.

35 Francis Fukuyama, "China's 'Bad Emperor' Problem", *The American Interest*, 28 May 2012.

36 *Handelsblatt*, 22 November 2004.

37 Quoted in Allison *et al.*, *Lee Kuan Yew*, 148.

38 When Robert Mugabe took power in 1980, Tanzanian President Julius Nyerere told him: "You have inherited a jewel. Keep it that way." (Quoted in *AP*, 22 November 2017.) In his early years the Marxist guerrilla Mugabe was seen in Africa and the world as a liberator. But botched land reforms, corruption and other poor decisions left Zimbabwe destitute. Suffering from hyperinflation, the country's GDP almost halved from 1998 to 2008.

39 In the words of historian Claude Nicolet: "Augustus, having learned the lessons of thirteen more years of civil war, realised that one must go masked, neither saying nor permitting to be said the word 'king' or 'dictator'; and he was able to reign and even found a monarchy ... by affecting to be a plain citizen." In "Dictatorship in Rome", Peter Baehr & Melvin Richter (eds), *Dictatorship in History and Theory: Bonapartism, Caesarism, and Totalitarianism* (Cambridge: Cambridge University Press, 2004), 275.

40 Quoted in Christopher Clarke, *Time and Power: Visions of History in German Politics, from the Thirty-Year War to the Third Reich* (Princeton, NJ: Princeton University Press, 2019), 206.

41 Clarke, *Time and Power*, 205.

42 When Napoleon ousted the republican Directoire in the Brumaire coup of 1799, it was easily argued that the nation needed a single-minded sovereign ruler, a strongman, who would establish the conditions of normalcy under which the ideals of the revolution could thrive. Arguing it needed a new king, however, was another matter. Napoleon assumed the Roman-sounding title of "First Consul". Later he elevated this title to "First Consul for Life". In 1804, Bonaparte crowned himself Napoleon I, Emperor of France, but he still rejected the divine right of kings.

43 *The Guardian*, 26 October 2017.

44 Interview with Erdogan in *Der Spiegel*, 29 March 2010.

CHAPTER 3

1 Marc Bloch, *Feudal Society* (London: Routledge Classics, 2014); see also F. L. Ganshof, *Feudalism* (Toronto: University of Toronto Press, 1996).

2 Bloch, *Feudal Society*, 170.

3 Alena V. Ledeneva, *Can Russia Modernise? Sistema, Power Networks and Informal Governance* (Cambridge: Cambridge University Press, 2013); and Henry E. Hale, *Patronal Politics: Eurasian Regime Dynamics in Comparative Perspective* (Cambridge: Cambridge University Press, 2015).

4 Richard Sakwa, *Putin and the Oligarch: The Khodorkovsky-Yukos Affair* (London: I. B. Tauris, 2014), 13–14.

5 Mikhail Zygar, *All the Kremlin's Men: Inside the Court of Vladimir Putin* (New York: Public Affairs, 2016), 55.

6 Arkady Ostrovsky, *The Invention of Russia: From Gorbachev's Freedom to Putin's War* (London: Penguin, 2017).

7 For this period and the so-called "oligarch wars", see David E. Hoffman, *The Oligarchs: Wealth and Power in the New Russia* (New York: PublicAffairs, 2011).

8 Zygar, *All the Kremlin's Men*, 48.
9 "Arctic Russia Travel: Adventures in the Extreme North", at http://www.arcticrussiatravel. com/chukotka/.
10 Quoted in *The Guardian*, 7 May 2004.
11 *Daily Telegraph*, 5 December 2010.
12 Bloch, *Feudal Society*, 223.
13 *Moscow Times*, 18 April 2013.
14 Bloch, *Feudal Society*, 245.
15 See the account in David Pendleton & Simone Foxman, "Freed Saudis Resurface Billions Poorer after Prince's Crackdown", Bloomberg, 2 February 2019.
16 Quoted in *China Daily*, 22 January 2013.
17 Quoted in Reuters, 19 March 2014.
18 *The Independent*, 25 April 2013.
19 Diego Gambetta, *The Sicilian Mafia: The Business of Private Protection* (Cambridge, MA: Harvard University Press, 1993).
20 Respectively European Commission vice president Frans Timmermans, in the *Financial Times*, 25 September 2017, and Emmanuel Macron in his Sorbonne speech, 26 September 2017.
21 Quoted in the *Financial Times*, 16 August 2016.
22 "Sepp Blatter Calls Predecessor Joao Havelange a 'Teacher', 'Like a Brother'", *ESPN* 16 August 2016.
23 *The Independent*, 4 June 2015.
24 BBC News, 29 May 2015.
25 BBC Sport, "FIFA President Sepp Blatter Likened to Jesus and Nelson Mandela", 16 April 2015.
26 Quoted in *The Guardian*, 24 May.
27 Quoted in the *New York Times*, 2 June 2015.
28 See Denis Tull & Claudia Simons, "The Institutionalization of Power Revisited: Presidential Term Limits in Africa", *Africa Spectrum* 52:2 (2017), 79–102.
29 Quoted in Elaina Plott, "Inside Ivanka's Dreamworld", *The Atlantic*, 12 April 2019.
30 Quoted in *The Guardian*, 10 March 2020.
31 "Fancy Sausages and a $2 Million Bribe: A Trial Uncovers Kremlin Infighting", *New York Times*, 15 December 2017.
32 Reported by BBC News, 7 March 2018.
33 Quoted in Reuters, 6 June 2019.
34 See for example Leonid Ragozin in "When Russian Officials 'Nightmare' Your Business, You Can Lose Everything – Even Your Life", Bloomberg, 29 January 2018.
35 Reuters, 7 June 2019.
36 Quoted in *The Guardian*, 10 June 2019.

CHAPTER 4

1 *The Guardian*, 6 September 2012.
2 Bueno de Mesquita & Alastair Smith, *The Dictator's Handbook: Why Bad Behaviour is Almost Always Good Politics* (New York: Public Affairs, 2012), 25.
3 Quoted in Andrew Roberts, *Napoleon the Great* (London: Penguin, 2015), 206.

4 Catherine Fieschi, *Populocracy: The Tyranny of Authenticity and the Rise of Populism* (Newcastle upon Tyne: Agenda Publishing, 2019).

5 *Leviathan*, chapter 10, part I (London: Penguin Classics, 1985), 150.

6 Most famously John Rawls, *A Theory of Justice* (Cambridge, MA: Harvard University Press, 1999) and T. M. Scanlon, *What We Owe to Each Other* (Cambridge, MA: Harvard University Press, 2000).

7 John Searle in *The Construction of Social Reality* (New York: The Free Press, 1995).

8 Tinubu did not quite get away with his "coup", reportedly provoking an angry response from Buhari that he was not *the* but only *one* of the party's National Leaders. See the *Vanguard*, 23 October 2016.

9 *The Telegraph*, 12 April 2018.

10 France 24, 27 April 2018.

11 Mass protests, political scientists note, are now the greatest challenge to autocratic regimes. In the twentieth century, most frequently dictators were toppled in military coups staged by officers. Today, they are more likely to be brought down by protests and elections that follow them. See Andrea Kendall-Taylor, Erica Frantz & Joseph Wright, "The Digital Dictators: How Technology Strengthens Autocracy", *Foreign Affairs*, March/April 2020.

12 Reuters, 4 July 2019.

13 *Daily Mail*, 6 November 2017.

14 Bueno de Mesquita & Alastair Smith, *The Dictator's Handbook*, 129.

15 See Richard Pipes, *Communism: A History* (New York: Modern Library, 2003), 67.

16 A raft of similar executions by anti-aircraft guns – and according to some sources by flame thrower – is said to have taken place since Kim took power in 2011. CNN reported on 29 December 2016 that the number of executions stood at 300, citing research by the South Korean Institute for National Security Strategy.

17 Tom Holland, *Dynasty: The Rise and Fall of the House of Caesars* (London: Abacus, 2015), 69–70.

18 See Paul Zanker, *The Power of Images in the Age of Augustus* (Ann Arbor, MI: Michigan University Press, 1990).

19 BBC News, 17 July 2017.

20 Quoted in Jacopo Barigazzi, "The Russian Stalinist Who Invented Europe", *Politico*, 22 March 2017.

21 Barigazzi, "The Russian Stalinist".

22 Alexandre Kojève, *The Notion of Authority* (London: Verso, 2014).

23 Kojève, *The Notion of Authority*, 55.

24 Quoted in Roberts, *Napoleon the Great*, 208.

25 The comment is Vyacheslav Nikonov's, cited in Peter Baker & Susan Glasser, *Kremlin Rising: Vladimir Putin's Russia and the End of Revolution* (New York: Scribner, 2005), 61.

26 Gleb Pavlosky, one of the Kremlin's spin doctors at the time, says: "He was not a leader in the beginning. He did not look like a leader ... In the beginning, Putin was asked to act more roughly. He was a more polite man. He could not make himself speak rudely, so he had to be asked to act more rudely." Pavlosky adds: "He is very flexible inside. He can change. If he has a feeling that you are irritated, he will change immediately. He will start looking for the right way to approach you, and he does it very easily." In "Frontline Interview", *PBS*, 13 July 2017.

27 Quoted in *The Independent*, 18 June 2017.

28 *The Guardian*, 14 November 2014.

29 *The Independent*, 10 August 2010.
30 Kojève, *The Notion of Authority*, 28.
31 Kojève, *The Notion of Authority*, 14.
32 Oliver Hotham, "Portraits to Inspire and Intimidate: North Korea's Omnipresent Leaders", *The Guardian*, 4 September 2015.
33 Zygar, *All the Kremlin's Men*, 4.
34 *The Guardian*, 25 January 2016.
35 Vladimir Putin, "Speech at the Celebration of Pyotr Stolypin's 150th Birthday", at http://archive.government.ru/eng/docs/15878/print/.
36 Kojève, *The Notion of Authority*, 19.
37 Vladimir Putin, "Russia at the Turn of the Millennium", 30 December 1999, in *First Person: An Astonishingly Frank Self-Portrait by Russia's President Vladimir Putin* (London: Hutchinson, 2000), 209–19.
38 Quoted in the *Financial Times*, 5 October 2011.
39 Dmitry Medvedev, "Go Russia!", 10 September 2009, at http://en.kremlin.ru/events/president/news/5413.
40 Quoted in *The Guardian*, 1 October 2019.
41 Justin McCarthy, "Trump Approval Inches Up, While Support for Impeachment Dips", 18 December 2019, at https://news.gallup.com/poll/271691/trump-approval-inches-support-impeachment-dips.aspx.

CHAPTER 5

1 *The Guardian*, 11 June 2018.
2 Tweet, @realDonaldTrump, 8 August 2017
3 Woodward, *Fear*, 281.
4 Associated Press, 24 May 2018.
5 Tweet, @realDonaldTrump, 11 June 2018.
6 *Financial Times*, 12 June 2018.
7 Quoted in the *New York Times*, 15 June 2018.
8 *The Economist*, "The Strange Love-in Between Donald Trump and Recep Tayyip Erdogan", 14 November 2019.
9 Janan Ganesh, "Trump, Xi and Other Nationalists are Less United than Ever", *Financial Times*, 22 April 2020, and for the same argument see his earlier article, "The Myth of a Unified World", *Financial Times*, 11 September 2019.
10 The idea of the state as a person has all but disappeared from contemporary political theory, even if its importance is certainly no less than when modern states first began to emerge in Europe. The idea that states or groups can ever be persons is held to be at odds with liberalism, in particular the assumption that things can only be good or bad insofar as they are good or bad *for individuals*. For attempts to recover the theory of personhood, see Quentin Skinner, "A Genealogy of the Modern State", British Academy Lecture, 13 May 2008, *Proceedings of the British Academy* 162, 325–70; and Hans Kribbe, *Corporate Personality: A Political Theory of Association* (Ann Arbor, MI: UMI Dissertation Publishing, 2002), which theorizes the person of the state as a practical and normative prerequisite of liberal order, political obligation and the rule of law.
11 Edmund Burke, *Reflections on the Revolution in France* [1790] (Oxford: Oxford University Press, 2009).

12 Quoted in Oleg Kharkhordin, "What is the State? A Russian Concept of Gosudarstvo in the European Context", at https://eu.spb.ru/images/rector/what-is-the-state.pdf.

13 "When the king dies, the kingdom remains, like a ship whose captain has perished", Conrad II of Germany (990–1039), quoted in Bloch, *Feudal Society*, 430.

14 "Distinct from both the ruler and the ruled", as Skinner puts it in "A Genealogy of the Modern State".

15 As Kissinger rightly insists in *Diplomacy* (New York: Simon & Schuster, 1994), these principles of diplomacy must not be thought of as laid down in documents or as a set of formal rules. They grew organically as codes of conduct, as an informal ethos imbedded in the practice of foreign diplomacy that over time became accepted by its participants.

16 See David Reynolds, *Summits: Six Meetings that Shaped the Twentieth Century* (London: Penguin, 2008), which argues that personal diplomacy and "summitry" only began to flourish with the advent of the modern state and its diplomatic codes. Before this, those undertaking personal diplomacy and summits carried the very real risk of being murdered.

17 Samuel P. Huntington, *The Clash of Civilizations and the Remaking of World Order* (London: Touchstone, 1997).

18 *The Guardian*, 5 September 2016.

19 CNN, 17 November 2017.

20 "Remarks by President Trump at 5th U.S.-ASEAN Summit", 13 November 2017, at https://www.whitehouse.gov/briefings-statements/remarks-president-trump-5th-u-s-asean-summit.

21 Quoted in the *New York Times*, 13 November 2017.

22 Quoted in Reuters, 15 November 2012.

23 Interview with *Die Zeit*, November 2017.

24 Associated Press, 12 March 2018.

25 Quoted in the *South China Morning Post*, 2 August 2019.

26 Quoted in the *Daily Mail*, 6 September 2015.

27 Quoted in Reuters, 9 August 2013.

28 *Politico*, 7 October 2019.

29 *The Guardian*, 17 October 2019.

30 Quoted in NBC News, 18 October 2019.

31 Woodward, *Fear*, 151.

32 *South China Morning Post*, 13 April 2017.

33 *Washington Post*, 9 November 2017.

34 *Quartz*, 9 November 2017.

35 Quoted by CNN, 10 November 2017.

36 Schmitt launched his concept *Großraumordnung* in "The Großraum Order of International Law", first in the form of a lecture in April 1939. It suggested that Germany, like the US, was entitled to its own Great Space, its own sphere of influence. The link to Hitler's ambitions for a Greater German Reich in Europe was easily made. However, Schmitt's theory of the *Großraum* still offended the Nazis in other ways. The "political idea" that America stood for, he argued, was multiethnic democracy, the melting pot. By contrast, the rival idea of a German *Großraum*, as he saw it, was that of a patchwork quilt of national cultures and peoples that would retain and celebrate their unique identities. It fell disappointingly short of the ideals of racial purity the Nazis propagated. See Carl Schmitt, *Writings on War*, ed. Timothy Nunan (Cambridge: Polity, 2011).

37 Winston Churchill, *Memoirs of the Second World War* (Boston, MA: Houghton Mifflin, 1987), 885–6.

38 Townsend Hoopes and Douglas Brinkley argue in *FDR and the Creation of the U.N.* (New Haven, CT: Yale University Press, 1997), that following the failure of the League of Nations, US President Roosevelt concluded that "responsibility for world peace depended exclusively on the few nations that possessed real power and that they must 'run the world' for an indefinite transitional period after victory" (207).

39 Tweet, @realDonaldTrump, 3 January 2018.

40 See Amitai Etzioni, "Spheres of Influence: A Reconceptualization", *Fletcher Forum of World Affairs* 39:2 (2015).

41 Quoted by NBC News, 18 October 2019.

42 Quoted in *Slate*, 19 November 2013.

43 "2019 State of the Nation Address", http://kremlin.ru/events/president/news/59863.

44 John Bolton, "Speech to the Federalist Society", 10 September 2018, at https://american-rhetoric.com/speeches/johnboltonfederalistsociety2018.htm.

45 Quoted by Jeffrey Goldberg in *The Atlantic*, 11 June 2018.

46 Schmitt, *The Concept of the Political*, 54.

47 Quoted in *RT*, 11 February 2018.

CHAPTER 6

1 *euobserver*, 7 May 2009.

2 "It's not going to be called that", Clinton added. "It's going to be called a customs union, it will be called Eurasian Union and all of that. But let's make no mistake about it. We know what the goal is and we are trying to figure out effective ways to slow down or prevent it." Quoted in the *Financial Times*, 7 December 2012.

3 *The Guardian*, 22 September 2013.

4 *euobserver*, 23 September 2013.

5 European Commission, "Statement on the Pressure Exercised by Russia on Countries of the Eastern Partnership", 11 September 2013.

6 European Commission, "Statement on the Pressure Exercised by Russia".

7 *Frankfurter Allgemeine Zeitung*, 30 November 2013.

8 *Euractiv*, 29 November 2013.

9 *Le Figaro*, 29 November 2013.

10 *Der Spiegel*, 24 November 2014.

11 Agence France Presse, 29 November.

12 About the EU's rejection of a three-way deal, Pierre Vimont, secretary general in the EU's External Action Service at the time, later reflected: "What strikes me is when we ask is this really incompatible as it's really said, we discover, discussing with our experts, that maybe it's not exactly that, and we can find a common ground … What strike[s] me is that we had our whole bureaucracy saying we should not do things that way." Quoted in *Euractiv*, 14 March 2014.

13 *Der Spiegel*, 5 December 2013.

14 *Daily Telegraph*, 3 February 2017

15 *The Guardian* 29 January 2014

16 "Transcript of Nuland-Pyatt Call", BBC News, 7 February 2014.

17 "Agreement on the Settlement of the Crisis in Ukraine", 21 February 2014, at https://archive.is/20140223081530/http://www.president.gov.ua/ru/news/30117.html.

18 *New York Times*, 3 January 2015.

19 Agence France Presse, 26 February 2014

20 *The Independent*, 28 February 2014.

21 OSCE, "Election Observation Mission Final Report", Warsaw, 28 April 2010.

22 News24 Archives, 4 March 2014.

23 *The Guardian*, 24 February 2014.

24 Reuters, 27 February 2014.

25 *RT*, 2 March 2014.

26 *New York Times*, 3 March 2014.

27 See Carl Schreck, "From 'Not Us' to 'Why Hide It?': How Russia Denied Its Crimea Invasion, then Admitted it", *RFERL*, 26 February 2019.

28 It was a phrase he repeated to Gorbachev on at least three occasions, according to Svetlana Savranskaya and Tom Blanton in "NATO Expansion: What Gorbachev Heard", *National Security Archives*, 12 December 2017, sarchive.gwu.edu.

29 "Address by President of the Russian Federation", 18 March 2014, at en.kremlin.ru/events/president/news/20603.

30 *Süddeutsche Zeitung*, 14 March 2014.

31 As over a thousand leaked private emails later revealed, the general ran a deliberate PR campaign aimed at goading Europe and the Obama White House into a military response. His public statements about Russian troop movements proved difficult to verify and some cases even contradicted NATO's own intelligence reports. See *Der Spiegel*, 28 July 2016.

32 Reuters, 30 August 2014.

33 *The Guardian*, 3 September 2014.

34 *Quartz*, "Telephone Diplomacy: Six Months of World Leaders' Phone Calls to Putin about the Crisis in Ukraine", 22 July 2014.

35 Reuters, 7 February 2015.

36 *Süddeutsche Zeitung*, 9 February 2015.

37 Sir Simon Fraser, former Foreign Office permanent secretary, and earlier chief of staff to EU Trade Commissioner Peter Mandelson, said: "With hindsight we might have foreseen in 2013 that the combination of formally signing a deep free trade agreement [with Ukraine], with the internal unrest facing President Putin on his return to office, and the perception that had arisen of greater reticence in western foreign policy, could result in a more aggressive Russian response in Ukraine, and opportunism in Syria". Quoted in *The Guardian*, 24 October 2016.

38 *New York Times*, 8 December 2011.

39 *The Guardian*, 8 December 2011.

40 Michael McFaul, Nicolai Petrov & Andrei Ryabov, *Between Dictatorship and Democracy: Russian Post-Communist Political Reform* (Washington, DC: Carnegie Endowment, 2004).

41 *International Herald Tribune*, 19 January 2012.

42 In his memoirs *From Cold War to Hot Peace: An American Ambassador in Putin's Russia* (New York: Houghton Mifflin Harcourt, 2018), McFaul argues Putin needed foreign enemies to restore Russia's political cohesion. While it certainly was expedient for the Kremlin to paint the political opposition as McFaul's stooges, there is little to suggest that the Kremlin did not genuinely believe the West was really pulling the strings, or at least trying to.

43 Comments made on MSNBC, 14 February 2017.

44 Tweet, @guyverhofstadt, 13 June 2018.

45 See the *New York Times*, 16 February 2018. Prigozhin is further said to finance a shadow army of mercenaries, known as the Wagner Group, active in eastern Ukraine, Syria and

more recently Libya. See also Joshua Yaffa in "Putin's Shadow Army Suffers a Setback in Syria", *New Yorker*, 16 February 2018.

46 *Die Presse*, 4 June 2018.
47 *The Guardian*, 27 March 2019.
48 *The Guardian*, 26 April 2019.
49 Buzzfeed, "No Deal: How Secret Talks With Russia to Prevent Election Meddling Collapsed", 8 December 2017.

CHAPTER 7

1   Quoted in *Der Spiegel*, 9 February 2016.
2   Quoted from the minutes of the meeting, leaked to Greek news site euro2day.gr.
3   *The Telegraph*, 10 October 2019.
4   Tweet, @eucopresident, 11 October 2019.
5   "Speech at Conference Held in Memory of Helmut Kohl", Budapest, 16 June 2018, at http://www.miniszterelnok.hu/prime-minister-viktor-orbans-speech-at-a-conference-held-in-memory-of-helmut-kohl/.
6   In the Middle Ages, Le Goff writes in *The Birth of Europe* (Oxford: Blackwell, 2005), "[f] rontiers of the modern linear kind, indicated by a line of posts or boundary markers, were to be found only here and there, appearing late on, associated with the constitutions of states". What passed for borders back then, as he puts it, were only "pseudo-frontiers", characterized by "indeterminacy" and "permeability". Or, as Eduardo Manzano Moreno writes: "the whole territory of medieval Europe was, in itself, a frontier"; see "The Creation of a Medieval Frontier: Islam and Christianity in the Iberian Peninsula, Eighth to Eleventh Centuries" in Daniel Power & Naomi Standen (eds), *Frontiers in Question: Eurasian Borderlands, 700–1700* (London: Macmillan, 1999), 36.
7   Speech by Commissioner Olli Rehn, "Europe's Frontier a Dynamic Concept", Brussels, 19 March 2007.
8   Quoted in *euobserver*, 8 October 2019.
9   Article 49 of the Treaty of the European Union (TEU) states: "Any European State which respects the values referred to in Article 2 and is committed to promoting them may apply to become a member of the Union".
10 As German politician Ralph Brinkhaus argued, addressing the Bundestag: "Europe is a community of values ... Europe is a peace project. Europe is an economic project. Whoever reduces Europe to a continent hasn't understood anything at all." Cited on *Deutschlandfunk*, 21 November 2018.
11 Speech by Commissioner Olli Rehn, "Europe's Frontier a Dynamic Concept", Brussels, 19 March 2007.
12 Quoted in Power & Standen, *Frontiers in Question*, 9.
13 Quoted in *Der Spiegel*, "Stille Revolution", 36/2003.
14 *The Economist*, 16 September 2004.
15 In 2004, when it was decided to open accession talks with Turkey, "ready" meant meeting the EU's "Copenhagen criteria" agreed in 1993. Europe's leaders had decided in 2002 that once these criteria had been met, the start of negotiations would follow "without delay". See "Copenhagen European Council, 12–13 December 2002, Presidency Conclusion", at https://www.consilium.europa.eu/media/20906/73842.pdf.

16 Quoted in *euobserver*, 15 January 2007.

17 To avoid that plebiscites would impede the Union's enlargement in the Balkans, which Sarkozy deemed less objectionable, it was considered – though ultimately rejected – that such referenda would not be compulsory for candidate states with less than 5 per cent of the EU population, effectively singling out Turkey.

18 Kostiantyn Yelisieiev, deputy chief of staff to Ukrainian President Petro Poroshenko, put his finger on the problem in an article in *euobserver*, 15 November 2017: "What Ukraine ultimately wants is a simple message: 'Once you're ready – you're in'. Ukraine's task would be to get ready. The EU's task would be to decide if or when Ukraine was ready." But given Russia's position, Europe could no longer limit its role to that of mere examiner. It needed to remain free to take its own sovereign decisions, and not solely on the basis of Ukrainian "readiness", a factor beyond its control.

19 In *The Concept of the Political*, Schmitt claimed that it is precisely the ability to decide who "the other" is – who is "in" and "out" – that makes a community "political". As he argues (49): "For as long as a people exists in the political sphere, this people must ... determine itself the distinction of friend and enemy. Therein resides the essence of its political existence. When it no longer possesses the capacity or the will to make this distinction, it ceases to exist politically."

20 See Olli Rehn, "Turkey's Best Response is a Rock-solid Commitment to Reforms", Speech, Ankara, 3 October 2006.

21 *Euractiv*, 27 November 2005.

22 *The Guardian*, 9 December 2006.

23 Vincent L. Morelli, "European Union Enlargement: A Status Report on Turkey's Accession Negotiations", *Congressional Research Service*, 5 August 2013.

24 Katynka Barysch, "Absorption Capacity – the Wrong Debate", *Centre for European Reform – Insights*, 9 November 2006.

25 Michael Emerson, Senem Aydin, Julia De Clerck-Sachsse & Gergana Noutcheva, "Just what is this 'Absorption Capacity' of the European Union?", *CEPS Policy Brief*, November 2006.

26 Emerson *et al.* "Just what is this 'Absorption Capacity'".

27 Absorption capacity, the Commission further tried spinning it, only referred to the EU's obligations to get its own house in order, to reform its institutions and policies, and even to persuade its citizens of enlargement's benefits, so that when Turkey was eventually "ready" it could promptly be "absorbed".

28 "We must avoid making enlargement hostage to a theological debate about the final borders of Europe", Rehn cautioned. But of course, only in civilizational terms did the notion of a final boundary invite "theological" debate. In political terms, it would only have required a simple decision. Quoted in Emerson *et al.* "Just what is this 'Absorption Capacity'".

29 Quoted in Emerson *et al.* "Just what is this 'Absorption Capacity'".

30 BBC News, 28 April 2007.

31 The investigations were aimed at a secret and clandestine organization called "Ergenekon" (2007), which purportedly aimed to overthrow the government, and "Operation Sledgehammer", an alleged coup attempt dating back to 2003. Both investigations later collapsed, following claims that evidence had been tampered with. By 2015 most of the accused had been acquitted.

32 *The Economist*, 16 August 2014.

33 *New York Times*, 25 December 2013.

34 The Committee to Protect Journalists declared Erdogan the world's worst jailer of journalists. See its report "Hundreds of Journalists Jailed Globally Becomes the New Normal", 13 December 2018, at https://cpj.org/reports/2018/.
35 Jean-Claude Juncker, "State of the Union Address 2017", at https://europa.eu/rapid/press-release_SPEECH-17-3165_en.htm.
36 Quoted in Reuters, 1 October 2017.
37 *NOS*, "Reconstructie Rotterdam: Zelfs Agenten Moesten Dekking Zoeken", 14 March 2017.
38 According to opinion polls, around two thirds of Turks living in the Netherlands support Erdogan. Among young Turks that number is even higher, as reported by *De Volkskrant*, 15 April 2017. In presidential elections in 2018, no fewer than 72.8 per cent of Turkish voters living in the Netherlands voted for Erdogan, *De Standaard* reported on 25 June 2018.
39 *De Volkskrant*, 28 December 2017.
40 Interview with *Der Spiegel*, 16 April 2007.

CHAPTER 8

1 In Henry Kissinger, *On China* (New York: Penguin, 2012), 308.
2 Xi Jinping, "Jointly Shoulder Responsibility of Our Times, Promote Global Growth", speech at the Opening Session of the World Economic Forum Annual Meeting, Davos, 17 January 2017.
3 Xi Jinping, "Speech at the Road to Rejuvenation", 29 November 2012.
4 Sun Tzu, *The Art of War*, I, 23 (London: Duncan Baird Publishers, 2005).
5 Xi Jinping, "Promote Friendship Between our People and Work Together to Build a Bright Future", speech 8 September 2013.
6 Reported by respectively the *South China Morning Post*, 21 February 2019, and China's state news agency Xinhua, 18 April 2019.
7 Xi Jinping, "Work Together to Build the Silk Road Economic Belt and the 21st Century Maritime Silk Road", speech delivered at the first Belt and Road Forum for International Cooperation in Beijing, 14 May 2017.
8 Quoted in the *New York Times*, 28 January 2018. See particularly Bruno Maçães, *Belt and Road: A Chinese World Order* (London: Hurst, 2018), which points out that the Belt and Road is neither belt nor road but China's alternative to what we know as "the West", as well as Alice Ekman (ed.) "China's Belt and Road and the World: Competing Forms of Globalization", *Etudes de l'IFRI*, April 2019.
9 For example, Howard French, *Everything Under the Heavens: How the Past Helps Shape China's Push for Global Power* (New York: Vintage, 2018), and on the influence of imperial thinking on modern China's foreign policy, Kissinger, *On China*.
10 Wang Yiwei, *China Connects the World: What Behind the Belt and Road Initiative* (China Intercontinental Press, 2016), 68–9.
11 For the importance of hierarchy and power asymmetry to "All under Heaven", see Yuan-kang Wang, "Explaining the Tribute System: Power, Confucianism, and War in Medieval East Asia", *Journal of East Asian Studies* 13 (2013).
12 *Financial Times*, 18 August 2018.
13 Tanner Green, "One Belt, One Road, One Mistake", *Foreign Policy*, 6 December 2018.
14 *Financial Times*, 25 July 2019.
15 Quoted in Reuters, 7 August 2019.
16 *Financial Times*, 22 November 2018.

17 *South China Morning Post*, 20 November 2019.

18 See *The Economist*'s Intelligence Unit, "China's Reboot of the Belt and Road initiative", 29 April 2019.

19 See Peter Frankopan, *The New Silk Roads* (London: Bloomsbury, 2019), 129–35.

20 For Schmitt's theory of *Großräume*, see his "The Großraum Order of International Law" in *Writings on War* and Chapter 5 of this book.

21 Quoted in the *South China Morning Post*, 12 May 2017, in an article with the telling title: "We're Still Figuring Out China's Belt and Road: European Diplomats Confess they Don't Know Much About Xi's Trade Plan".

22 Quoted in Stephen Sestanovich, *Maximalist: America in the World from Truman to Obama* (New York: Random House, 2014).

23 Quoted in Reuters, 8 January 2018.

24 Reuters, 16 July 2018.

25 Quoted in Keith Johnson, "In Odyssey for Chinese, Greece Sells Its Fabled Port of Piraeus", *Foreign Policy*, 8 April 2016.

26 "China en de strategische opdracht voor Nederland in Europa", ed. Luuk van Middelaar, *Adviesraad Internationale Betrekkingen*, 78, n.230. English edition at https://www.advisorycouncilinternationalaffairs.nl/documents/publications/2019./06/26/china-and-the-strategic-tasks-for-the-netherlands-in-europe.

27 *Seatrade Maritime News*, 18 July 2018.

28 Aleksandar Vucic, "Guest Post: The Serbia–China Friendship Bridge", *Financial Times*, 25 December 2014.

29 Jacob Mardell, "China's Belt and Road Partners Aren't Fools", *Foreign Policy*, 1 May 2019.

30 Mardell, "China's Belt and Road Partners".

31 François Godement and Abigaël Vasselier write: "Most actual business is transacted bilaterally, and summits are largely venues for strings of bilateral meetings". In "China at the Gates: A New Power Audit of EU–China Relations", *European Council on Foreign Relations*, 2017, 65–6. The authors further note a "distinct asymmetry between both sides" and observe that China has "clearly sought to amend the format where it sees benefit to itself".

32 *Financial Times*, 10 April 2019.

33 Quoted in Reuters, 16 July 2018.

34 Jonathan E. Hillman, "China's 'Belt and Road' Court to Challenge Current US-led Order", *Financial Times*, 24 July 2018.

35 Quoted in Reuters, 18 June 2017.

36 See "China en de strategische opdracht voor Nederland in Europa", ed. Luuk van Middelaar, 31.

37 Quoted in *The Diplomat*, 9 September 2017.

38 Quoted in the *Financial Times*, 9 August 2016.

39 Quoted in *AFP*, 22 February 2018.

40 Quoted in the *South China Morning Post*, 18 October 2017.

41 "Commission Reviews Relations with China, Proposes 10 Actions", press release, 12 March 2019.

42 Interview with the *Financial Times*, 16 January 2020.

43 Quoted in Noah Barkin, "The US is Losing Europe in its Battle with China", *The Atlantic*, June 2019.

44 Quoted in Reuters, 22 March 2019.

45 *Financial Times*, 20 September 2015.

46 *Financial Times*, 15 September 2016.
47 Mike Pompeo, "Thatcher Lecture 2019", delivered at the Centre of Policy Studies, 8 May 2019.
48 Richard Grenell, Trump's envoy to Berlin, wrote a letter spelling out the same consequences to German authorities. Allowing Chinese firms to be involved in the roll-out of 5G in Germany would mean America scaling back its intelligence cooperation. Reported in the *Wall Street Journal*, 11 March 2019.
49 *Financial Times*, 6 February 2020.
50 "Remarks by Vice President Pence at the 2019 Munich Security Conference", 16 February 2019.

CHAPTER 9

1 Interview with Fox News, 1 July 2018.
2 "Remarks by President Trump at the White House Business Session with our Nation's Governors", 10 February 2020, at https://www.whitehouse.gov/briefings-statements/remarks-president-trump-white-house-business-session-nations-governors.
3 Interview with CBS, 14 July 2018.
4 Kissinger, *Diplomacy*, 54.
5 Tweet, @eucopresident, 15 July 2018.
6 BBC News, 22 November 2016.
7 *The Independent*, 24 January 2018.
8 See Paul Waugh, "Why a No-Deal Brexit is Now Theresa May's Fallback Plan to Save Her Party – And Herself", *The Huffington Post*, 11 February 2019.
9 Lord Ricketts, letter to *The Times*, 31 January 2017.
10 Quoted in Bloomberg, 24 January 2018.
11 *Financial Times*, 27 January 2017.
12 The latter term was used by Liam Fox, May's international trade secretary, in his "Speech at the Manchester Town Hall", 29 September 2016, at: https://www.gov.uk/government/speeches/liam-foxs-free-trade-speech.
13 As May confirmed in a bylined article in German newspaper *Die Welt*, 19 September 2018: "We will still be neighbours, we are still all part of the European family of nations and we all still champion the same beliefs. We all stand for freedom, democracy and the rule of law, underpinned by a rules-based global order – in a world in which these are increasingly under threat."
14 Tweet, @realDonaldTrump, 30 November 2017.
15 Tweet, @realDonaldTrump, 8 July 2019.
16 Tweet, @realDonaldTrump, 8 July 2019.
17 Tweet, @realDonaldTrump, 3 June 2019.
18 Quoted in *The Guardian*, 7 June 2019.
19 Tweet, @realDonaldTrump, 23 July 2019.
20 Quoted in *The Independent*, 9 December 2015.
21 Gideon Rachman, *Financial Times*, 31 January 2017.
22 *The Guardian*, "Merkel 'Explains' Refugee Convention to Trump in Phone Call", 29 January 2017.
23 See Susan Glasser, "How Trump Made War on Angela Merkel and Europe", *New Yorker*, 17 December 2018.

24 CNBC, 17 March 2017.

25 See James P. Rubin, "The Leader of the Free World Meets Donald Trump", *Politico*, 16 March 2017.

26 Interview with *Der Spiegel*, 1 February 1994.

27 Quoted in René Pfister, "Will Merkel be Followed by Darkness?", *Der Spiegel*, 28 May 2019.

28 Quoted by CNN, 9 June 2018.

29 Tweet, @realDonaldTrump, 8 May 2018.

30 Quoted in *Breibart*, 3 June 2018.

31 Tweet, @realDonaldTrump, 18 June 2018.

32 *Journal du Dimanche*, 27 May 2017.

33 *Financial Times*, 28 June 2017.

34 *USA Today*, 14 July 2017.

35 Reuters, 2 March 2018.

36 Politico, 28 April 2018.

37 Quoted in the *Financial Times*, 21 August 2019.

38 Reuters, 11 November 2018.

39 *Washington Post*, 28 June 2018.

40 *Independent*, 29 June 2018.

41 Reuters, 7 June 2018.

42 "Remarks by President Trump and NATO Secretary General Jens Stoltenberg at Bilateral Breakfast", at https://www.whitehouse.gov/briefings-statements/remarks-president-trump-nato-secretary-general-jens-stoltenberg-bilateral-breakfast/.

43 Tweet, @realDonaldTrump, 11 June 2018.

44 Tweet, @realDonaldTrump, 11 June 2018.

45 "Remarks by President Trump before Marine One departure", 10 July 2018, at: https://www.whitehouse.gov/briefings-statements/remarks-president-trump-marine-one-departure-9/.

46 Reuters, 26 September 2018.

47 Quoted in the *Financial Times*, 7 November 2018.

48 *Financial Times*, 5 October 2018.

49 *Financial Times*, 5 October 2018.

50 Interview with *RT*, 11 November 2018.

51 "Remarks by President Trump and President Juncker of the European Commission in Joint Press Statements", 25 July 2018, at https://www.whitehouse.gov/briefings-statements/remarks-president-trump-president-juncker-european-commission-joint-press-statements/.

52 *The Guardian*, 25 July 2018.

53 Quoted in Reuters, 14 June 2018. Later, in an interview with *Bild Zeitung*, 2 June 2019, Juncker added: "I knew how to get along with him – like killers do".

54 *The Guardian*, 25 July 2018.

CHAPTER 10

1 On improvisation as a mode of politics, see van Middelaar, *Alarums and Excursions*.

2 Quoted in Jackson, *De Gaulle*, 568.

3 The other reason why the other EU founders rebuffed de Gaulle's vision of a multipolar world was that the world was obviously bipolar. The US and Europe – including de Gaulle's

France – were deeply united in their opposition to the Soviet Union and communism. The need for a sovereign Europe did not really arise.

4 Josep Borrell, "Address to the European Parliament", 7 October 2019, at https://www.europarl.europa.eu/news/en/press-room/20190926IPR62260/hearing-with-high-representative-vice-president-designate-josep-borrell.

5 Vladimir Chizhov, Russia's ambassador to the EU, quoted in *Tass*, 24 October 2019.

6 The EU's power as a global rule and standard setter for business is what Anu Bradford calls the "Brussels effect". See her *The Brussels Effect: How the European Union Rules the World* (Oxford: Oxford University Press, 2020). The ability to set global business standards is understandably a source of European pride. That said, regulatory hegemony is only global hegemony to the extent that rules matter.

7 BBC News, 6 November 2018.

8 Arendt, *The Human Condition*, 192.

9 Quoted in the *Financial Times*, 3 December 2018.

10 European Commission, "Connecting Europe and Asia – Building Blocks for an EU Strategy", 19 September 2018.

11 Reuters, 22 March 2019.

12 Quoted in the *Financial Times*, 5 December 2019.

13 Quoted in *Politico*, 30 October 2019.

14 *Irish Times*, 19 April 2019.

15 So far, the EU maintains that it will only offer reconstruction aid once "a comprehensive, genuine and inclusive political transition is firmly under way". See https://eeas.europa.eu/headquarters/headquarters-Homepage/59417/eu-and-crisis-syria_en.

16 European Commission, "Artificial Intelligence: Commission Takes Forward its Work on Ethics Guidelines", press release, 8 April 2019; and in the European Commission blog post, "Ambitious New Strategy to Make Plastic Fantastic", at https://ec.europa.eu/environment/efe/news/ambitious-new-strategy-make-plastic-fantastic-2018-03-16_en.

17 Martin Selmayr, "A Conversation with Secretary-general of the European Commission Martin Selmayr", *Brookings Institution*, 6 March 2019, at https://www.brookings.edu/wp-content/uploads/2019/02/fp_20190306_eu_selmayr_transcript.pdf.

18 *The Economist*, 7 November 2019.

19 Quoted in Reuters, 3 December 2019.

20 See Reuters, 24 August 2019.

21 Quoted in Bloomberg, 19 July 2019.

22 Sara Stefanini & Nicholas Hirst, "Hungary's Russian-built Nuclear Plant Powered by Politics in Brussels", *Politico*, 22 November 2017.

23 For a discussion of how hesitatingly China's political class embraced the language of strength, and how the ideal of rejuvenation needed to be rooted in the experience of national humiliation, see Orville Schell & John Delury, *Wealth and Power: China's Long March to the Twentieth Century* (London: Little Brown, 2013).

24 Reuters, 27 November 2019.

25 United States Senate, "Letter to Allseas CEO", 18 December 2019.

26 Quoted in the *Financial Times*, 12 December 2019.

27 Joschka Fischer, "The Day After Nato", in *Project Syndicate*, 4 December 2019.

Index

Note: numbers in brackets preceded by *n* refer to notes.

227